The Europa Library of Business Biography
Series Editor: Neil McKendrick

Sir Alfred Jones
Shipping Entrepreneur Par Excellence

Sir Alfred Jones (1845–1909)

Sir Alfred Jones

Shipping Entrepreneur Par Excellence

P. N. Davies

London
Europa Publications Limited

Europa Publications Limited
18 Bedford Square, London, WC1B 3JN

© P. N. Davies, 1978
ISBN: 0 905118 17 0

Printed and bound in England by
STAPLES PRINTERS LIMITED
at The Stanhope Press, Rochester, Kent.

Contents

Abbreviations

ASP	African Steam Ship Company Papers
CO	Colonial Office Papers
E & OP & SC	Report of the Committee on Edible and Oil Producing Nuts and Seeds
FO	Foreign Office Papers
HTP	Henry Tyrer Papers
JHP	John Holt Papers
RCSR	Royal Commission on Shipping Rings
RNCP	Royal Niger Company Papers

Note: Full details of these abbreviations and of all other works cited in the footnotes are given in the bibliography.

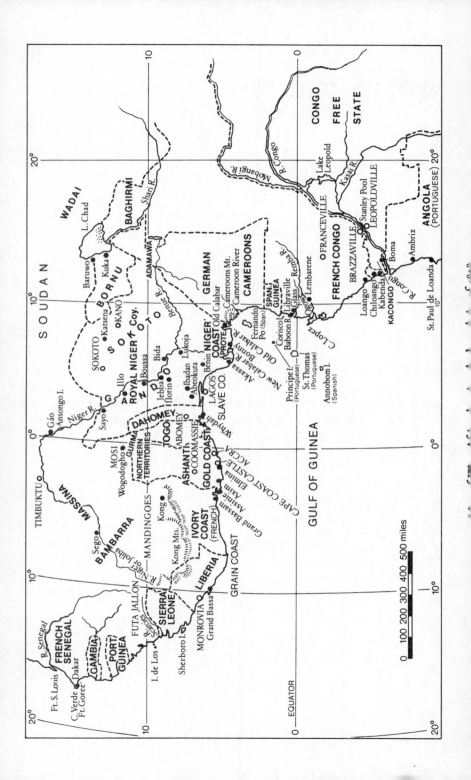

Literary Luddism and the Businessman

Neil McKendrick

THAT THERE IS AN UNACCEPTABLE FACE of capitalism is not in doubt. What has often seemed more in dispute is whether there can be an acceptable one. The generalizations concerning the low esteem of industry and businessmen are as easily available as weeds in an untended garden – so much do they flourish as almost to choke any profitable discussion of why they are there; so rank is their growth as to conceal almost completely the virtues of those involved in business. Few have questioned the Schumacher proposition that 'the prestige carried by people in modern industrial society varies in inverse proportion to their closeness to actual production'.[1] Many indeed regard it as a basic sociological law. It is, in consequence, not surprising that it is easier to construct a hierarchy of business vices than it is to draw up a catalogue of business virtues. Corruption, pollution, monopoly, oligopoly and political extremism spring more readily to most commentators' pens than do energy, resource, the creation of wealth or the benefits of commercial enterprise.

Verbal associations can be revealing and it is clear to me from reading hundreds of Cambridge undergraduate essays on the subject that to many – indeed, until recently, to most – industry equals environmental pollution, factory efficiency equals worker alienation, businessman equals expense account amorality, provincial businessman equals *nouveaux riches* vulgarity, the boardroom battle equals the rat-race, competition goes with cut-throat, and profits go with excess. Sadly

---

[1] E. F. Schumacher, *Small is Beautiful: A Study of Economics as if People Mattered* (1973), p. 125.

the responses are, of course, all too often all too justified. The danger lies in regarding them as virtually universally so. And it is an alarming comment on the likely career choice of the young and the likely profits of our future industries if excess comes to be so much the matching adjective for profits that it excludes all but the most fleeting and reluctant recognition of their life-enhancing effects in helping to finance schools and universities and hospitals and housing and roads and the social welfare which should accompany any humane society.

Those who argue, very properly, that the prosperity of the working people is a true measure of a country's advance are often a little short on how to encourage the creation of wealth so that that prosperity can be increased.

Those who drop out rarely try to explain who is to provide the money to run the hospitals to cure them when they are sick, to pay for the schools to educate their children, to provide the sewers to carry their effluent, or the services to carry their water, clear their roads or provide their electricity. To be truly self-sufficient in a modern industrial society is about as possible as it is to be a truly orthodox Jew outside the social conditions of the nomadic tribes which produced the Talmudic laws: possible, that is, only by reliance on a host of others to break the rules to provide the necessities of life for the purist élite. This is not to fail to recognize the aspirations of the self-sufficient – nor indeed their possible usefulness. They are often among the most enterprising elements in our society and their future role may be an important one. Their survival – like the survival of uneconomic breeds of animal which can survive in more hostile conditions – may provide an important genetic resource, not to mention a fund of invaluable techniques, should our society and economy ever collapse. But it is a sad comment on that society that such creative enterprise is so often reacting against it from outside rather than improving it from inside.

Even more disturbing is the increasingly common attitude of those who *do* operate inside – even those who operate *directly* inside industry. What has recently been described as 'the double life of the graduate in industry' or 'the half-life of the executive' sums up this attitude of mind with startling clarity.[2] Paul Greengrass, a recent Cambridge graduate, has suggested that although '*Business* has become a general area' for the graduate 'which *must be entered for the purpose of securing a salary*', it has almost wholly failed to capture his allegiance. It breeds,

[2] Paul Greengrass, 'Double Life of the Graduate in Industry', *The Times*, 18 July, 1977, p. 16.

he tells us, no common identity of purpose. Both its means and its ends are unattractive – even at times repellent. The very language it uses to recruit him appals him by its 'dead mechanical and impersonal' tone. So the graduate 'while accepting jobs in business' fails to 'identify with the values of the business world. That is to say they *remain profoundly unconvinced of the efficacy of the profit motive* as it applies to large corporations'.

Many, many graduates are now choosing a half-life; by day fulfilling the demands of the executive to the barest minimum, and retreating at nights and weekends, to view quite objectively and dispassionately their career 'half'.

This is *a quite new managerial schizophrenia which has mingled a private, radical disavowal of a business career with a public acceptance of market necessity, and its full ramifications have yet to be seen.*[3]

Such managerial schizophrenia is not as new as Mr. Greengrass thinks; although it may have grown more intense. A similar attitude was being complained of in an issue of *The Director* in 1954, and there are those who have seen similar symptoms as early as late Victorian England. A Cambridge debate in the early 1960s between M. M. Postan, then Professor of Economic History, and G. R. S. Kitson Clark, then Reader in Modern English History, provided a nice illustration of this point: Professor Postan was describing what he called the entre-preneurial absenteeism of much of late Victorian business, when Dr. Kitson Clark, who clearly felt that his recent ancestors – the Kitsons of Leeds – were being impugned, interrupted to deliver a defensive panegyric on Victorian businessmen. He praised their hard work, long hours and unremitting sense of duty. They might have preferred to be in their estates shooting their game, organizing their gardens or tend-ing their social life, he concluded, but they remained at their works from dawn to dusk, chained there by a sense of loyalty to the family firm and a stern moral sense of their responsibilities. 'Precisely', said Postan, with sibilant speed, 'precisely. Psychological absenteeism!'

There are many reasons for this attitude to business which has so often been described as characteristic of English culture, but one of the most often-cited influences (along with the English class system, the English public school system and the English value system) has been

[3] Greengrass, *op. cit.* p. 16 [my emphases]. Significantly Mr. Greengrass graduated in English. His comments represent a public echo of many similar private confessions.

the emotional Luddism of so much of English fiction during the last hundred and fifty years.

This is not to say that business lacked its critics before the nineteenth century. Montesquieu said that when financiers were given honour all was lost; Goldsmith echoed him when he wrote that 'Honour sinks where commerce long prevails';[4] and one could compile a dictionary of quotations to show that business and businessmen have always had denigrators.[5] But such literary stepping stones (unless very comprehensively selected) would conceal many interesting changes of tone, and many revealing concentrations of adverse comment. A true index of animadversion against business would show a heavy concentration in the last two centuries and a disproportionate concentration in the English language.

In *The Path to British Decadence* Noel Annan has recently argued that 'What is interesting is not the cultural opposition of Leavis, Orwell and others to Bloomsbury and the Oxford wits, but the way they share one major common assumption.' 'That assumption,' he goes on, 'is that *the life of the professional classes is alone supportable and that of industry and commerce degrading*. . . . Whether it is Eliot or Forster, Lawrence or Leavis, Tawney or Herbert Read, *the world of commerce, advertising, speculation, automation, management and enterprise, became so hateful* that some of these sages praised those who wanted to return to the world of the wheelwright and the blacksmith. . . . The life of pontificating, explaining, recommending, analysing and advising other men how to run their affairs rose in esteem, while *the actual business of management was not so much denigrated as ignored and left to lesser fellows.*'

'*The shift in Britain out of business and industry and into the new bureaucracies* of higher education, broadcasting, journalism, research organizations, social welfare, planning and the plethora of commissions, committees, boards, regulatory agencies designed to restrain evil and promote virtue, seems to be a direct response to what their sages have been telling the British since before 1914.'[6]

It is worth quoting Lord Annan at length, for not only does he accurately describe the symptoms of what has been called the English disease, but he points to some chilling conclusions.

[4] Oliver Goldsmith, *The Traveller* (1765).
[5] See Neil McKendrick, General Introduction to R. J. Overy, *William Morris, Viscount Nuffield* (1976), pp. xxiv–xxxix.
[6] Noel Annan, 'The path to British decadence', *The Sunday Times Weekly Review*, 22 May 1977, p. 34.

For the rejection of the world of industry is not a universal phenomenon. As Lord Annan points out 'this did not happen in France. There,
despite the fact that for years the intelligentsia has been *marxisant* and
the student revolt actually challenged government, the doctrine of
Enrichissez-vous has lost little of its appeal. In West Germany, Grass,
Böll and *Der Spiegel* satirize the culture of the *Wirtschaftswunder*; and
murderous revolutionary groups attempt disruption. But the trade
unions . . . still put their faith for a better life in the policies of hard
work and discipline.'

'Yet in Britain, the message of our teachers – that we should seek
social justice and exercise compassion – has been all too effective. As a
result we now run the risk of a decline in productivity so steep that it
will leave an ailing industry – its weakness masked by the profits of
North Sea oil – unable to support a vast well-intentioned bureaucracy.'[7]

The singular strength and effectiveness of literary Luddism in
Britain has, of course, been noted before. But in Britain alone life seems
to have adopted the values of its art. And it is worth investigating
briefly how these literary attitudes to industry grew up. It is worth
asking how universally Luddite English literature has been during the
last two hundred years. It is worth examining whether English
Luddism is distinct from that of other countries, and, if not, enquiring
into its singular effectiveness.

It is almost always assumed that English literature is wholly hostile
to men of business. There has been an enormously influential dynasty
of critics from Ruskin and Arnold down to Herbert Read and F. R.
Leavis whose hostility to industry and most of its practitioners is
unquestioned.[8] And it is certainly not difficult to find evidence of
literary hostility. From the early nineteenth century onwards it is
embarrassingly abundant, and vividly memorable. The literary critics
of the industrial system did not pull their punches. Coleridge's verdict
was that the poor were being 'mechanized into engines for the manufacture of new rich men'. In his view 'the machinery of the wealth of
the nation was made up of the wretchedness, disease, and depravity of
those who should consistitute'[9] its strength.

[7] Ibid.

[8] Herbert Read finds some virtue in a select few industrialists, like Josiah Wedgwood, who promoted art through industry, but the mass of businessmen are
condemned along with the social and economic consequences of their endeavour.

[9] S. T. Coleridge, *On the Constitution of the Church and State*, ed. H. N. Coleridge
(3rd ed. 1839), p. 63.

Shelley was equally bitter in his judgement, writing that 'one of the vaunted effects of this system is to increase the national industry, that is, to increase the labours of the poor and those luxuries of the rich which they supply'.[10]

And there was little in the later poetic condemnation of industrialism which Blake did not anticipate. His hostility to the machine has been as influential as any other single poet. As Bronowski pointed out 'to his mind, the machine became one with the mechanics of Newton and the mechanical society of Locke',[11] part of that scientific rationalism which dared to explain the mysteries of life, soul and universe, in mechanistic terms, which in Blake's words 'turned that which is Soul and Life into a Mill or Machine'.[12] In Blake's *Milton* the identification of Satan with the new powers of industry is quite explicit, and the identification was made visual when the painter John Martin illustrated *Paradise Lost* in 1832 and took so many of his designs from industry.[13]

Those critics, like Arnold, who peered into the 'fatal glooms' of Thomson's 'cities of dreadful night', or Blake's new world where work was at best 'sorrowful drudgery to obtain a scanty pittance of bread', and at worst an 'Eternal Death with Mills and Ovens and Cauldrons',[14] found little to reassure them. 'The pale weaver ... thrice dispirited' was an unhappy substitute for those who bloomed in health in the pastoral idyll they preferred to look back to. Even worse was the sight of Wordsworth's 'little children, boys and girls ... offered up to Gain, the master idol of the realm, (as) Perpetual sacrifice';[15] or Elizabeth Barrett Browning's 'Little outcasts from life's fold ... lean and small, Scurf and mildew of the city'; or even more movingly, the 'pale and sunken faces' of her 'young, young children' ... (who) ... 'are weary ere they run'- [16]

---

[10] Shelley, *A Philosophical View of Reform*, (1820), ed. T. W. Rolleson (1920), p. 42.

[11] Jacob Bronowski, *A Man Without a Mask* (1944), p. 86.

[12] William Blake, *The Four Zoas* (1804). See Jeremy Warburg, op. cit., p. 8.

[13] F. D. Klingender, *Art and the Industrial Revolution* (1947), p. 105.

[14] He was in fact willing to work for the new industrialists himself and provided illustrations for Wedgwood's catalogues. But until late in life his knowledge of industry was based only on hearsay – having seen very little of it himself.

[15] William Wordsworth, *The Excursion*, Book VIII, II, 181–5.

[16] Elizabeth Barrett Browning, *A Song for the Ragged Schools. The Poetry of the Brownings: An Anthology*, compiled by Clifford Bax (1947), p. 54.

For, all day, we drag our burden tiring
Through the coal-dark, underground –
Or, all day, we drive the wheels of iron
In the factories, round and round.[17]

Lesser voices added their condemnation of evils, which

. . . would make a Monarch groan! a Brougham weep!
Were these things known, the Premier could not sleep!

They identified the cause –

Curs'd avarice, the cause of all their woes.

They identified the victim –

With limbs deformed, her symmetry destroyed,
For sixteen hours full oft she is employed.

They identified the villain –

Some masters are so merciless and mean
Thirst so for gold, and so to avarice lean,
That they will keep the children on their feet
For any length of time they fancy meet.[18]

---

[17] Elizabeth Barrett Browning, *The Cry of the Children* (1844) in *The Poetical Works of Elizabeth Barrett Browning* (1904 edition), pp. 232–3. Her poem is all the more effective since she recognized so clearly the dangers of the prelapsarian myth, and the poet's fatal tendency to 'cry for togas and the Picturesque',

> every age
> Appears to souls who live in't (ask Carlyle)
> Most unheroic. Ours, for instance, ours!
>
> . .
>
> I do distrust the poet who discerns
> No character or glory in his times,
> And trundles back his soul five hundred years.
>
> *Aurora Leigh* (1856)

[18] *The Factory Child: A Poem* (1831) (anon), pp. 614–39. The victims are usually factory girls:

> Her little hands, besmear'd with dye and oil,
> Depict the drudgery of her infant toil,
>
> . .
>
> Born to a life of pain, to slave and toil,
> Beyond her power.

They identified the seat of the crime in

> . . . the receptacle for dreary woe,
> The Factory Mill . . .
> . . . that dreary place
> (Where squalid suffering meets his shrinking gaze).[19]

It mattered little that the condemning voices included those of manufacturers, like John Fielden, who wrote bitterly in *The Curse of the Factory System* (1836) 'as her little nimble fingers are useful to us; as they conduce to our prosperity, add to our wealth, and assist us in rivalling all other nations of the world in the worldly race for riches, we cannot dispense with her labour; and, as she is a "free labourer", the Parliament cannot interfere to protect her from labour which is an overmatch for her body: Oh, MOLOCH! MOLOCH!'[20] Some poets recognized and even named the virtuous few, but they served only to heighten the condemnation of the many. If the Wedgwoods, Owens and Fieldens could prosper through benevolent paternalism (or better) how much worse that the evil majority should seek to profit through heartless tyranny – that was the unmistakable message. It had a powerful emotional appeal, and, of course, considerable justification.

Little wonder that poets turned back to the delights of the pastoral life as an antidote to the evils of industry.[21]

It would be best, William Morris urged his readers, to

> Forget six counties overhung with smoke,
> Forget the snorting steam and piston stroke,
> Forget the spreading of the hideous town
> Think rather of the pack-horse on the down[22]

Most Victorian poets were only too happy to draw

> . . . backward from the coarse town sights
> To count the daisies upon dappled fields.[23]

---

[19] Caroline Norton, *A Voice from the Factories*, subtitled *In Serious Verse* (1836), pp. 1–40.
[20] John Fielden, *The Curse of the Factory System* (1836), p. 31.
[21] Elizabeth Barrett Browning, *The Cry of the Children*, op. cit., p. 232:
Go out children, from the mine and from the city,
Sing out, children, as the little thrushes do;
Pluck your handfulls of the meadow cowslips pretty.
[22] William Morris, Prologue to *The Earthly Paradise* (1868–70).
[23] Elizabeth Barrett Browning, *Aurora Leigh*, VI, II, 139.

Their elegies for rural life, their nostalgia for the rural past, were the products of a violent reaction to the ugliness of the new industrial society. They saw only 'the ugliness which the new conditions of industry were forcing people into'.[24] Their inherited concept of beauty was at war with what Herbert Read called 'the purely mechanistic element of machine production'.[25]

Little wonder that Jeremy Warburg has been able to conclude that 'most poets have recoiled from the mechanistic habit of mind and from the world it has created. They recoiled from what they regarded as the profitable dirt, the profitable smoke, the profitable slums, the profitable ignorance, and the profitable despair of a materialistic society – a "gold-crushed hungry hell".'[26] Profit, and the speculation which so often promised it in vain, were damned as false gods: in Tennyson's *Maud*, for example, it is only necessary to mention that 'a vast speculation had failed' to indicate long perspectives of dishonesty and even criminality.[27]

In their disgust some turned away completely, complaining like Ruskin, 'I have written fifty times, if once, that you cannot have art where you have smoke'.[28] But with familiarity, the images of industry were inevitably absorbed and domesticated: so that Rupert Brooke could recognize 'the keen Unpassioned beauty of a great machine',[28] and it could be conceded by Spender that some machines 'effect their beauty without robbery'.[28]

Indeed once poets could be nostalgic about machinery it was usually safe from outright condemnation. It is interesting to note that nineteenth century farm machinery which now attracts the most fervent admiration from those in reaction against modern industry was once bitterly deplored. Charles Tennyson Turner might sing the praises of 'The Steam Threshing Machine' as early as 1868 and wish to 'catalogue in rich hexameters the Rake, the Roller and the mystic Van'[28] but he was very much the exception – standing in stark contrast to Wordsworth, Blake, Cowper and Clare who deplored the impact of industry and mechanization on the countryside.[28]

[24] Geoffrey Tillotson, 'William Morris and Machines', *Essays in Criticism and Research* (1942), p. 144.
[25] Herbert Read, 'Machine Aesthetic', *A Coat of Many Colours* (1946), p. 322.
[26] Jeremy Warburg, *The Industrial Muse: The Industrial Revolution in English Poetry: An Anthology* (1958), p. xxii. This is an excellent anthology to which I am much indebted.
[27] John R. Reed, *Victorian Conventions* (1975), p. 178.
[28] Warburg, passim.

However, although the majesty of machinery was eventually acknowledged in metaphor,[29] the verdict on industrialists and their impact on their society remained unforgiving. An impressive anthology has accumulated testifying to a world where

all is seared with trade; bleared, smeared with toil.[30]

But if the final verdict, which most educated Englishmen have inherited, was unambiguously hostile, the poets' reaction to industry had not always been so damning. In the early days of the Industrial Revolution there were poets, at least in the industrial provinces, willing to welcome industry and to praise – even to eulogise – those who ran it. Men such as Boulton and Watt, Wedgwood and Bentley, Brindley and Bridgewater were heroes to many in the late eighteenth century. As early as 1777 Thomas Bancroft wrote:

Such are England's true patriots, her prop and her pride;
They draw wealth from each state while its wants are supply'd;
To mankind all at large they are factors and friends;
And their praise with their wares reach the world's farthest ends.[31]

[29] It required what C. Day Lewis called 'a further process of digestion in the individual poetic organs'. After that had happened, a point was reached when he commented, 'It is no longer accepted by the poet that a factory has not the qualifications for poetic treatment possessed by a flower'. C. Day Lewis, *A Hope for Poetry*, p. 61. Not surprisingly the familiarity with machinery came earlier to the working class poets, and they found no difficulty in absorbing the technicalities of technology. They even combined the metaphor of the machine with overt sexual imagery. One would need to be blind to miss the implications of 'The New Bury Loom' first published in 1804:

My shuttle run well in her lathe, my treadle it worked up and down,—
My level stood close to her breast-bone, the time I was reiving her loom.—
The cords of my lams, jacks and treadles at length they began to give way.
The bobbin I had in my shuttle, the weft in it no longer would stay.
Her lathe it went bang to and fro, my main treadle still kept in tune.
My pickers went nicketty-nack all the time I was squaring her loom.—
My shuttle it still kept in motion, her lams she worked well up and down.
The weights in her rods they did tremble; she said she would weave a new gown.
My strength now began for to fail me. I said: It's now right to a hair.
She turned up her eyes and said: Tommy, my loom you have got pretty square.

See Martha Vicinus, *The Industrial Muse: A Story of Nineteenth Century British Working Class Literature* (1974), pp. 40–1.

[30] Gerard Manley Hopkins, 'God's Grandeur', *Poems*, ed. W. H. Garner (3rd ed., 1948), p. 70.

[31] Quoted in Witt Bowden, *Industrial Society in England Towards the End of the Eighteenth Century* (New York, 1925), p. 136.

Erasmus Darwin was as admiring as Bancroft. His enthusiastic prophecies for the achievements of 'UNCONQUER'D STEAM' have been preserved for posterity mainly by parody, but they once represented a very real optimism for what science and industry could together achieve. It should not be forgotten that Darwin's attempts 'to inlist Imagination under the banner of Science' (as they were described in an advertisement of his *Poetical Works*) were extremely well received at first.[32] Nor should it be forgotten that his optimism was shared by others. Anna Seward's tribes of 'fuliginous chemists' and their 'troops of dusky artificers' were all active servants of Britain's 'rich inventive Commerce'. Canals, factories and above all the steam engine all had their rapturous admirers. They were to be the harbingers of a better future:

> Blessings on Science, and her handmaid Steam!
> They make Utopia only half a dream;
> And show the fervent, if capacious souls,
> Who watch the ball of Progress as it rolls,
> That all as yet completed, or begun,
> Is but the dawning that precedes the sun.[33]

Charles Mackay had no doubts about the virtues of 'Steam's triumphal car', and little use for those who could not see them:

> No poetry in Railways! foolish thought
> Of a dull brain, to no fine music wrought.[34]

Ebenezer Elliott was equally trenchant

> Ill it becomes thee, with ungrateful sneer,
> The trade-fed town and townsmen to dispraise
> Why rail at Traffic's wheels, and crowded ways?[35]

[32] Erasmus Darwin, *The Economy of Vegetation*, 1, (1782), 1, 289. They simply never recovered from the brilliant parody published as 'The Loves of the Triangles' in 1798:

> Drags the long *chain*, the polish'd axles glow
> While slowly circumvolves the piece of beef below.

Poetry of the Anti-Jacobin (2nd ed., 1800, p. 119).

[33] Charles Mackay, 'Railways 1846', *Voices from the Crowd* (1846); see his *Poetical Works* (1876), p. 214.

[34] Ibid.

[35] Ebenezer Elliott, 'Steam at Sheffield', written in the mid-1830s and later published in his *Poetical Works*, ed. Edwin Elliott (1876), vol. 1, pp. 352 ff.

He saw a glorious harmony in 'this Tempestuous music of the giant
Steam'; and his admiration for its creator was unstinted

> Watt! and his million feeding enginery!
> Steam miracles of demi-deity.

He had no doubts about its beneficial powers

> Engine of Watt! unrivall'd is thy sway
> Compared with thine, what is the tyrants power?
> His might destroys, while thine creates and serves
> Thy triumphs live and grow, like fruit and flower.

To Elliott, the great engineers of the Industrial Revolution were to be
admired and emulated.

> How oft of Brindley's deeds th'apprenticed boy
> Would speak delighted, long ere freedom came!
> And talk of Watt! while, shedding tears of joy,
> His widow'd mother heard, and hoped the name
> Of her poor boy, like theirs, would rise to fame.[36]

If there were few as ecstatic as Elliott, there were many others who
struggled to recognize the marvellous benefits of progress along with
its dreadful costs. In 1833 Wordsworth wrote

> Nor shall your presence, howsoe'er it mar
> The loveliness of Nature, prove a bar
> To the Mind's gaining that prophetic sense
> Of future change, that point of vision, whence
> May be discovered what in soul ye are.[37]

When he later decided that the costs outran the benefits he referred
back to these earlier lines, writing 'Once and for all let me declare that
it is not against Railways but against the abuse of them that I am
contending. How far I am from undervaluing the benefit to be expected
from railways in their legitimate application will appear from "Steamboats, Viaducts and Railways".'[37] But it is of course such later eloquent
disavowals as 'Proud were ye, Mountains' which are best remembered

---

[36] Ibid.
[37] See Jeremy Warburg, op. cit., p. 27. William Wordsworth's 'Steamboats,
Viaducts and Railways' was written in 1833 and published 1835.

> Hear YE that Whistle? As her long-lined Train
> Swept onwards, did the vision cross your view?
> Yes, ye were startled; and, in balance true,
> Weighing the mischief with the promised gain,
> Mountains, and Vales, and Floods, I call on you
> To share the passion of a just disdain.[38]

Many were only too willing to do so. Indeed many went further. For the characteristically remembered voice of the Victorian reaction was as much polemical condemnation as 'just disdain'.

The much quoted voice of Ernest Jones has been described as 'sample Chartistry'. Sentenced to two years hard labour in 1848 for sedition, he wrote prolifically for *The Labourer* and the *Northern Star* and his political verse was widely popular. He made no pretence at impartiality and his verses have the splendid appeal of unqualified conviction.

> The factories gave forth lurid fires
> From pent-up hells within their breast;
> E'en Etna's burning wrath expires,
> But *man's* volcanoes never rest.
>
> Women, children, men were toiling,
> Locked in dungeons close and black,
> Life's fast-failing thread uncoiling
> Round the wheel, the *modern rack*!
>
> For the reeking walls environ
> Mingled groups of death and life:
> Fellow-workmen, flesh and iron,
> Side by side in deadly strife.
>
> On the lealands slept the cattle,
> Freshness through the forest ran –
> While, in Mammon's mighty battle,
> Man was immolating man! . . .
>
> Young forms – with their pulses stifled,
> Young heads – with the eldered brain,
> Young hearts – of their spirit rifled,
> Young lives – sacrificed in vain:

[38] 'Proud were ye, Mountains' was published on 17 December 1844 in the *Morning Post*. See Jeremy Warburg, *op. cit.*, p. 27.

There they lie – the withered corses,
With not one regretful thought,
Trampled by thy fierce steam-horses,
England's mighty *Juggernaut*! . . .

Thinner wanes the rural village,
Smokier lies the fallow plain –
Shrinks the cornfields' pleasant tillage,
Fades the orchard's rich domain;

And a banished population
Festers in the fetid street: –
Give us, God, to save our nation.
Less of *cotton*, more of *wheat*.

Take us back to lea and wild wood,
Back to nature and to Thee!
To the child restore his childhood –
To the man his dignity![39]

Jones's *The Factory Town* was the authentic voice of political protest. But it reveals many common characteristics with the work of less politically inspired Victorian poets. Their Luddism, like Jones's, was expressed in general, not specific terms. The potential for personal attack on the entrepreneur was exploited largely at the level of implication. For most it was enough to write movingly of the horrors of the new industrial system, and the moral responsibility of the masters could be left to proclaim itself. Even those who did indict those responsible did so largely by attacking anonymous targets. They attacked 'the Masters' as a group. Individual businessmen were not named. The system was condemned, and the faceless men of business who ran it were, by implication, condemned with it. In fact the characteristic response was to attack the MACHINE, to identify the VICTIMS of its "cold metallic motion",[40] and to condemn the MASTERS largely by association. Over the years the early machines have been largely vindicated (rescued by the nostalgia gap), the victims – or at least their descendents – have been rescued from the worst evils by the Unions and the Welfare State, and the industrialists and their system have been left to bear the burden of guilt. Modern technology is still attacked, the factory is still deplored, and the victims

---

[39] Ernest Jones, *The Factory Town* (1855).
[40] Elizabeth Barrett Browning, *The Cry of the Children*, op. cit., p. 233.

of the system are still recognized.[41] Auden, for instance, unambiguously felt that 'Man's advance in control over his environment is making it more and more difficult for him, at least in the industrialized countries . . . to lead a naturally good life, and easier and easier to lead a morally bad one', but his criticism is more subtle, more oblique, than that of the Victorians. The tone is less emotional, less melodramatic. The machines are less ogrish. The victims are the victims of prosperity as much as of poverty, trapped as colourless cogs in a subtle system of industrial power. Auden's victims here are passive products of the industrial machine – ground into insipid acceptance of manipulated attitudes:

> He worked in a factory and never got fired
> . . .
> When there was peace, he was for peace; when
> there was war he went.[42]

The tyrant can of course still be crudely identified by other poets:

> Not Satan but a booted merchant stood
> God-fearing, God-important, in this street:[43]

The poets' verdict is, in fact, more hostile in received opinion than the actual record will support. If quality alone was our criterion then the record would be largely one of condemnation, but once admit the lesser poets and the versifiers, and admirers can be found. Even the greater poets were not unremittingly hostile, not even universally Luddite. Both Wordsworth and Tennyson invested in the railways. Both invested their hope that progress would be possible and beneficial. But when Wordsworth's valleys were invaded and Tennyson's shares devalued; when the new economy proved highly unstable, when Britain was plunged into terrible depressions, then the disillusion was very deeply felt. Greed, famous swindles, spectacular bankruptcies – all well publicized – bred further dismay. Exploitation and the human misery it caused provided the final condemnation. It was then that the continuing legend of literary Luddism was born.

But it has always had an internal hierarchy of moral disapproval – not all aspects of industry and commerce were equally deplorable.

[41] See, for example, W. H. Auden. *I Believe*, quoted in Warburg, op. cit., pp. 141–4.
[42] W. H. Auden, *I Believe* (1941), p. 21.
[43] John Pudney, 'Industrial Landscape', *Ten Summers* (1944). Quoted in Warburg, op. cit., p. 131.

Literary Luddism amongst the poets embraced a vast range of attitudes, and those attitudes did not develop simultaneously or unanimously. The Mechanical Muse was at first admiring, then condemning and has settled into uneasy ambivalence – half suspicion and half nostalgia. The Industrial Muse was at first doubtful but prepared to be impressed, then, with odd exceptions, violently hostile when the promised progress was blighted by industrial squalor and commercial exploitation; and this hostility has, on the whole, been well sustained. The Commercial Muse, when not silent, has rarely deviated from hostility; the Business Muse is barely perceptible; the Entrepreneurial Muse is almost non-existent.

Poets could, on occasion, sing in praise of the mechanic and the inventor – Watt actually achieved semi-divine status in verse, and Brindley was held up as an example for British youth to emulate – but the poets never sang in praise of profit, and profit achieved by commercial ingenuity alone was always highly suspect.

Here the decision was moral, not aesthetic. One would not expect a poet to find much magic in the manufacturer of ball bearings, but it is significant that he would find much less in those who sold them. Production was allowed certain modest virtues. Selling was allowed none. Prospering through the mere manipulation of money was even worse: Tennyson's 'vast speculation' typified greed and dishonesty.

Where there was a love-hate relationship, hate usually surfaced as the dominant emotion. In this the poets both reflected social attitudes and strengthened them. They gave voice to a disappointment which was widespread amongst the most influential classes in Britain. Not all of that disappointment was humanitarian. Much of it was financial. It should not be forgotten that the vast speculative manias owed much to the greed of the powerful few: 'A return called for by Parliament, to show the number of persons who had subscribed more than £2,000 in railway undertakings, included the names of 900 lawyers, 364 bankers, 257 clergymen and 157 Members of Parliament besides large numbers of noblemen, merchants and manufacturers.'[44] Wordsworth and Tennyson were in good company, and the disappointment and anger they felt when the speculative bubbles burst was very widespread.

But this was an area which they left to the novelist to dissect in detail and to apportion blame. They left the novelist to particularize. Where the poets accused, the novelists have convicted. The novel

[44] R. S. Lambert, *Railway King* (1934), pp. 166–7.

offered greater potential for exploring in detail the motives and moral responsiblities of the businessman. And the Victorians amply exploited that potential. As with the poets, though, there was an early phase of appreciation – more patronising and less ecstatic than Erasmus Darwin or Ebenezer Elliott but nevertheless aware of the businessman's important economic role.

In the first heady days of the Industrial Revolution there was a very real excitement about the potentialities of industry. The early show-piece factories like Etruria were enthusiastically inspected by troops of visiting aristocracy. There was even an active market in romantically drawn prints of such prestigious seats of industry as Coalbrookdale. Bridges, canals and viaducts received the awed admiration which we reserve for cathedrals. The men responsible for these marvels were looked at with both respect and admiration: these men had 'ten times the endurance, energy, and mind of the old type', said Henry Adams later.[45] Their own optimism and self-confidence in their powers were infectious.

Even some of the literary world was prepared to be impressed. 'I shall never forget Mr. Boulton's expression to me: "I have here, Sir, what all the world desires to have – POWER",' recorded Boswell in his life of Johnson.[46]

And that most didactic form of literature – children's books – was full of the authors' instructive admiration of industry and manufacture. Little children were solemnly informed that 'there is much more entertainment in seeing a pin made than in many fashionable diversions': they were further advised that 'if you see extensive manufacture in any nation you can be sure it is a civilized nation'.[47] The authors of these improving works took what solace they could from the eighteenth century poets, and quoted Thomson to show how INDUSTRY improved the lot of MAN, as it

> Tore from his limbs the blood polluted fur
> And wrapt him in the woolly vestment warm.

More prosaically they instructed the young that 'mechanics and chemistry' were 'the two sciences which most assist the manufacturer'. They kept the infant reader informed about significant industrial

---

[45] Henry Adams, *The Education of Henry Adams* (1964), p. 297.
[46] James Boswell, *Life of Johnson* (1963 edition), p. 704.
[47] Mrs. Barbauld and Dr. Aiken, *Evenings at Home or the Juvenile Budget Opened* (Dublin, 1794). I am indebted to Mr. Peter Oborne for this reference.

breakthroughs: 'by chemistry an ingenious gentleman has lately found out a way of bleaching a piece of cloth in eight and forty hours, which by the common process would have taken a great many weeks'.[48] In these books fathers directed their sons' attention to the great industrialists like Josiah Wedgwood and Sir Richard Arkwright whose achievements deserved their admiration.

> *Father:* 'You have heard of Sir Richard Arkwright who . . . invented, or at least perfected, a machine by which one pair of hands may do the work of twenty or thirty; and, as in this country everyone is free to rise by merit, he acquired the largest fortune in the country, had a great many hundreds of workmen under his orders, and had leave given him by the King to put Sir before his name[49] . . . Arkwright used to say, that if he had time to perfect his inventions, he would put the fleece of wool into a box, and it should come out broadcloth.'
>
> *Son:* 'What did he mean by that; was there any fairy in the box to turn it into broadcloth with her wand?'
>
> *Father:* 'He was assisted by the only fairies which have the power of transformation, Art and Industry: he meant that he could contrive so many machines, wheel within wheel, that the combing, carding, and other various operations should be performed by mechanism, almost without the hand of man.'[50]

When the preternaturally dutiful son asks 'What are the chief Manufactures of England', he was doubtless relieved when his honest as well as well-informed father concedes 'We have at present a greater variety than I can pretend to enumerate'. Nevertheless he still gets a brisk lecture on the merits of Manchester and the wonder of Birmingham, and as a finale a detailed tribute to Josiah Wedgwood ('an excellent chymist, and a man of great taste') who together with his partner Thomas Bentley ('another man of taste') 'has made our clay more valuable than the finest porcelain of China. He has moulded it into all the forms of grace and beauty that are to be met with in the precious marbles of the Greek and Etruscan artists. . . . In short, he has given to our houses a classic air, and has made every saloon and every dining-room schools of taste.'[51]

---

[48] This was, in fact, one of the most significant advances in the textile industries which can properly be attributed to chemistry.

[49] One rather warms to the son, who asked 'Did that do him any good?'

[50] Mrs. Barbauld and Dr. Aiken, *Evenings at Home.* . . .

[51] Ibid. The information was impressively accurate, even down to the source of Wedgwood's designs and the extent of his exports. As an instructive treat the son is promised a visit to Wedgwood's showrooms.

Adult fiction felt less inclined to inform its readers of the wonders of our burgeoning industries, and even less to sing the praises of the first great entrepreneurs. Little of this early admiration and respect penetrated the English novel before 1830. The Industrial Revolution itself was rarely mentioned in fiction and there are very few full length portraits of industrialists in this period. As Gossman has shown, Jane Austen was not alone in her preference for the social problems of the old order.[52]

But it is significant that in the few early examples – whether actually written early or written later but written about the early period of industrialization – the industrialist fares probably better than any time during the last two hundred years. In John Galt's *Annals of the Parish* (1821), Mr. Cayenne, his cotton lord, 'exists in a golden age of manufacturing, a time in which he does not meet with the kind of resistance that was to come a generation later from both the working classes and the landed interests.'[53] Galt feels no need to account for the failings of the new class and Mr. Cayenne emerges as a mixture of choleric humour and benevolence, much in the eighteenth century literary tradition of the typical country squire.

When Mrs. Craik set her novel *John Halifax, Gentleman*, which was published in 1856, in the first quarter of the nineteenth century, she felt able to produce a truly sympathetic, almost heroic industrialist – a gentleman not by the accident of birth, but by virtue of the moral absolutes. *John Halifax, Gentleman* was a Victorian best seller. Its sales – 250,000 by 1897 – were an eloquent tribute to the existence of a need for an alternative to the Luddite view.[54] Her novel became 'to many a draughtsman, tradesman and hard-handed toiler, on both sides of the Atlantic, a dear companion and a household name'.[55]

When James Kay-Shuttleworth set *Scarsdale* (1974) in the 1830s, he includes both the general run of manufacturers who 'are men risen from the ranks, illiterate, of a coarse mould, contracted ideas and selfish habits', and an admired élite of the 'highest and most intellectual' manufacturers.[56] Among these the Holtes were cast as the protégés of

---

[52] Norbert Gossman, 'Political Social Themes in the English Popular Novel, 1815–1832', *Public Opinion Quarterly*, 20 (1956), pp. 531–41.

[53] Melada, *The Captains of Industry in English Fiction, 1821–71*, p. 91.

[54] Louisa Parr, 'Dinah Mulock (Mrs. Craik)' in *Women Novelists of Queen Victoria's Reign* (1897), p. 248.

[55] W. M. Parker, Introduction to *John Halifax, Gentleman* (1961), p. vii. Quoted Melada, p. 172.

[56] *Scarsdale*, p. 47.

[56] *Scarsdale*, p. 47. Quoted Melada, p. 20.

the aristocracy. They were patronised but they were approved of. They deserved 'the success of their honest endeavours'. They were 'the chief manufacturer of the district', but they knew their place. However admirable their son he was not fit for Sir Guy's daughter – and Holte with his 'quiet confidence but . . . marked deference' recognized the fact.[57] The social message of the novel is that 'England's role as an industrial power depended on the manufacturing classes, but the landed gentry still had an important function . . . which the early captains of industry would have done well to emulate'.[58] The message of most of Victorian fiction was less accommodating and the verdict on the manufacturer much less flattering than those of Galt, Craik and Kay-Shuttleworth.

The social gap recognized by Kay-Shuttleworth was in many cases to widen not close, and one of the reasons appears in another novel of his. In *Ribblesdale*, or *Lancashire Sixty Years Ago* (1974), it was religious non-conformity, which kept the classes even further apart. 'If to these distinctions were added Puritanical non-conformity . . . the causes of repugnancy were complete between a family of humble origins engaged in trade, and one like that of Sir Hubert Noel, proud of its long line of ancestry'.[59] That was a mild condemnation when compared with Lancelot Smith's denunciation in Charles Kingsley's novel *Yeast* (1848) of the 'frantic Mammon-hunting which has been for the last fifty years the peculiar pursuit of the majority of Quakers, Dissenters and Religious Churchmen . . . Puritanism has interdicted them to all art, all excitement, all amusement – except money making. It is their *dernier resort*, poor souls'.[60]

This was a characteristic prejudice, but there were more potent objections than those of the manufacturers' religion. By the 1840s even being or becoming an Anglican could not save the industrialist from the charge of being responsible for destroying the old patriarchal feudal order, for causing untold human mistery in the factories, and for causing the panics which followed the collapse of the recurrent financial manias of the nineteenth century.

Perhaps the most potent objection of all however, certainly the most persistent and pervasive objection was that of social snobbery. This was always one of the major obstacles for the industrialist to overcome.

[57] Quoted Melada, op. cit., p. 21.
[58] Melada, op. cit., p. 24.
[59] *Ribblesdale*, p. 42.
[60] Charles Kingsley, *Yeast: A Problem* (1848), pp. 36–67.

What has been called the 'horror of parvenuism' existed throughout the whole period. It was rampant in Victorian England, and apparent even in the late eighteenth century. Even James Watt, who was more respected than most, complained that 'Our landed gentlemen ... reckon us poor mechanics no better than the slaves who cultivate their vineyards';[61] another complained that 'the proud and bigoted landowners look down with contempt on the merchant and the manufacturer';[61] and Thomas Gisborne condemned 'the aristocratic prejudices and the envious contempt of ... [those] ... proud of their rank and ancient family, who even in these days occasionally disgrace themselves by looking down on the man raised by merit and industry from obscurity to eminence'.[62] Even before the economic disasters of the nineteenth century which so damaged their reputation there were those who were reluctant to accept them. Their titles were often the labels of sarcasm: as when Cobbett derisorily played on the term 'cotton lords' in an address to 'My LORDS SEIGNEURS of the Twist, sovereigns of the Spinning Jenny', or mocked the 'great Yeoman of the Yarn', 'the Lords of the Loom', and the 'iron Gentlemen'.[63]

The examples of snobbery are legion. They are too well known to need repeating. But one feels that the industrialist might more easily have overcome *this* objection if it had not been for the arrival of others. It was the consequences of the slumps and depressions of the nineteenth century which the novelists could not forgive. The social consequences of unemployment, the child and female labour, the long hours and the foul factory conditions bred humanitarian concern for the working classes; falling prices, dividends and profits bred financial concern for themselves by the middle and upper classes. Together they bred an emotional indictment of industry and business which is with us still.

The slump of 1839–42 was as traumatic an experience as the unemployment of the 1930s: both scarred the social consciences of a generation. And the events of the second quarter of the nineteenth century left as indelible an impression on the moral sensibilities of Victorian writers and critics as the events of the second quarter of the twentieth century have left on the folk memory of the unions and on modern industrial relations.

[61] Witt Bowden, op. cit., pp. 155 and 35.
[62] T. Gisborne, *Enquiry into the Duties of Men in the Higher and Middle Classes of Society in Great Britain* (1794).
[63] *The Opinion of William Cobbett*, ed. G. D. H. Cole and Margaret Cole (1944), p. 171.

It is in the great depression of 1839–42 that the British industrialist first really earned the black literary reputation that has stuck to him to this day. The great novels may have come rather later but the lasting attitudes were formed for many in the polemical controversy which grew out of the terrible sufferings of the workforce at this time. There was in any case no need to wait for the verdict of the great. The lesser lights leapt more nimbly into print.

Women novelists were amongst the first to deliver society's censure; and Mrs. Trollope, Mrs. Tonna and Mrs. Stone all delivered powerful contributions to the condemnation of the manufacturer between 1839 and 1842. Mrs. Stone was the most balanced of the three. In her novel *William Langshawe, the Cotton Lord* (1842), there were vulgar tyrannical manufacturers like John Balshawe with sensual sons like John Balshawe Junior 'a low-lived libertine, carrying, in the indulgence of his brutal pleasures, shame and sorrow to the lowly hearths of those whom his father was bound by every tie of decency and morality to protect and cherish'.[64] But there was also Mr. Ainsley, 'a self-made gentleman' who 'acquired his hard-earned accomplishments entirely in the intervals of a laborious business'.[65] In between there were William Langshawe who although vulgar and ostentatious was both liberal and kind 'in his domestic establishment' and just 'in his mercantile one'. 'His operatives respected him, his domestics loved him'.[66] But for all Mrs. Stone's good intentions the memorable portrait, and usually the quoted one, is that of the licentious John Balshawe Junior.

Mrs. Stone's work was a deliberate and self-avowed attempt to avoid a partisan attitude. Mrs. Trollope and Mrs. Tonna had no such scruples. Both were inspired by powerful Tory nostalgia for the past and they had no doubts that the 'millocrats' (Mrs. Trollope first coined the phrase) were the chief enemies of the old order. They struck a welcome political chord for many then, and they strike it for many still, which doubtless accounts for their contemporary popularity and their later survival – it is difficult to think that literary merit could account for it.

Mrs. Trollope went straight for the jugular. Her millowners are monsters of depravity. They differ mainly only in the way their wickedness expresses itself. Sir Matthew Dowling in *Michael Armstrong* (1839–40) is given his deserts by Mrs. Trollope when he lies on his

[64] Elizabeth Stone, *William Langshawe, the Cotton Lord*, pp. 124–5.
[65] Ibid., p. 68.
[66] Ibid., p. 125.

deathbed, bankrupt both morally and financially, 'haunted by the dangling broken limbs of all the factory children maimed and killed in his employ'.[67] Lady Clarissa delivers a splendidly wifely epitaph when she says of him that he is 'abominable, wicked, low-born, brutal, treacherous', a 'pitiful, cheating, brutal, manufacturing savage'.[68] It provides a nice touch that the aristocratic Lady Clarissa saved up the word 'manufacturing' as the final telling stroke in her crescendo of hate against her dying husband.

Mrs. Tonna saved herself from the dangers of creative fiction by copying down the worst abuses unearthed by the Factory Inspectors and proclaiming them typical. Mrs. Tonna did not believe in impartiality. She believed in polemic. A perfect example of the proponent of the prelapsarian myth, she longed for a golden past – 'a patriarchal, agrarian England wherein the country squire and not the cotton lord was the master of man'.[69] Her *Helen Fleetwood* has been called 'a sermon addressed to a nation going to the devil'[69] and there was little doubt who was cast in that satanic role. As a French critic wrote it was 'Une dissertation, non une oeuvre d'art . . . une traité d'apologétique chrétienne, où Satan prend la forme du manufacturier'.[70]

Instead of the idyllic patriarchal relations of old England, the factories had introduced hotbeds of sedition and false religion. In them 'the blight of Popery noiselessly spreads';[71] souls 'perish(ed) while their poor bodies are worn out by hard and cruel labour to swell his unholy gains';[72] sexual evil flourished unchecked (the heat of the factory rooms was held to hatch abominable vices, and the close proximity of the sexes to encourage some pretty ordinary ones); but worst of all 'the unutterable curse of socialism' was spread in them by men 'of whom it is hard to think otherwise than as of an actual incarnation of Satan'. Words almost fail her, but, 'It will suffice to say that some half dozen of the young men in the mill had become Socialists. Beyond that it was impossible to go – Socialism is the *ne plus ultra* of six thousand years' laborious experience on the part of the great enemy of man – it is the moral Gorgon upon which whomsoever can be compelled to look must wither away: it is the doubly denounced woe upon the

[67] *Michael Armstrong* (1839–42), p. 345.
[68] Ibid.
[69] Melada, op. cit., pp. 96–101.
[70] Louis Cazamian, *Le Roman Social en Angleterre, 1830–1930* (Paris, 1934), p. 157.
[71] Charlotte Elizabeth Tonna, *Helen Fleetwood* (1839–40), p. 170.
[72] Ibid., pp. 91–2.

inhabitors of the earth – the last effort of Satanic venom wrought to the madness of rage by the consciousness of his shortened time'.[73] On Judgement Day, Mrs. Tonna required the Lord to use capital letters to ask 'WHO SLEW ALL THESE?', but she was sure that He would already know that only Satan could preach that fate worse than death – a belief in socialism.

Mrs. Tonna's solution was to restore power to the landed aristocracy. They in turn would restore their idyllic patriarchal relations with their workers which the millowners had destroyed.[74] Curiously enough she had powerful allies on the left. For the *Communist Manifesto* also held the new industrial class responsible for putting 'an end to all feudal, patriarchal, idyllic relations. It has pitilessly torn asunder the motley feudal ties that bound man to his "natural superiors" and has left remaining no other nexus between man and man than naked self-interest, the callous "cash-payment". It has drowned the most heavenly ecstasies of religious fervour, of chivalrous enthusiasm, of Philistine sentimentalism in the icy water of egotistical calculation.'[75]

Caught between the cross-fire of those who fervently condemned from the Right, and those who bitterly accused from the Left, and those who expressed their disappointed humanitarianism from the committed centre, 'Not against TOIL, but TOIL's excess we pray',[76] the reputation of the industrialist as harbinger of progress had little hope of survival. The ogre of the factory was firmly established. Dickens's Gradgrind and Bounderby ensured that it would never be forgotten. Whether portrayed in terms of Bounderby bullying or Gradgrind's cold reasonings, or Dombey's moral bankruptcy, or Merdle's financial manoeuvres, Dickens's men of business greatly enriched the Luddite tradition. It mattered little if he exaggerated, for however melodramatic the monster, however atypical of the industrialist classes, the critics insisted upon the truth behind the caricature. Dickens was right, declared Ruskin: his readers 'will find much that is partial and because partial, apparently unjust; but if they

---

[73] Ibid., p. 168.

[74] The rural idyll was the popular contemporary alternative to the intolerable situation in the industrial cities. In the country 'poverty could still be honest'. It is true that emigration was the alternative in Mrs. Gaskell's *Mary Barton* or Paul Pimlico's *The Manufacturer* but they were the exceptions.

[75] Marx and Engels, *The Communist Manifesto*, pp. 9–10. They did not, of course, agree with Mrs. Tonna's cure.

[76] Caroline Norton, *A Voice from the Factories*.

examine all the evidence on the other side, which Dickens seems to overlook, it will appear, after all that trouble that his view was finally the right one, grossly and sharply told.'[77] When Dickens attempted to give the good employer his due by portraying the Cheeryble brothers of *Nicholas Nickleby* (1838–39), the critics reacted by denouncing them as 'monstrosities of benevolence'. They are variously dismissed as 'stupid', 'gruesome', 'nauseous' and 'thoroughly tiresome'.[78] Finally they are 'incredible'. Despite the fact that they were explicitly based on the Brothers Grant, Manchester calico printers (a fact which Dickens confirmed in convincing detail), the critics refused to believe that such 'babies could ever have been successful in business'.[79] The Cheeryble brothers did not 'fit' the Luddite view so they were rejected. Not surprisingly they proved more attractive to the Smilesian tradition and in Smiles they are duly honoured, as reflections of their factual counterparts, the Grants.

If the grinders of the industrial poor took a well recorded and well remembered drubbing in Victorian fiction, the financial speculators, the railway promoters, the entrepreneurs behind the great joint stock companies kept them ignominious company.

The titles of joint stock companies leave little doubt about the authors' attitudes. Dickens's 'United Metropolitan Improved Hot Muffin and Crumpet Baking and Punctual Delivery Company' is too indulgently comic to really strike home; in Samuel Warren's 'Gunpowder and Fresh Water Company' and the 'Artificial Rain Company' the satirical edge is sharper; and Charles Lever's 'The Grand Glengariff Villa Allotment and Marine Residence Company' sounds suitably phoney;[80] and Dickens's later 'Eden Land Corporation' or the 'Anglo-Bengalee Disinterested Loan and Life Assurance Company' or George Gissing's 'Irish Dairy Company' all have that right note of dishonest promise which lured the investors in.[81]

The names of those who masterminded these companies offered equally clear pointers to their likely moral standing: Sir Sharper Bubble, Davenport Dunn, Sir Gavial Mantrap, Mr. Lassmann of

---

[77] John Ruskin, 'A Note on Hard Times', in *The Dickens Critics*, ed. George H. Ford and Laurent Lane, Jr. (Ithaca, N.Y., 1961), pp. 47–78.

[78] Melada, op. cit., pp. 107–8.

[79] Ibid.

[80] Dickens in *Nicholas Nickleby* (1838–39); Warren in *Ten Thousand a Year* (1841); and Lever in *Davenport Dunn: A Man of Our Day* (1857–59).

[81] Dickens in *Martin Chuzzlewit* (1843–44), and Gissing in *Demos* (1880).

Grapnell and Co.[82] Those who were not actually labelled as swindlers and cheaters, usually announced it pretty quickly by their actions or their words. 'We companies are all birds of prey', says Dickens's Montague Tigg, 'mere birds of prey'.[83] The golden hearted were not difficult to recognize either. When Wilkie Collins has one of his characters condemn, in *Fallen Leaves* (1878–79), those 'organized systems of imposture, masquerading under the disguise of banks and companies . . . with the shameless falsification of accounts, and the merciless ruin of thousands on thousands of victims' it comes as little surprise to learn that his name is Amelius Goldenheart. In their dealings with men of business and finance, the Victorian authors did not insist on over-subtlety.

The Victorian reader came so to identify evil with such activities that Thackeray has only to mention a company in *The Newcomers* (1853–55) to alert them to their correct responses. When the expected disaster occurs Thackeray admits to his readers 'Yes, sir or madam, you are quite right in the opinion which you have held all along regarding the Bundelcund Banking Company in which our Colonel has invested every rupee he possesses', and tells them that 'whenever I have had occasion to mention the company I have scarcely been able to refrain from breaking out into fierce diatribes against that complicated, enormous, outrageous swindle'.[84]

The businessman's image became so tarnished that his appearance in fiction, like the demon king on the stage, was usually the cue for public hostility, but in case they were taken in by apparent virtue, the Victorian readers were repeatedly warned to be on their guard against the spurious respectability conferred by conventional signs of recognition and worldly success. Davenport Dunn is honoured by the government as 'a man of successful industry', his political and financial power is immense, but his real worth is revealed by the heroine who describes him as 'a man of nothing . . . trading on the rich man's hoard and the poor man's pittance, making market of all, even to his patriotism'.[85]

---

[82] In respectively Samuel Warren's *Ten Thousand A Year* (1841), Charles Lever's *Davenport Dunn* (1857–59), and George Eliot's *The Impressions of Theophrastus Such* (1879) and *Daniel Deronda* (1876).

[83] In *Martin Chuzzlewit* (1843–44). Another novelist announced her intentions in the title of her novel: Miss Braddon: *Birds of Prey* (1867).

[84] Quoted in John R. Reed, *Victorian Conventions* (1975), p. 178.

[85] Ibid., p. 181.

Even when the author's intention was to attack his readers' *own* greed and *their* commitment to Mammon, the character who symbolizes that greed by exploiting it almost inevitably carried the odium into posterity. Charles Lever's intention was to criticize the misplaced values of a whole nation which 'intending to honour Industry . . . had paid its homage to Money';[86] Robert Bell's intention in *The Ladder of Gold* (1850) was to warn the public against its own greed and gullibility when faced with the apparent financial wizardry of Richard Rawlings;[87] Dickens's intention in *Our Mutual Friend* (1864–65) was to indict the general lust for gain and society's uncritical admiration of money making – if men of no moral stature could command respect simply by the possession of shares, he argued, then 'Have no antecedents, no established character, no cultivation, no ideas, no manners; have Shares. Have shares enough to be on Boards of Direction in capital letters, oscillate on mysterious business between London and Paris and be great. Where does he come from? Shares. Where is he going? Shares. Has he any principles? Shares. . . . Sufficient answer to all; Shares.'[88]

Their intentions may well have been achieved. Society may well have felt guilt at its own greed. Those who galloped so eagerly into the railway manias, or helped to inflate the bubble companies, may have recognized their own folly. But they were also provided with a scapegoat. They were given someone to blame. They were only too willing to do so: since in the last third of the nineteenth century investors lost their money in one of every three bubble companies, and limited liability enabled the financial entrepreneurs to fleece the middle class investors.[89] Many of the Victorian reading public must have identified eagerly with the fictional victims of the frantic pursuit of easy profits. The novelists helped to concentrate their rage and their disappointment on to an easily identifiable target. Their self pity helped to focus their prejudices on those incarnations of Mammon-worship – the entrepreneur and the man of business. The ultimate condemnation of Victorian society was put into the mouth of Dickens's Mr. Morfin when he said 'We are so d . . . . d business like'.[90]

[86] Quoted Melada, p. 45.
[87] Rawlings was based on George Hudson, the railway king.
[88] *Our Mutual Friend* (1864–65), pp. 136–7.
[89] See H. A. Shannon, 'The Limited Companies of 1866–1883', in *Essays in Economic History*, ed. E. M. Carus Wilson (1954).
[90] *Dombey and Son* (1848). Quoted in Reed, op. cit., p. 184.

This is not, of course, the whole story. Even at the height of the businessman's unpopularity Mrs. Gaskell produced a highly sympathetic portrait of a manufacturer in the dynamic character of John Thornton in *North and South* (1855). Significantly Mrs. Gaskell felt the need to ease her readers into the unusual position of having an industrialist to admire by allowing her heroine, Miss Hale, to voice the standard genteel objection to 'all who have something tangible to sell',[91] and to ask indignantly 'What in the world do manufacturers want with classics, or literature, or the accomplishments of a gentleman?'.[92] Eventually her haughty dislike softens into admiration and love, but Thornton's metamorphosis, under *her* influence, is more dramatic. The millowner, symbol of the industrial North, is given an education in sensibility by the Hales, representatives of the cultural and moral values of the agricultural South. Thornton 'sheds his ideas of economic individualism for a sense of social responsibility'.[93] The strike breaker, the exponent of the need to undersell, the proud self-made man with his contempt for the poor is transformed into a firm but sympathetic employer genuinely concerned for the welfare of his men and conducting progressive experiments in industrial relations. Mrs. Gaskell's final verdict is unquestionably favourable, and Thornton is allowed to become one of the most attractive industrialists in British fiction.[94]

There was, of course, an alternative tradition – albeit a weaker one – outside fiction. There were apostles of the self-made man, there were political economists who fully recognized the value of the industrialist, and there were political apologists ready and willing to justify his role.[95] My intention here is merely to point out how small a part that tradition played in the mainstream of English literature, and how influential that literature and its Luddite convictions have been·in forming our cultural and moral attitudes to business and the businessman.

What is significant is how much less dominant and how much less

---

[91] The nice distinctions observed between production and selling is provided by her father, 'Don't call . . . manufacturers, tradesmen, Margaret. . . . They are very different'. *North and South*, p. 59.

[92] Ibid., p. 34.

[93] Melada, op. cit., p. 147.

[94] The tradition of the ironic panegyric was cunningly exploited by some novelists to allow their readers to enjoy, say, Dickens's encomium on Merdle's greatness without recognizing the irony.

[95] Some general introductions have already been published as preludes to this piece. Further introductions are planned as sequels. Together they will, I hope, fill some of the gaps in this discussion.

influential literature and the literary critics of industrialization have been in other cultures. For Britain is not, of course, alone in possessing a Luddite tradition – it is a recognizable element in most European literatures. Balzac could be as devastating in his dissection of men of business as could Dickens; and the French poets travelled much the same route to disillusion as did the English. One can parallel the rejection of Mammon in the disdainful reaction to 'le Dieu de l'or'. One can echo the sense that too much was being attempted too soon in Alfred de Vigny's reaction to the railway

> Sur ce taureau de fer qui fume, souffle et beugle
> L'homme a monté trop tôt.

One finds the same feeling that industrial man has overreached himself

> Nous nous sommes joués à plus fort que nous tous.[96]

In Germany too the Luddite tradition is easy to identify. In recent years its satirical version has flourished and its exponents gained an international reputation, but it had managed to co-exist with an alternative tradition. Where Ruskin and Arnold and Leavis have seemed determined to crush their utilitarian opponents, the Germans have been content to mock theirs. The intensity of the fight to control the schools and the universities, and the values they instil, has seemed less grim.

Perhaps as a result, just as the *Grandes Ecoles* system allows for the necessity of vocational training at the highest levels of French education, so Germany has designed a system which allows the Luddite and the utilitarian traditions to co-exist.

Where in England the public schools and the grammar schools were divided on essentially class lines and monopolized most of the available talent,[97] the German system was divided functionally – the more purely

---

[96] Alfred de Vigny, 'La Maison du Berger' in *Les Destinées* (ed. by V. L. Saulnier, 1967), p. 45. In fact de Vigny reacted much as the Victorian poets of Britain did, 'la haine des cités étouffantes et de certain progrès industriel, invitant à la retroite rustique'. Ibid., p. 19. The only consolation which de Vigny found in the railways was hardly economic!

> Béni soit le Commerce au hardi caducée,
> Si l'Amour que tourmente une sombre pensée
> Peut franchir en un jour deux grandes nations.

[97] Both systems offered incidentally a very similar syllabus, and those grammar schools which aped the public school (and they were the majority) attempted to instil very similar values. The syllabus despised the utilitarian, the purer the science the better, but better no science at all; the values strongly favoured the mandarin society and not the industrial.

academic went to the *Gymnasium*, and those seeking more vocational training went to the *Realschule* and the *Oberrealschule*. The gap in esteem is still very small. In the same way the *Technische Hochschule* provided a prestigious alternative to the traditional university pre-occupation with the purer disciplines. Even Victorian commentators envied the flow of trained chemists and engineers who gave Germany such a decisive lead in the new high technology industries at the turn of the century. Even more important their achievements kept alive the esteem of the world of business. Any educational system which absorbs much of the country's academic talent will keep its prestige.

The Law Schools and the Business Schools performed a similar important function in America. So many of the best minds go to them that they simply cannot be denied. Where in Britain the ablest and the most ambitious head unerringly for the prestigious slots in the mandarin world, in America many more enter industry or those professions which allow an easy interchange with business.

The evidence suggests that where a prestigious alternative system exists the Luddite values will not be automatically accepted. The corrective voice of the Luddite tradition has not gone unheard in these countries. It has thundered against the evils of an uncritical acceptance of the profit motive, it has mocked the values of corporate man, it has alerted society to the dangers of pollution, it has informed the consumer of the perils of built-in obsolescence, it has acted as an aesthetic conscience bewailing the worst that industrial design can inflict upon us, but it has not persuaded its readers that 'the life of . . . industry and commerce is degrading', best 'left to lesser fellows'.[98]

What is so striking is that although Mark Twain's *The Gilded Age: A Tale of Today* (1873), and William S. Dean Howell's *The Rise of Silas Lapham* (1885) provide an American counterpart of Trollope's *The Way We Live Now* (1874–75), American literary Luddism has never managed to deprive the American entrepreneur of his status and esteem. It was certainly not for want of criticism either then or now. As a class American businessmen were typified, in a novel published in 1903, as 'case-hardened, supremely selfish . . . fouled with the clutchings and grapplings of the attack, besmirched with the elbowing of low associates and obscure allies'. They set their 'feet towards conquest . . . now in merciless assault, beating the fallen enemy underfoot; now in repulse, equally merciless, trampling down the auxiliaries of the day before, in a panic dash for safety'. Frank Norris's final verdict

[98] Annan, loc. cit.

on the businessman was unambiguously hostile: he was 'always cruel, always selfish, always pitiless'.[99] Later the attack was on his faceless impersonality, like J. P. Marquand's portrayal of Willis Wayde as 'a type interchangeable with any photograph on the financial pages of the *New York Times*. It was hard to tell about these people, who had all been processed in the same way, but he was essentially an American type'.[100] Even more recently he has been criticized by making him seem absurdly comic, as in J. P. Donleavy's *A Fairy Tale in New York City*[101] where Cornelius Christian blows, and is blown, through the corridors of American business in a marvellously effective satire. Whether selling death or car batteries, the businessmen are no match for our cultivated, articulate and witty hero. He has on occasion to associate with them to earn his bread between bouts of frenzied sexual endeavour. But his superiority, his separateness, his immunity from their ideology is always clear. He caps their jokes, seduces their wives, laughs at their values, is effortlessly (almost unintentionally) better at what they try so hard and so earnestly to do. He floats through life in mocking triumph at their pathetic dedication to making money and their even more pathetic belief in the value of doing so. In Donleavy's company we have travelled a very long way from Dreiser's Frank Algernon Cowperwood, the man of business who stalked like a hungry wolf through the defenceless folds of those he so ruthlessly exploited.[102] But whether the subject of bitter attack as merciless robber baron,[103] of subtle send up as 'the bland leading the bland', or of hilarious satire, the American businessman has retained much of his status: 'a stream of unfavourable portraits from Charlie Anderson to Babitt has not made any noticeable effect on American youth. They have swallowed both the success books and the novels of protest, and gone on to business school.'[104]

Lewis and Stewart conclude that 'the public image of the American businessman seems little affected by the novelist', but the fact is that in America the novels of protest and satire are running against a fundamental American belief that 'business remains, by and large, the

[99] Frank Norris, *The Pit: A Story of Chicago* (London, 1903).
[100] J. P. Marquand, *Sincerely Willis Wayde* (1955).
[101] Published in 1976.
[102] See Theodore Dreiser, *The Financier* (1912, new edition 1968), p. 441.
[103] For a fuller discussion of this point, see Neil McKendrick, 'General Introduction' to R. J. Overy, *William Morris, Viscount Nuffield* (1976), pp. xxvii–xxxi.
[104] Ray Lewis and Rosemary Stewart, *The Boss: The Life and Times of the British Business Man* (1958), p. 214.

American way of life and private enterprise the right system for God's own country'.[105] In America there *are* major and prestigious business schools to go to. In America the success books *are* ubiquitously presented as an effective antidote. The American business man has been better served by the American historians than his British counterpart. He has been far better served by the press – 'the businessman in America is presented by the press as the embodiment of the success which the average Americans would like to achieve'.[107] And 'because the Americans like business they like reading about it too . . . there is nothing in Britain to compare with . . . *Fortune* or *Harvard Business Reviews*'.[108] They even like hearing about some of them, and there is a rich literature of folk song recalling and celebrating the achievements of the American railway engineer and his role in opening up the country.

For all the controversy which surrounds the American man of business few Americans doubt his importance. The contrast with Britain is difficult to avoid: 'Every perceptive European visitor to America perceives that, in a society lacking Europe's aristocratic and medieval distinctions the captain of industry is a hero-type for adult men and women.'[109]

In Britain the Luddite values of so much of our literature are reinforced by the predominant attitudes of our class system, our schools

[105] Lewis and Stewart, op. cit., p. 215.
[106] Benjamin Franklin was one of the earliest Americans to write such a success book modelled on the examples of past men of business. He has had plenty of followers: from A. McCurdy's *Win Who Will*, or *The Young Man's Key to Fortune* (1872), through Walter R. Houghton's *Kings of Fortune* (1889) and James Burnley's *Millionaires and Kings of Enterprise* (1901); right up to the modern *How to Win Success before Forty* and the famous *How to Win Friends and Influence People*. There was a similar tradition in Britain between 1850 and 1880 but like so many voices praising the entrepreneurial ideal, it has grown very faint compared with the influential organs of the Luddite tradition. See Neil McKendrick, 'In Search of a Secular Ideal, op. cit., p. xvi.
[107] Lewis and Stewart, op. cit., p. 206. See also Sigmund Diamond, *The Reputation of the American Business Man* (1955).
[108] *Fortune* was reputed to be read by 38 per cent of top executives in 1957 and the latter by 24 per cent: see 'New Dimensions in Top Executive Reading', *Harvard Business Review*, Sept./Oct. 1957.
[109] Graham Hutton, *We Too Can Prosper* (1953), p. 40. 'The American businessman is . . much more part of the main stream of American life – indeed he is the parent river. He mixes with, and often interchanges with, diplomats, defence chiefs, and professors. An interchange which is comparatively rare in Britain.' See Lewis and Stewart, op. cit., p. 205.

and our universities. Literary Luddism was primarily a symptom not a cause of our disenchantment with business and industry. But with so many effective allies it is nearing the status of an additional cause. For it is, of course, a very potent source of confirmation of values and beliefs. It is imbibed at an early age and the values it teaches are difficult to alter – or even refine. There are very few antidotes available in Britain. Historians have done little to redeem the balance. Indeed some would say that the historical tradition is as Luddite as the critical tradition. The massively influential voices have seen little merit in industry. Not since Macaulay has there been a really effective trumpeter of the value of progress. And 'in the eyes of a generation which learnt economic history from the Hammonds, every business man is the grandson, or great-grandson, of Mr. Gradgrind'.[110] There sometimes seems to have been the same unholy alliance between the Left and the Right to denigrate industry in history as in literature: the Left inspired by political opposition to capitalism and the Right inspired by nostalgia for a golden rural age in which men knew their place and were kept firmly in it by the unquestioned authority of the landed classes. But the more influential and committed voice has been that of literature and the literary critics. In the propaganda war the businessman has been heavily out-gunned. The instant backlash against any attempt to sing the praises of technology, or to point out the value of those involved in the creation of wealth, has been startling in its strength and intensity. Mild attempts to point to the importance of science, technology or industry, persuasive appeals to the need for a healthy economy to support the values most of us hold dear, were met, and still are met, by a violent attack on what Leavis called 'the technologico-Benthamite civilisation'. For many literature must remain not only the supreme value but almost the only value. Apparently threatened by expanding departments of science and technology it was only natural and proper that the arts should offer a defence of their values, but the method of defence was all too often that of virulent attack – the tone of which was characterized by the Leavis assault on C. P. Snow. Any suggestion that our universities were ultimately dependent on the wealth created by our industries was, for instance, fiercely resisted: 'By a logical slide, the implication arose that the arts were now parasitic upon the new world that scientists were in process of building.[111]

[110] Lewis and Stewart, op. cit., p. 39.
[111] Philip Hobsbaum, 'From Collaboration to Prophecy: On Leavis', *Encounter* (March, 1977), p. 76.

This, to a world which had accepted what has been called 'the sanctification of literature', was simply not acceptable. Poetry for many had become the repository of all those psychological needs and interests which had once been expressed by such terms as soul, spirit, morality and God.[112] The first great statement of this view has often been taken to be Matthew Arnold's famous 1880 essay on 'The Study of Poetry'. Arnold is characteristically authoritative.

'More and more mankind will discover that we have to turn to poetry to interpret life for us, to console us, to sustain us. Without poetry, our science will appear incomplete; and most of what passes with us for religion and philosophy will be replaced by poetry.'[113] A few have recognized the potential dangers and the heavy responsibilities of such a view. As Lionel Trilling said of these words 'never, perhaps, has such a tremendous burden been placed on secular poetry'. But they have been enormously influential. 'For close on a hundred years, poets, critics and educators have consciously or unconsciously been purveying this doctrine'.[114] They have purveyed it so successfully that even those arts graduates who do join industry carry with them a set of values which they feel are threatened, if not actually contradicted by industrial values.

It has become a characteristic complaint that British businessmen regard their business careers as 'a rather distasteful way of acquiring the wherewithal to conduct their real life, their private life, according to the civilized and serious ritual which expresses the values that are considered really important.'[115]

This is what distinguishes British attitudes so clearly from those of her economic rivals. As Lord Annan has so trenchantly argued, 'There is nothing in the least odd about writers loathing industry, or the left preaching that if social relations are to be humanised, the structure of society must be massively changed. This is the stock in trade of modern consciousness. The post-war intelligentsia of France and West Germany, the Dutch and the Swedes and American liberals, held similar views.

[112] Harold Fisch, 'The Sanctification of Literature', *Commentary*, vol. 63, no. 6 (June 1977), pp. 63–9.

[113] For an eloquent and influential statement of this view see I. A. Richards, *Science and Poetry* (1926). Poetry he tells us will 'take the place of the old order'.

[114] Harold Fisch, op. cit., p. 63. He goes on to say 'It is part of the grand secular religion of the 19th century, of a piece with Gothic railway stations and town-halls with dreaming spires. But while fashions in building have changed, the underlying assumption about the sacred task of poetry has remained.'

[115] *The Director* (September 1954), quoted by Lewis and Stewart, op. cit., p. 205.

What is so odd is that *in Britain alone life began to imitate art.* E. M. Forster reminded his readers in *Howards End* that cultivated, liberal minded families such as the Schlegels depend for their livelihood on the money making families such as the Wilcoxes; but he left them in no doubt which of the two is to be preferred. *In Britain today we all want to be Schlegels.*[116]

Foreign observers have seen the point even more clearly than Forster and certainly expressed it more forcefully: 'Ah, Forster', said Cavafy, half in jest, 'You English! Watch that you never lose your money.' The Alexandrine poet knew well that art is manured by money. And so, in the end, is a more just and humane society.[117]

But if such characteristic British attitudes to business are well entrenched in British society, they are not irremovable. It is important not to be too pessimistic about the possibility of change. All too often explanations of past failure are interpreted as predictions of future failure. But blueprints for success can, in my view, be drawn from past stratagems for disappointment. Stark necessity can breed a welcome sense of reality. Values can change remarkably quickly given the right inducements.

The values instilled by education lie at the root of many of these attitudes and educational priorities are capable of surprisingly rapid adjustment. Science, for so long a second class subject in the schools, has successfully emerged from the shadows; applied science has successfully made inroads on pure science; classics have lost their long dominance over more modern languages; economic history has shown that it can successfully challenge constitutional history. The resistance to such changes is always great. The vested interests are powerful. But change can, and has been, achieved.[118]

Quite significant changes of attitude have occurred even within the last decade. In the early nineteen-sixties Cambridge colleges openly recognized the quality gap between the vocational and the non-vocational subjects: lawyers needed to be less well qualified than men

[116] Noel Annan, 'The path to British decadence', *The Sunday Times Weekly Review*, 22 May 1977, p. 34. My italics.

[117] Ibid., p. 34.

[118] It is impossible not to regret some of the values lost, but it is important to recognize the potential gains. The prestige which attaches to the pure as against the applied subjects, to the non-vocational as against the vocational, was often an artificially maintained prestige. Once the most brilliant schoolboys and undergraduates started switching from the pure to the applied, then the prestige switched with them.

reading English or History; engineers less well qualified than mathematicians; medical scientists were notoriously dimmer than natural scientists. In order to fill their medical quota colleges had to offer places to men with significantly lower examination qualifications than the norm.

The situation is now dramatically different. Now the most competitively fought for places go to medical students. From being regarded, intellectually speaking, as the scrapings of the educational barrel, they are now the *crème de la crème*. The change is not confined to Cambridge. It is nationwide, and the quality of our future doctors should be spectacular.

There is no reason why our businessmen should not improve too. For years our ablest undergraduates have shunned industry.[119] Appointments Boards have bewailed the lack of interest: Cambridge was not alone when in 1976 it 'expressed its disquiet at the fact that numbers entering industry, actually fell for the second successive year'.[120] This makes it all the more welcome that in 1977 they reported 'a positive change in attitude towards work in industry'.[121] They identified 'a much more active interest in industry, a much more general feeling that it is important as the wealth-generating sector, and a greater tendency on the part of undergraduates to include manufacturing in their list of worthwhile and useful work'.[122]

Work in industry has been for so long so low on the list of jobs attractive to graduates that one year's evidence is far from conclusive. A more instructive pointer to the future (and one which points in the same direction) can be found in the statistics of *applicants* for unversity places. Here startling changes have occurred in the last few years. The new popularity of vocational studies is faithfully reflected with medicine (12,015)[123] the most popular subject, law (8,924) second, followed by

[119] See for further discussion of this point Neil McKendrick, 'In Search of a Secular Ideal', A General Introduction to R. C. Trebilcock's *The Vickers Brothers: Armaments and Enterprise, 1854–1914* (1977), pp. xxi–xxiii.

[120] *Annual Report of the University of Cambridge Appointments Board for 1976* (24 February 1977), p. 1.

[121] Ibid.

[122] Ibid. The rapture of *The Times Higher Education Supplement* which headlined 'a doubling of Cambridge graduates entering industry' seems a little premature: the 'doubling' was, in fact, a rise from 6.4 per cent of graduates to 10.5 per cent. One feels that industry could with advantage take far more than that.

[123] For the first time in many years the medical applicants fell slightly last year, and those applying to study dentistry (the subject which has grown most

combinations of social, administrative and business studies courses (8,261) in third place and civil engineering (5,570) in fifth place.[124]

The most dramatic increase in individual subjects came in business studies. The number of applicants for degree and diploma courses in business management studies have doubled during the last five years, 'Business management courses now top the list of courses which are increasing most in popularity.'[125] In 1972 business studies was the twentieth most popular subject: in 1976 it had rocketed to twelfth as an individual subject, and third as a combined course.[126] It is all the more important given this surge in interest and this dramatic rise in numbers that these courses are given an adequate historical under-pinning, a proper awareness of the problems businessmen have faced and overcome in the past. Studies of business success and failure are still in short supply, and it is one of the aims of this *Europa Library of Business Biography* to remedy that shortage.

Larger numbers, as so many educational experiments have sadly shown, are not a sufficient answer. When the critics plead for univer-sities to teach 'designing, making, marketing and managing which [will] ensure products are economic, usable, reliable and safe',[127] one can be confident that schools of Industrial Technology and Manage-ment will write indignantly to say that is exactly what their courses are designed to do.[128] Such courses have their value and so have those who graduate from them, but if the most prestigious university centres, which still produce so many of our national leaders, continue

---

rapidly in the preceding five years) also fell. But these falls are almost certainly a reflection on the intense competition for entry and a reaction against very well qualified candidates being rejected rather than any real fall in popularity. See *Universities Central Council on Admissions Statistical Supplement to the fourteenth report 1975–76.*

[124] Ibid. English is in fourth place (with 6,085) but its popularity is declining, whilst business studies and civil engineering are still moving up.

[125] Diana Geddes, 'Business Studies are more popular with students', *The Times*, 10 September 1977, p. 2.

[126] *UCCA Statistical supplement . . . 1975–76.* Business management studies attracted 3,282 applicants last year, compared with 1,627 in 1972, and the latest forecast for applicants starting courses this autumn (1977) is that the figure will rise to 4,300.

[127] Peter Wilby, 'Sacred Cows: The British Universities', *The Sunday Times Supplement*, 14 August 1977.

[128] See George Lowrison, of The University of Bradford, *The Sunday Times*, 21 August 1977.

to generate the attitudes of mind which Lord Annan identifies and Mr. Greengrass confesses, then they will fight an uphill battle.

At the moment, in the words of Jo Grimond, a Balliol first, 'The climate in our universities – especially Oxford – . . . turns the thoughts of its students away from industry and commerce . . . it has done the country much harm'.[129] The dons should, he thinks, ask some of their 'Firsts in Greats to go out and bend their talents to industry and trade', and he regrets that some of 'the richest and most expensively educated of my generation certainly did not grapple with problems of production'.[130] Both cause and consequence is, he concludes, that 'Intellectuals revere *navvies*, not entrepreneurs to engage them in new and useful enterprises. And it is reverence . . . which moves intellectuals.'[131]

When men like Dr. Joseph Pope argue 'It is our history we have to live down',[132] he is right. Many of us carry an accumulation of prejudices and guilt, some of which was never justified and much of which no longer is. British industry itself too often adopts an apologetic stance. The defensive note so often comes through in its advertisements even when it is trying to be brave. The contrast between a recent French advertisement for graduates and an English one illustrates the point: the English one took a whole page of *The Times* for a brief dictionary definition of the word entrepreneur followed by the boast 'Entrepreneur is not a dirty word with us'; the French one proudly proclaimed, 'If you were a General we would offer you an army. Become an engineer, and we will offer you the World.'[133]

It is important that this new interest in business is properly nourished and informed. Many students will already have digested much of the Luddite literary tradition, and they will need a powerful corrective vision if they are not to man British industries with the 'managerial

[129] He makes the familiar point that Oxford 'encourages rather a commitment to the professions and what is peculiarly called "public service" ', and adds universities 'should be breeding grounds for something better than bureaucrats. They should teach science and technology against the background of morals. They should care for the future and cherish the past. From the universities should flow an informed public, capable of judgement, and with some notion of the common good.' See *My Oxford*, ed. by Ann Thwaite (1966), 117–8.

[130] *ibid.*

[131] *ibid.*

[132] J. Pope, 'Report on the Education of Engineers by the British Association for the Advancement of Science' (1977).

[133] See Michael Nally, 'Job Opportunities', *The Observer*, 11 September 1977, p. 16.

schizophrenia' described by Paul Greengrass; 'the psychological absenteeism' diagnosed in their late Victorian forebears by Professor Postan; or the emotional Luddism of the literary world described by Lord Annan.

If British industry cannot promote an acceptable image for itself, it is all the more important for historians to present a more balanced version of the past than is provided by the persuasive values of the literary tradition. The fall of man did not occur with the Industrial Revolution. The catastrophe theory of industrialization is not an adequate verdict. For too long the young have been reared on too one-sided a diet. For although there is an alternative tradition few would claim that it is much read or promoted.

The problem is not simply that when Luddite fiction took real life models they preferred to chose such spectacular rogues as George Hudson.[133] It was not simply that the critics were reluctant to accept their offerings as real or credible when they chose the benevolent Grant brothers. It was that the results of their efforts was to make all business-men objects of moral suspicion. They were expected to be evil. They certainly were not recognized as essential parts of the economy and valuable assets to society. It was hardly worth examining the facts about such 'lesser fellows'. The verdict was delivered before the evidence was examined.

Industry has long changed its spots. When the Luddite tradition was born, there was much to deplore, and, of course, there still is. But the social snobbery of upper class Luddism is absurdly anachronistic, the prejudice against the non-conformist pioneers is even more so, the reaction against the financial short cuts which led to so many disasters was justified for far too long but no longer is so. The horror at con-

---

[133] Robert Bell's Richard Rawlings in *Ladder of Gold* (1850) was explicitly based on Hudson. In Ouida's novel *The Masserenes* (1897), William Masserene is partly based on Hudson, and Dickens's Merdle has been variously associated with Hudson, John Sadlier, the Irish banker speculator who committed suicide, and Leopold Redpath, the clerk of the Great Northern Railway who embezzled something like a quarter of a million pounds. The Victorian novelist was well supplied with novelogenic rogues. D. M. Evans, *Facts, Failures and Frauds*, published in 1859, was a rogue's gallery for them to plunder. John Wilks of the forty-five bubble companies was at one time almost as notorious as his famous namesake. And it is fair to say that just when the industrial entrepreneur might have risen above the novelists' initial prejudices, as John Thornton did, the image of the financial entrepreneur came so to preoccupy fiction's imagination that the whole business class was damned by association.

ditions of work, the moral outrage at the exploitation of women and children, the indignation at the size of profits would all be difficult to maintain in the face of modern industrial behaviour.

Yet the Luddite tradition lingers on. Until the boredom of monotonous industrial labour is lightened, until the danger to the environment is significantly lessened, until corruption is reduced, it will always survive. But many of its prejudices are ludicrously out of date. Many of its most sustaining beliefs need to be challenged by an alternative tradition. There *is* an entrepreneurial ideal and its virtues need to be stated. There is an entrepreneurial role and its importance needs to be recognized.

One major prejudice they will need to overcome is the particular disdain felt for the entrepreneur who prospers without even the fig leaf of respectability provided by invention, the man whose quick perception of the needs of the market allows him to prosper far beyond those who could merely invent the machinery to supply that demand; the man whose ruthless drive turned a potentially valuable invention into a productively profitable innovation, the man whose commercial skill and cunning created wealth, not simply machinery. This prejudice is one which the Luddite tradition in literature has nurtured, and which historians have done little to correct. A prize example of this prejudice at work can be found in Mantoux's description of the contrast between Crompton and Arkwright.

Crompton had many attractive features. He was modest, shy, highly intelligent and tolerably cultivated. But for the Luddite tradition he had other attractions: he failed to profit from his mechanical ingenuity and, despite £5,000 grant from Parliament, he died poor. He rejected an offer of a partnership from Sir Robert Peel, he failed to keep his best workmen, and Mantoux admits that he lacked 'the gift of organisation', he lacked 'leadership', and he had 'very little talent for business'. In short he was just such a man as the Luddite tradition could take to their hearts. Arkwright, who made a fortune, was not.

'The contrast between his [Crompton's] life and that of Arkwright shows the difference there is between original research and discovery, and their clever adaptation to practical ends. In the South Kensington Museum the portraits of the two men hang side by side. Arkwright, with his fat vulgar face, his goggling heavy-lidded eyes, whose expressionless placidity is belied by the vigorous line of the brow and the slight smile on the sensual and cunning lips, is the matter-of-fact businessman, who knows how to grasp and master a situation without too many qualms of conscience. Crompton, with his refined and emaciated profile, his fine forehead, from which his brown hair is tossed back, the austere line of his mouth and his large eyes, both enthusiastic and sad, combines the features of Bonaparte in his younger days with the expression of a Methodist preacher. Together they represent invention and industry, the genius which creates revolutions and the power which possesses itself of their results.'[134]

A tradition, which can perceive such little merit in Sir Richard Arkwright, would not be likely to find much merit in Sir Alfred Jones. Jones made his fortune by manipulating the commercial potential of Liverpool shipping. As a mercantile entrepreneur he was even farther removed from the inventive mechanical genius who, almost alone, could be admired in the literary tradition which has dominated British culture. As a result he has been largely ignored by posterity. Like so many British businessmen he has suffered a fate worse than criticism, he has risen without trace.

The swelling notes of Khatchaturian's theme music have introduced millions to the dramatic possibilities of Victorian shipping lines. Through the rugged agency of James Onedin's adventures they have witnessed the fight to the death between steam and sail, the profits and pitfalls of a price war in freight rates, the politics and betrayals of attempts at price fixing, the intricate strategy of shipping take-overs, the fate of the less perceptive or less enterprising or less cunning or less ruthless owners in their fight for economic survival and aggrandisement, and the remorseless emergence of the dominant entrepreneurial personalities.

All this, and more, have been revealed to an enviably wide audience. They have been able to observe the violent reaction to the arrival of steam – the romantic attachment to sail fighting the shrewd recognition of the realities of speed and regularity. The likely outcome – so inevitable to those with the benefit of hindsight – was vigorously debated by contemporaries, and even for those who had no doubts about the future winner, there were nice problems of timing one's decision to switch out of sail. There were fine points of judgement like the need to gauge any short term profits which might be taken from buying in discarded ships whose ultimate obsolescence often disguised a temporary value; there were interesting alternative avenues for profit opened up by the need for a regular supply of coal; and there

[134] P. S. Mantoux, *The Industrial Revolution in the Eighteenth Century* (1928), p. 242.

was, of course, the major problem involved in raising massive new capital in order to buy the steamships.

The problems, as in all business, required, therefore, accurate but flexible judgement. They required access to capital (however varied and various that access might be). They required shrewd timing, good judgement, an adequate supply of luck and, perhaps more than anything else, the desire to succeed. Ambition, need-achievement, the hunger for power and recognition, the psychological hunger to dominate, the simple desire to excel one's fellow man in one's chosen field – call it what you will, this unmistakable quality emerges over and over again in the business studies of the successful. Fascinating as it is to watch such phenomena in a fictional setting,[135] for many this is not enough. There is a powerful need for authentication, for the confirmation of historical fact, for the certainty that such things actually occurred in the way that fiction claims. What gave *Roots* its special excitement was the claim that it was true; what gave Rowland Parker's *House on the Green* its particular flavour was in its firmly researched foundation in fact; what explains the recent flurry over the discovery of a factual namesake (a real, living James Onedin who sailed ships out of Liverpool in the nineteenth century) is this hunger for reality.

The career of Sir Alfred Jones provides it. His career provides in microcosm a vivid picture of the world of Victorian shipping and the way a shrewd and determined entrepreneur could manipulate it to his advantage. His career displays in detail the process of the acquisition of power, the methods of obtaining ever-increasing control, the mechanics of building up his capital base and then remorselessly extending it.

---

[135] It is an interesting straw in the wind to note that several of Britain's most popular television series have not only cast themselves against a commercial background but have presented the heroes of those series in a tolerably admiring light. The ruthlessness of James Onedin or those involved in Hammond Transport is not disguised but there is also a greater recognition and tacit approval of those qualities needed for success than is usually found in the English fiction of the last hundred years. The main interest of their massive audiences no doubt depends on the soap-opera element of the series, but the very fact that that interest takes place in a business setting is not without interest. The novels of high seriousness (and even many of pretty low seriousness) reach a very restricted audience when compared with television audiences. Most serious novel readers can probably still be counted on to reflect the values of the educated mandarin society. Those values are less prevalent and less dominant amongst the far larger audience for a popular television series.

Jones's career offers more than just the conventional appeal of a success story. It provides an unusual psychological case study as well. The success story itself is compelling enough: an expatriate Welshman who started his working life in Liverpool as a cabin boy at the age of fourteen, he rose to a position of enormous economic power and influence. As such he attracted the attention of even the greatest men of his time.

Churchill was an admirer of Jones and defended his conference system when it was attacked in parliament. But he was shrewd enough to penetrate Sir Alfred's characteristic false *bonhomie*, which worked so well to charm his less perceptive contemporaries, and he was powerful enough to say so – 'Sir Alfred Jones . . . is . . . a candid man, and never so candid as when he tries to conceal his thoughts.'

Lloyd George, in equally characteristic vein, settled more accurately on one of Jones's greatest strengths when he wrote 'his energy is only comparable to the Atlantic Ocean: ruthless and absolutely restless, in fact he is not a man, but a syndicate. Let me assure you, even Wales can only turn out one Sir Alfred in a generation.'

Others thought that perhaps Wales had managed two, and described Jones as a 'Lloyd George of business'. Certainly there were similarities in their dynamic energy, in their ruthless fight to the top of their chosen careers, in their personal magnetism. Neither is ever likely to be chosen as a moral exemplar, but whereas Lloyd George was one of the most accomplished rams in British politics (and his competition, even if limited to prime ministers, is formidable), Jones died, as far as we know, a virgin. Certainly he never married, and no breath of sexual scandal has surfaced in the records. Like many successful businessmen he channelled all his energies into his work and it is there that his moral peccadilloes (and they were many) revealed themselves.[136]

His climb to power was remarkable for although his origins were less humble than many have suggested, he certainly started with few

---

[136] It may be simply ignorance (for businessmen are notoriously less well observed than politicians, and notoriously less well recorded by historians), it may be that the business world demanded, as it still demands, a greater sense of public propriety, it may be simply that they chose less interesting mistresses, but in terms of the historical record British businessmen are simply not in the same class as British politicians when it comes to sexual conquest. Doubtless there will be those who take this as a further index of their lack of status and appeal in British society, but for want of evidence I shall leave such conclusions to others.

advantages. Most crippling of all, it might be thought, for a man seeking power in the control of a shipping empire he lacked capital. Inevitably, therefore, his first steps towards affluence were modest. He needed to establish a base – either a financial base, or a power base, or at the very least, a base of competence which was of value to others. His earnings provide an illustrative index to his progress. Starting at 2s. 6d. a week (where so many traditional rags to riches stories seem to start) he had reached only £1 a week by the age of twenty. His wages then rose steadily but undramatically to nearly £5 a week by the age of 33 when he set up independently. He later claimed that in his first year on his own he earned more money than in all the previous seventeen years put together – which if true, means that he earned more than £2,000 in that year. A further year later he had been lured back into a junior partnership with the firm of Elder Dempster. Five years later, in a remarkable coup, he had levered both Elder and Dempster out of the control of their own company, but it is difficult to argue that his net assets could have been more than £10,000 at that stage. Yet some twenty years later his estate was conservatively estimated at some £600,000. Even given light taxation that is a prodigious rate of capital accumulation, yet given his enormous power and influence it surprised many by being so small. In fact the sale of his assets was conducted in such a way as considerably to undervalue his estate, but nevertheless Jones had operated his enormous financial empire from what Dr. Davies calls 'a relatively small capital base'.

For by then his sphere of influence was such that even 'a considerable fortune rapidly acquired' seemed an inadequate reflection of his commercial reach. And it was. For by extensive use of debentures, by exploiting to the full the possibilities of mortgage facilities, by the cunning use of the deferred rebate system Jones always had command of funds far in excess of his own wealth.

Indeed his capital raising techniques explain much of his success. He could be diverted from profit, and even be willing to sustain a loss, by the lure of a knighthood but when there were no such diversions his financial judgement was exceptionally secure. Like many good games players with peripheral vision, good businessmen seem to focus very quickly on financial problems from however unexpected an angle they arrive. They seem to have, as it were, extra time to take their decisions and to play their shots. And in explaining Jones's success it is difficult to avoid putting particular stress on his control of finance. But he had many other business strengths.

His ousting of Elder and Dempster from their own firm and his callous treatment of Holt when once he had him at his mercy were important steps in his rise to power: they were strokes of ruthlessness. His choice of Ross, to run the Liverpool School of Tropical Medicine which he had initiated, was taken against the advice of many – it was thoroughly vindicated by the award of the Nobel Prize to Ross in 1902: that was a characteristic stroke of good judgement. His withdrawal from competition with the Canadian Pacific Railway and his decision to come to terms with the German rivals rather than attempt to fight them, show that he knew when to withdraw – they were strokes of discretion. The way in which he introduced bananas into the diet of the northern working classes was his stroke of flamboyant salesmanship – he imported costermongers from London and supplied them with free bananas until the popular demand had been created. The way he tried to popularize the mongoose in Britain to control rats was a typically imaginative absurdity – worthy of a Churchill or many a creative entrepreneur of the Lipton or Selfridge or Wilkinson type. His decision to diversify, to press on when once he had dominated the West African trade, showed that he was a man of uncommon perspective – they were his strokes of high competence as well as high ambition. But his stroke of early genius was the deferred rebate system and the conference system – they were the cornerstones of his success. The ruthless first Rockefeller might have admired them for their virtual exclusion of future competition. He still needed to be extremely adroit but they provided him with immensely powerful weapons in his fight to the top – and apart from anything else the rebate system greatly eased his need for working capital, because he always now had in his hands a sum equal to 10 per cent of nine months' freight receipts – a perpetual interest-free loan which could only grow in proportion to the growth of the carrying trade.

The way he constantly extended his empire reveals a characteristic ambition which never seemed to be fully satisfied. Having won control of his own company, having eliminated the British opposition and come to terms with the German, having consolidated his position in the carrying trade, he began to diversify. In Dr. Davies' words, he 'gained control of the boats necessary for the loading and unloading of cargo; he set up the Bank of British West Africa to control the credit structure of the area; he acquired mines, collieries, hotels, plantations, ships' chandlers, cartage companies, and oil mills; and he created subsidiary firms with existing merchant houses.'

Having diversified economically, he then spread geographically, but despite his interests in the Canaries, Jamaica and Canada, it was in West Africa that Jones dominated. No man – not even Joseph Chamberlain, Sir George Goldie, John Holt or Sir Frederick Lugard – can claim to have played a larger role in the economic development of West Africa. And of all the titles he acquired, and all the honorary positions, few more picturesquely albeit inadequately sums up his career than 'Consul for the Congo'.

He enjoyed titles and honours because they were symbols of his power. He had the common entrepreneurial characteristic of wanting complete personal control and where better to control than from the chair of all his various interests. But hunger for control can co-exist with charm – albeit of a somewhat rough-edged type. For all his ruthlessness he possessed remarkable powers of persuasion, and sufficient personal magnetism to retain the essential good will of many whom one would have expected to detest him heartily. It was an important ingredient in his success.

Jones accumulated many of the legends that stick to a successful businessman like burrs. He was reputed to have sacked a man for walking too slowly up the office stairs, and dismissed another for looking idly out of the window. He maintained a reputation for ceaseless work by dictating to his secretaries through breakfast, on his way to work, and through lunch and dinner. When he travelled to London a number of his staff travelled with him and at each stop, one would get off and return to Liverpool with his master's instructions. Urgent messages were telegraphed to these stations and replies would often be dictated before the train moved on. The *Liverpool Echo* was properly appreciative and publicized such energy when it reported a speech of Lord Derby:

> Sir Alfred Jones is a man who travels about with four shorthand writers and disposes smartly of his business letters on a railway station platform while the guard is making wild and frantic signals. Such a man who takes time by the forelock and holds on to it is sure to promote the trade of the world.[137]

Such whirlwind activities are the conventional attributes of a successful entrepreneur, but it would be a mistake to think that Jones's success was just a matter of stamina. He was as prolific in ideas as he was spendthrift in energy. As Lord Scarbrough said of him: 'Sir Alfred is at the centre of a whirl of ideas – an incubator in fact'. Some of them

[137] See Davies, below, p. 102–3.

were exceptionally good ones which left a profound and lasting impression on the economies of West Africa and the Canaries.

But not everyone was as grateful for his attentions as the inhabitants of the Canaries. Making money on the scale which Jones made it has often required the kind of ruthlessness which his dealings with his colleagues reveal. It is often an unappealing spectacle. And it is one of the important tasks of business history to distinguish between the unattractive and the unacceptable, between legitimate business ambition and the hunger for success which took men beyond the law. The great swindles have after all played an important part in generating and feeding the suspicion of business which literary Luddism has kept alive and well.

Very often the differences between ruthless, self-aggrandizing entrepreneurs who stayed within the law, and those who went beyond it has seemed morally very small. But the distinction is an important one, which it is easy to overlook. The striking similarities have often been pointed out between the characters of successful entrepreneurs and those who are successful until they are discovered to be frauds. Kreuger, Bottomley, Hudson, Hatry, Insull and Bishurgian all possessed the hall-marks of the entrepreneurial success story – marked ability, massive ambition, sustaining optimism, a successful idea, the discernment of a need and the ability to raise the funds to supply it. They had 'confidence, application, determination – everything but integrity';[138] and for many commentators the mystery has been 'why so few of them did not stop in time. In most cases it would have been possible long before the crash and disclosure to retire from the ardours and anxieties of high finance and cultivate a leisured garden'.[139] In explanation it has been suggested that 'all suffered from *folie de vitesse*. Products of an acquisitive society they typified – in extreme degree – its madness'.[140] Another explanation is that the distinguishing characteristic of the legitimate businessman was not simply moral superiority but superior skill. He did not have to break the rules. He could succeed – even to the point of excess – within them.

Whether Sir Alfred Jones would have possessed the moral scruples to resist the temptation to break the law, had it proved necessary, is not a question the historian can answer. What it can show is that such were his legitimate skills that he never had to face the temptation.

[138] Lewis and Stewart, op. cit., p. 105.
[139] A. Vallance, *Very Private Enterprise* (1955), p. 11.
[140] Ibid.

Dr. Davies, that rare breed of business historian who has actually run his own business, makes an ideal guide through the business realities of this consummate entrepreneur. Sir Alfred Jones had obvious faults – he was too ruthless and too brash – but he deserves our attention. He loomed very large indeed in the economy of Liverpool. He dominated West African shipping. Yet he is pre-eminently the kind of businessman which the Luddite tradition has belittled, and when not belittled, ignored.

Gonville and Caius College, Cambridge.

Foreword

MY FIRST KNOWLEDGE OF ALFRED LEWIS JONES came in 1961 at a time when I was examining the various topics that were available to a potential post-graduate research worker. Under the guidance of Professor F. E. Hyde, the Department of Economics at the University of Liverpool developed a major interest in the economic history of the shipping industry and he together with Dr. Sheila Marriner had produced a number of studies of individual firms.[1] My original intention was to follow their example and when a preliminary survey showed that little had been written on the West African shipping trade I approached the major operator on that route.

Unfortunately (or so it seemed at that moment) Elder Dempster Lines were understandably reluctant to commit their history to some-one without experience and, furthermore, they indicated that their records (particularly for the period before 1932) were extremely limited. At the suggestion of Berrick Saul,[2] therefore, I turned my attention to an almost forgotten individual who, it was alleged, was the real force behind the growth of the predecessors of the present firm.

Somewhat to my surprise I found that Alfred Jones was virtually a classic example of the entrepreneur as defined by Schumpeter and that he was not only of prime importance in building up Elder Dempster

---

[1] See F. E. Hyde, *Blue Funnel (A History of Alfred Holt and Company, Liverpool, 1865–1914)*, Liverpool University Press, 1957; S. Marriner, *Rathbones of Liverpool*, Liverpool University Press, 1961; S. Marriner and F. E. Hyde, *The Senior. John Samuel Swire*, Liverpool University Press, 1967; F. E. Hyde, *Shipping Enterprise and Management – Harrisons of Liverpool*, Liverpool University Press, 1967; and F. E. Hyde, *Cunard and the North Atlantic, 1840–1973*, Macmillan Press Ltd., London, 1975.

[2] S. B. Saul was than a lecturer in the Department of Economics at the University of Liverpool. He is now Professor of Economic History at the University of Edinburgh.

and Company but that he also played a vital role in the economic development of British West Africa.

Schumpeter identified five cases of entrepreneurship, including the introduction of a new good or quality of product; the innovation of fresh methods of production or of handling a commodity commercially; the opening up of a new market; the development or acquisition of control of raw materials or semi-manufactured goods; and the instigation of the reorganization of an industry.[3]

It is possible to identify Alfred Jones with most, if not all, of these characteristics of the entrepreneur.[4] He first gained a fundamental knowledge of the trade and then gained control of 'the means of production' and access to credit as prescribed by Schumpeter. Jones subsequently established a monopoly in the carrying trade of the Coast and consolidated this by creating a shipping conference which effectively precluded further competition during his lifetime. Having organized a firm base for his power via his control of West African shipping routes, Jones extended his monopoly into other areas and fields, and like all true entrepreneurs, did not simply respond to changes in customers' preferences – he actively educated his markets and thus promoted or extended new outlets for his enterprise.

From his earliest entry into the business world Jones's activities were characterized by an enormous appetite for work. As in Schumpeter's model, Jones was distinguished more by his will than his intellect though few would doubt his capacity. Similarly he achieved more by his determination and authority than by the use of original ideas – he was not an inventor, but a man who got things done. His motivation, like that of other entrepreneurs, was not merely the satisfaction of his wants – the impulse to succeed was of far greater importance than purely financial rewards.[5]

One aspect of Jones's character which demonstrates his superiority to many lesser mortals is that he was never content with his successes however great they may have appeared. Thus he continued to invest and innovate throughout his life and it is because of this characteristic

---

[3] J. A. Schumpeter, 'The Fundamental Phenomenon of Economic Development', in Peter Kilby (Ed.), *Entrepreneurship and Economic Development*, New York Free Press, 1971.

[4] I am indebted to Miss Janice Spicer, formerly an undergraduate in the School of Social Studies, University of Liverpool, for originally bringing this analysis to my attention.

[5] J. A. Schumpeter, op. cit., pp. 66–8.

that he qualifies for the title of 'entrepreneur par excellence'. Jones never relaxed into mere management and although he undertook a massive amount of administration he never failed to look for opportunities to diversify and increase his interests. This characteristic remained prominent until his last, fatal, illness for the achievement and exercise of power was his sole *raison d'être*.

In due course my study of this remarkable man led to the award of an M.A.[6] and provided a foundation which led to further work on West African shipping and to the achievement of a Ph.D.[7] A small part of this topic was published as *The African Steam Ship Company* in 1969[8] and I was then invited by Elder Dempster Lines to extend my research so as to provide an official history of their Company. This was published as *The Trade Makers, Elder Dempster in West Africa, 1852–1972*,[9] during 1973, and other, more specialized, aspects have appeared in recent years.[10]

Inevitably these publications have included many references to Alfred Lewis Jones but nowhere has it been possible to give full weight to his achievements nor to provide a detailed analysis of his motivation and character. It is my sincere hope that these omissions will have been rectified in this present work. This necessarily includes much that has been previously published but it should be appreciated that even a subtle change of emphasis, consequent on the acquisition of new evidence, can be as important as an original publication in a virgin field.

I would like to express my thanks to my colleagues and former colleagues in the Department of Economics (now Economic History) in the University of Liverpool for their constant support and constructive criticism. In particular I would wish to single out John Harris,[11] Sheila Marriner and Berrick Saul. I am also extremely

---

[6] *Sir Alfred Jones and the Development of West African Trade* (M.A. thesis, University of Liverpool, 1964).

[7] *British Shipping and the Growth of the West African Economy, 1910–1950* (Ph.D. thesis, University of Liverpool, 1967).

[8] Published in *Liverpool and Merseyside* (ed. J. R. Harris), Frank Cass & Co., London, 1969.

[9] Published by George Allen and Unwin Limited, London, 1973.

[10] P. N. Davies (Ed.), *Trading in West Africa*, Croom Helm, London, 1976; 'The Impact of the Expatriate Shipping Lines on the Economic Development of British West Africa', *Business History*, vol. XIX, no. 1, January 1977; 'Group Enterprise: Strengths and Hazards', in *Business and Businessmen*, a Festschrift in honour of Emeritus Professor F. E. Hyde, Liverpool University, 1977.

[11] J. R. Harris is now Professor of Economic History at the University of Birmingham.

grateful to Mrs. Florence Mocatta, a great niece of Alfred Jones, for making her family papers available to me; to Mr. G. P. Clifford of Fyffes Group Limited for permission to reproduce an item from his company's history;[12] to Mr. G. J. Ellerton of Ocean Transport and Trading Limited for permission to include references from *The Trade Makers*; to Mr. C. Harrison for the use of the records of Henry Tyrer and Company; and to Mr. F. D. H. Mather of John Holt and Company (Liverpool) Limited for authority to quote from the John Holt archives.

In addition, I would like to acknowledge, yet again, the kind assistance provided by Emeritus Professor Francis Hyde. Although retired he continues to provide his customary valuable advice and this study owes much to his impeccable judgement.

Finally, my gratitude must be expressed to my wife, Maureen, for her tolerance and forbearance. She has lived with Alfred Jones for many years!

P. N. DAVIES
University of Liverpool

[12] P. Beaver, *Yes! We have some. The Story of Fyffes*, Publications for Companies, Stevenage, 1976.

The Man and his Achievements

ALFRED LEWIS JONES BEGAN HIS ASSOCIATION with West Africa in 1859. He was then a cabin boy, aged fourteen, with the African Steam Ship Company, and from then until his death in 1909 his whole existence was bound up with the trade between Liverpool and the West Coast of Africa.

Though born in Carmarthen, Jones lived in Liverpool from the age of three, and it was in that city that he achieved such remarkable success in rising from office boy to shipping magnate. His progress in business was rapid, and by the time he was thirty-nine, Jones had become the senior partner of Messrs. Elder Dempster and Company. In the years that followed he transformed this relatively small firm of shipping agents into a mighty monopoly that controlled not only the shipping of West Africa, but many aspects of its trade and economy as well.

The West Coast trade in the nineteenth century had many peculiarities. Its comparative nearness to Britain enhanced its potential profitability, but the terrible climate and the lack of interest of the British Government had greatly retarded its development. In addition, almost the only method of internal communication was by water. This had the effect of encouraging the growth of a miniature port at the mouth of every navigable river and creek. Thus instead of a few large ports, the shipping companies had to provide a service to some eighty points of call and many of these possessed nothing better than an open beach.

Alfred Jones saw in the steamship the means of modifying the adverse geographical factors. But he felt that competition would have to be eliminated for this to be possible economically as well as technically. He achieved this monopoly by destroying his British rivals and making terms with his German ones. Then he maintained his hold by establishing a conference system, complete with deferred rebate, that ensured that any future competitor would find it difficult to obtain freight.

Jones then used his position of strength to build up his power still further. He gained control of the boats necessary for the loading and unloading of cargo; he set up the Bank of British West Africa to control the credit structure of the area; he acquired mines, collieries, hotels, plantations, ships' chandlers, cartage companies and oil mills, and he created subsidiary firms to compete with the existing merchant houses.

This virtual control of British West Africa gave Jones immense strength, and led in turn to many honorary positions which still further increased his authority. He became president of the Liverpool Chamber of Commerce, president of the British Cotton Growing Association, and consul for the Congo. Furthermore, Jones was not content with success just in Africa and, in time, he spread his shipping and commercial interests to include the Canaries, Jamaica and Canada.

It is the purpose of this study to show that Alfred Lewis Jones, entrepreneur par excellence, was the dominant figure in the development of the trade of West Africa. Joseph Chamberlain, Sir George Goldie, John Holt, Macgregor Laird and Sir Frederick Lugard all played important parts, but to Jones must go the prime responsibility for the way British West Africa assumed its place in the modern world.

P. N. DAVIES
The University of Liverpool

CHAPTER ONE

The Background to the West African Trade

I

A COMPLETE ANALYSIS OF THE TRADE AND HISTORY of West Africa from 1850 to 1910 would be a very lengthy and complicated undertaking, and in the present context an unnecessary burden for the reader. The intention in this first chapter is, therefore, to give only a general picture of the relevant geographical, historical, political and financial factors, and to indicate broadly how these were modified during Jones's lifetime. Such a survey is naturally concerned with the increasing demand for West African products in foreign countries and with the development of communications and organizations which enabled the supply to be enlarged.

In 1850, the British possessions in West Africa were the Gold Coast, Sierra Leone, the Gambia and what was later to become Nigeria. All these dependencies lay between latitudes 4 and 14 degrees North. By 1910, their populations totalled about twenty million people, and geographically each had many similarities. Parallel to the coast was a series of zones varying in depth; in many places that nearest to the coast consisted of mangrove swamps, then came a jungle forest zone, followed by the open savannah, and this in turn gave way to the Sahara Desert. For all practical purposes there were two habitable regions; the jungle with its hot, moist climate near the coast, and the savannah with its hot, dry climate in the interior. As these two areas were so different they had evolved two entirely dissimilar economies. The jungle natives were very backward, living in small clearings in the forest and engaged in ceaseless war with their neighbours. Under such conditions, economic progress was impossible and their only products consisted of such items as palm oil, palm kernels, kola nuts and rubber which could be gathered in the forest. On the other hand, the savannah natives lived in large communities and had made considerable economic progress. They had walled cities, schools and independent judges. Their products resulted from their own husbandry and included groundnuts, cotton and hides. Both areas were inhabited by a negroid population, but within each zone there were many differences in the mentality, character, physique and language of the inhabitants, and it has been said that the Hausa and the Munshi are less alike than the Slav and the Scandinavian.[1]

The whole area suffered from a lack of natural and artificial communications. Only the Gambia and Niger rivers and the coastal creeks of Nigeria provided a reasonable means of transport before the railways were introduced in the 1890s. Large regions were, therefore, completely dependent on native porters, it not being possible to use draught animals because of the presence of the tsetse fly.

The first Europeans to do business with West Africa were the Portuguese, but many other nations, including the French, Spanish, Danish, Dutch, Brandenburgers and English, disputed their right to an exclusive trade. By the seventeenth century the West Coast of Africa played an essential role in Britain's economy because it was the source of the slave labour needed for the West Indian sugar plantations. Although vast numbers of slaves were being sent to the mainland of America, as well as to the West Indies, it was not found necessary to establish formal colonies in West Africa to ensure an adequate supply. This was because the native rulers were well used to the idea of slavery and were quite prepared to trade with the European merchants: in fact the Coastal chiefs rapidly became very jealous of their rights and insisted that all trade with the interior must pass through their hands. The merchants of Liverpool were very active in the slave trade, and gradually acquired most of this business in the area of the Niger Delta.[2]

In 1807, the slave trade became illegal for British citizens, and although this had been expected it was still a severe blow to Liverpool. Large amounts of capital were tied up in ships, contracts and in credits given to the native suppliers.[3] Fortunately this occurred just when an

---

[1] Address to the Nigerian Legislative Council, 1920, p. 19, by Sir Hugh Clifford.
[2] John E. Flint, *Sir George Goldie & the Making of Nigeria* (Oxford University Press, London, 1960), p. 10.
[3] For a recent view of this situation see B. Drake, 'Continuity and Flexibility in Liverpool's Trade with Africa and the Caribbean', *Business History*, vol. 18, No. 1, Jan. 1976.

alternative to the export of men was presenting itself. This was the growth of the palm oil industry and the quantity imported into Liverpool rose from 55 tons in 1785 to over 1,000 tons in 1810 and to 30,000 tons in 1841.[4] Almost all this oil was from the coastal regions, as little attempt was made to penetrate to the interior.

At first, the oil was a poor substitute for the trade in slaves and the ensuing difficulties led to a complete reorganization of British commerce with West Africa. For two centuries the African Company had enjoyed many privileges in West Africa, particularly in the Gold Coast where it had a monopoly of trade, but its existence was ended in 1821. From that date all merchants enjoyed equal rights, but the heavy mortality from tropical disease, the paucity of the communication system and the lack of interest of the British Government continued to restrict the growth of trade.

II

By the time the trade in slaves was coming, officially at least, to an end British interests on the West African Coast were to be found in four distinct areas. The Gambia was settled on a permanent basis by English merchants in 1816 after several centuries of fluctuating trade in beeswax, ivory, hides, gold and slaves. The slave trade prevented any sustained growth of legitimate exports and it was not until the groundnut industry began to develop that economic progress could really begin. The first few baskets of these nuts were exported in 1830 and, by 1848, had risen to 8,600 tons valued at £104,000.[5]

Sierra Leone had been founded in 1787 as a colony for emancipated slaves who could not be returned to their former homes. At first it was organized by the Sierra Leone Company, but in 1807 the Crown assumed direct control. The colony was fortunate in having an excellent harbour at Freetown, and a number of small but navigable rivers which assisted in the bringing of produce to the Coast. In the earlier period, timber, groundnuts, ginger and a little coffee were the main exports, but by 1850 palm kernels and palm oil were of paramount importance.[6]

---

[4] Macgregor Laird, *Memorandum for the Committee on West African Trade and Slavery*, 1842, Parliamentary Papers, vol. XI, p. 575.

[5] Sir Alan Pim, *The Financial and Economic History of the African Tropical Territories* (Oxford Clarendon Press, 1940), p. 34.

[6] C. Fyfe, *A History of Sierra Leone* (Oxford University Press, London, 1962).

The Gold Coast '. . . was the special preserve of the successive African Companies from the days of James I to the times of George IV'.[7]

The Crown took over the government in 1821, but bad relations with the merchants, the terrible effects of the climate and their defeat by the Ashantis led the Home Government to decide to withdraw in 1828. This evoked so many protests from the English traders that a compromise was reached. A subsidy of £4,000 a year was granted for the merchants to man and maintain the coastal forts, and it was with this pitiful sum that George Maclean, appointed Governor in 1830, did so much. Under his guidance, trade and British influence increased to such an extent that in 1843 the Crown resumed direct control. From 1820 onwards palm oil exports grew rapidly, and was clearly the largest item when the Gold Coast became a separate colony in 1850.

The fourth region of British influence was in what is now Nigeria. In 1850, this was purely a trading area with the export of palm oil the most important consideration. As we have already seen, the merchants of Liverpool were very active in this region. They operated only in the coastal areas, receiving the oil from natives at various points near the sea or on the 'Oil Rivers'. In fact, it was not realized until 1830 that the 'Oil Rivers' were branches of the mouth of the Niger, whose outlet until then had been a mystery. This discovery, by the Lander brothers, led many people to hope that the Niger could now be used to penetrate to the interior of the continent for the great benefit of English commerce. It was also believed that a vast trade crossed the Sahara by caravan, and it was thought that these goods could profitably be carried by cheap sea transport provided by Britain.

III

Macgregor Laird, a member of the Birkenhead shipbuilding family, was the first to use steamships in West Africa. Inspired by the discovery of the mouth of the Niger, he joined with Richard Lander to form a company to seek ivory and spices up the Niger. Their expedition, however, was not a financial success and the death rate was extremely high. Consequently, Laird withdrew from West African affairs and rejoined his father's shipbuilding firm in Birkenhead. Nevertheless, Laird continued to maintain an interest in West African trade and by

[7] Allan McPhee, *The Economic Revolution in British West Africa* (George Routledge, London, 1926), p. 10.

4

1850 he was convinced that the size of the shipments was sufficient to justify a regular steam ship service. In 1852, he was able to persuade the Government to support a venture with an annual subsidy and thus the African Steam Ship Company came into being.[8]

The provision of a regular service by the vessels of the African Steam Ship Company led to a substantial increase in the trade of West Africa. The existing firms found it more convenient to utilize the new sailings to send urgently required merchandise and, in time, they tended to stop operating their own or chartered vessels. In addition, the facilities offered by the company meant that for the first time small traders could enter the trade. By using the scheduled services goods could be ordered and received promptly and the West African produce taken in exchange could be rapidly sent for sale in Liverpool. The African Steam Ship Company thus played an important part in opening up the trade of West Africa to a wider market: Macgregor Laird made some attempt to extend his activities into the interior by financing expeditions up the River Niger but the African Steam Ship Company took no part in this and built up its business by providing for the carriage of mail, cargo and passengers between West Africa and either the United Kingdom or Europe.

At first the African Steam Ship Company enjoyed somewhat fluctuating fortunes, partly because of the effect of the Crimean War, but by the 1860s it was well established and making reasonable returns on its capital.[9] For various reasons, however, it failed to expand with the demands of the trade and it paid the price when, in 1869, a rival line entered the trade.[10] This was the British and African Steam Navigation Company and much of the subsequent development of the West African shipping trade was to hinge on the co-operation of these two firms. It was, in fact, the situation brought about by the presence of these companies on the same route that was to give Alfred Jones his opportunity to achieve power in the West African trade and, eventually, to control them as well.

IV

The basis of the expansion of the two British lines lay in the existence of growing quantities of produce that could be profitably sold in the

[8] See below, chapter 2, p. 20.
[9] P. N. Davies, 'The African Steam Ship Company', in J. R. Harris (ed.), *Liverpool and Merseyside* (Frank Cass, London, 1969).
[10] See below, chapter 2, p. 24.

industrialized countries. From 1850 to 1910 the main exports of West Africa continued to be palm products. Together these formed from 43 to 96 per cent of the annual totals. The enlarged demand was due to two factors. Larger quantities of edible oil and fats had to be imported into England merely to maintain existing standards, because of the increase in the population. At the same time a new demand was growing for oils to be used in the manufacture of soap and candles, and for use in lubricating the machinery generated by the industrial revolution. A little later, the discovery that palm kernels could be used instead of animal fats in the manufacture of margarine gave this import a tremendous impetus. From 1855 to 1900, the average annual quantity of palm oil imported was about 50,000 tons. It would undoubtedly have been more, but the native producer was very sensitive to price movements and this was a period of falling prices:

	£	s.	
1856–60	43	6	per ton of palm oil[11]
1861–65	37	2	
1866–70	38	4	
1871–75	34	2	
1876–80	33	0	
1881–85	31	0	
1886–90	20	4	
1891–95	23	6	
1896–1900	21	4	

When the price fell too much the native tended to abandon cash crops and return to growing food for his own consumption. Thus it was fortunate that the world forces lowering prices were partially offset by a fall in freight rates. The reduction in price was begun by the competition of petroleum from the United States after 1860. Oil and seeds from India, and tallow from Australia later provided additional rivals. But the rising demand for tins and cans in the 1890s and the corresponding increase in the amount of palm oil used for tin plating then led to better prices being obtained.

In addition to palm oil and palm kernels, a third palm product was increasingly exported in about 1865. This followed the discovery that palm kernel oil had valuable keeping qualities, characteristics not shared by palm oil, and a ready market was stimulated by the demands of the German margarine manufacturers. The French, on the other

[11] 'Annual Abstract of the United Kingdom', quoted by McPhee, op. cit., footnote to p. 33.

hand, were much more interested in groundnuts for use in soap-making. As a result, exports of this crop from the Gambia rose from 12,000 tons in 1851 to an average of between 15,000 and 20,000 tons for the latter part of the nineteenth century.[12] Another crop of great export potential began to be grown during the 1880s. This was cocoa and, under the control and supervision of the local governments, production expanded at a tremendous rate:

	tons[13]
1900	536
1906	8,975
1912	38,647
1914	52,888

Other commodities of importance included cotton, which was greatly assisted by Alfred Jones as president of the British Cotton Growers' Association,[14] and timber.[15] The latter, especially hardwoods, had been exported for many centuries and although its relative significance declined in the period before 1914, this was due to the expansion of other items rather than its own decline. Rubber was yet another product that made a substantial contribution to the cargoes carried by the shipping lines. Its export began in the 1870s and reached a peak towards the end of the century. It was gathered in the forest areas, and little attempt was made to cultivate it. The plantations of Malaya were far more efficient, and as they came into production the demand for West African rubber declined. In more recent years there has been a trend towards more intensive development, and the export figures have again risen.

A great deal of gold was found by the earlier traders on the Coast, but this was the accumulation of many centuries of production. The amount mined each year was only small, so exports fell from £3.5 million in value in 1700 to only £400,000 in 1800. There was little attempt to introduce large-scale mining until about 1878, and the attempts made by European firms after that date failed because of the high cost of transport from the sea or river to the mines. It was not

[12] J. R. McCulloch, *Dictionary of Commerce* (1883), p. 965.
[13] Annual Reports for the Gold Coast (relevant years).
[14] See below, chapter 7, pp. 106–7.
[15] Department of Scientific and Industrial Research, *A Handbook of Empire Timbers* (HMSO, London, 1945).

until the railways reached the goldfields that output was enabled
to rise:

	oz.[16]
1903	71,000
1907	292,000
1915	462,000

The tin and coal industries did not begin serious production until
1909 and 1914 respectively for, like the goldmining industry, they
required rail transport to become viable producers. Many traditional
items such as hides, skins, furs, ivory, gum, wax and spices were always
present in any list of West African exports but they continued to be of
relatively minor importance.[17]

The character and scale of imports also changed significantly during
this period. In 1787 the main categories were as follows:

	£
Textiles[18]	408,000
Metal goods	97,000
Spirits	40,000
Arms and ammunition	39,000

During the next century, imports rose in volume and value, but the
chief items and their proportions of the total remained nearly constant.
Then, after about 1880, the growth of cash crops led to a large increase
in food imports. This was because the native population had to be fed
while producing crops for export, and the increasing number of
Europeans also required additional food and consumer goods of all
types. The Convention of Brussels in 1890 forbade the importation of
all arms except flint locks and smooth bore weapons. There were also
continuous attempts made to control the importation of spirits, but
apart from these two items it may be said that practically everything
else was imported without restriction. The range of imports covered
the many small goods necessary to preserve a European standard of
living on the Coast for the merchants and government officials. During
the period 1850 to 1941, these commodities rose in importance as
Western customs spread amongst the native inhabitants, and as the
numbers of Europeans resident in West Africa were increased.

[16] W. Page, *Commerce and Industry*, vol. II, p. 199.
[17] See appendix, table 1, p. 126.
[18] A. Anderson, *Annals of Commerce*, vol. IV, p. 154.

V

Practically the entire trade of British West Africa was in the hands of the English business houses throughout this period. There was little attempt by other European nationals to enter the business, and although the local inhabitants gradually came to take a fuller part, their relative importance was very small. The partnership was the customary method of organization, and it was only when a firm reached very large proportions that it became a joint stock company. The size of the typical concern rose steadily, as did the capital invested, but as the partnerships did not make their accounts public, no exact figures are available. It is very clear, however, that nearly all the capital invested in British West Africa up to 1914 was of external origin, and that an overwhelming proportion of this came from Britain.

The need for a standardized currency was felt chiefly for the payment of customs duties by the European merchants. Up to 1894, this was accomplished by the government of the colony concerned accepting bills issued by the larger houses on their home offices. This was a very inconvenient and clumsy method, and it had the added disadvantage of making it harder for the small trader to compete with larger rivals. Any firm which wished to import silver, the universally accepted means of exchange, could do so, but only the larger merchants in fact did so because of the capital required. This meant that in practice the smaller traders had to obtain their silver from the big firms, and frequently had to pay five per cent for the accommodation. This system was ended when, in 1891, the African Banking Corporation established a branch at Lagos. The corporation subsequently received a monopoly under which it alone could obtain new silver from the Mint, and in return guaranteed to re-export any coin that became redundant. Private merchants could still obtain silver from England and import it into West Africa, but it was not freshly minted and in many cases the Africans would only accept new and shiny coins.

After the African Banking Corporation withdrew from West Africa in 1893, merchants were again allowed to get new silver from the Mint on payment of one per cent plus the cost of a telegraph message. This practice was ended the following year when the Bank of British West Africa was established with the same privileges and responsibilities that its predecessor had enjoyed.[19] From then onward an

[19] Richard Fry, *Bankers in West Africa* (*The Story of the Bank of British West Africa Limited*) (Hutchinson Benham, London, 1976).

efficient system of credit was evolved. The manager of a firm's West African branch presented a bill (three days sight was customary) and received silver in exchange. One per cent was normally charged for this service, but a company that arranged in advance for all its requirements would be charged only half a per cent.[20]

The Manchester Chamber of Commerce was very reluctant to see the Bank of British West Africa receive the privileges of the African Banking Corporation. This was because the new bank was regarded by many merchants as a tool of the shipping companies, and in fact Alfred Jones controlled it for many years. The Manchester merchants later withdrew their objections, and at the Royal Commission on Shipping Rings in 1907, it was stated on their behalf that it was the unanimous opinion of them all that the bank was of great benefit. They did not wish to see the existing system altered in any way.[21] A rival bank was established in 1903. This was the Bank of Nigeria and was founded by a group of the larger African merchants, including Miller Brothers, to prevent the existing bank from assuming a complete monopoly. But it was not a financial success, and was taken over by the Bank of British West Africa in 1912. No serious challenger then presented itself until the advent of Barclay's Bank (DC and O) during the First World War.[22]

VI

The period between 1850 and 1910 also saw many new developments in the relationships between the European powers and their trading areas in West Africa. Both France and Germany took an increasing interest but, at first, this was ignored by the British Government in spite of the warnings given by her merchants. A brief summary of political events in West Africa at this time would seem to suggest that Britain was following a policy of dynamic expansion, but this is incorrect. In 1850, all the Danish interests in the Gold Coast were bought by the British Government for £10,000. In 1861, Lagos was annexed. Then in 1872 came the cessession of the Dutch forts, and the Ashantis were defeated in 1874. But at the same time many influential

---

[20] Royal Commission on Shipping Rings (RCSR), (HMSO, Cd. 4668–70, 1909), Q.9118 (Section 23), p. 330.
[21] RCSR, op. cit., Q.13260. Evidence given by Hutton and Zochonis.
[22] Sir Julian Crossley and John Blandford, *The DCO Story. A History of Banking in many Countries, 1925–1971* (Barclays Bank International, London, 1975).

people in England were against any expansion of British interests and, in 1865, a Parliamentary Committee counselled complete withdrawal from West Africa. While this was not acted on, the British Government ended its occupation of Ashanti and funds for West African projects became even more difficult to obtain.

In 1884, however, at the Congress of Berlin, the British Government was made to realize that if it took no action, France and Germany would take advantage of its lack of interest. A policy was then evolved to extend British sovereignty inland. This was designed partly to increase trade, but primarily to prevent the French and Germans from closing in on the British colonies on the Coast. But it believed that the public would not support the undertaking of new expenses and responsibilities in West Africa. It therefore adopted the expedient of creating a chartered company in 1886.[23] This was the Royal Niger Company, and it was given the duty of ruling as well as the privilege of exclusive trading in vast areas of the interior in the Niger Basin. But public opinion, aided by the activities of the West African merchants and shippers, was gradually altering and the position of the Government was also changing.

By 1895, Britain's new approach to its colonial territories was confirmed by the advent of Joseph Chamberlain to the Colonial Office, for he was known to be in favour of a more vigorous policy. One aspect of his work came to fruition in 1900 when the Royal Niger Company was replaced by the Crown, having played a large part in laying the foundations of modern Nigeria.[24] In other areas, too, the Colonial administration began to take an ever increasing interest in developing their resources and in providing a more comprehensive infrastructure. By 1910, therefore, the four British possessions in West Africa had in many ways assumed what was to be their final shape before independence in the 1950s and 1960s.

VII

From the foregoing sections it should be apparent that a number of specific factors had influenced the economic development of West Africa. A basic consideration was the geographical environment which

[23] John E. Flint, *Sir George Goldie & the Making of Nigeria* (Oxford University Press, London, 1960).
[24] Frederick Pedler, *The Lion and the Unicorn in Africa* (The United Africa Company, 1787–1931) (Heinemann, London, 1974).

made internal communication virtually impossible in many areas, and which had played a vital role in determining the existing forms of the local societies. A second essential aspect was the continuously rising demand for West African products and this applied equally well to the traditional exports like palm oil and timber, as to the new items such as palm kernel oil and cocoa. A third vital consideration was the change in the attitude of the Government to its West African territories. Here the desire to be rid of a liability became the expressed wish to enlarge and develop British colonies there as quickly as possible.

The development of British West Africa during the second half of the nineteenth century was thus conditioned by the three prime factors of geography, the demand for produce and the attitude of the British Government. In one way or another, these three factors were modified by the activities of Alfred Lewis Jones. He considerably eased the geographical difficulties by improving communications from Europe to the Coast. The technical innovation of the steamship had occurred long before he had achieved a position of responsibility, and regular services to West Africa had begun in 1852. But it was his activity in ending the rivalry between the two chief British companies, and in preventing a conflict with his German competitor that enabled him to continue to provide a fast and frequent service. Jones also supplied a coastal fleet which linked the minor stopping places with the main ports. This eliminated the need for the larger ships having to stop at every creek and river mouth, and thus made the service more efficient. His company buoyed the rivers, dredged the harbours, built quays and wharves, lighthouses and yards, and did everything possible to facilitate the movement of cargo and passengers. Jones encouraged the building of roads, and saw that his ships were refrigerated at an early date. This enabled fresh meat and vegetables to be made available at each port, and was of great assistance in varying the diet of the merchants and officials resident there. In turn, this helped in combating the incidence of tropical disease, and Jones was also the founder and constant supporter of the Liverpool School of Tropical Medicine which did so much to reduce the mortality from disease in West Africa.[25]

Jones was a keen agitator for the provision of railways in the British colonies. He led many deputations on behalf of the Liverpool Chamber of Commerce, all urging that railways be either started or extended. Between 1879 and 1893, there were many applications by private firms

[25] See below, chapter 7, pp. 107–8.

to build railways in West Africa, and most of these were sup̣
Jones. All these attempts failed, however, because the promote
the Government to guarantee their shareholders a fixed rate of interest.
The Colonial Office would not agree to this proposal. It wanted the
Government to undertake the construction in the areas it felt would be
profitable, and did not wish to help private firms in the other regions
because it thought they would be a continual burden. Lord Knutsford
got the preliminary surveys started in 1892, but it was not until 1895
that any further action was taken. Joseph Chamberlain was then
responsible for deciding that the colonial governments should undertake the construction of the railways. In this decision he was no doubt
influenced by the friendship which he shared with Jones. The following
year, railway building began in both Sierra Leone and in the colony of
Lagos. Construction in the Gold Coast started in 1898, but it was not
considered necessary to have a railway in Gambia as it was adequately
served by its central river.

In Sierra Leone, the main line was built from the port of Freetown
to Pendenbu in the East. A branch line was also built from Boia
Junction to Kamabai. In the Gold Coast, two lines were developed.
One started at the port of Sekondi, and ran via the gold fields to
Kumasi, the capital of Ashanti. The other began at Accra, and traversed
the cocoa growing area before meeting the first at Kumasi. Lagos
Colony, which was later to form the nucleus of Nigeria, began its
railway on the coast at Iddo in 1896. This ran 307 miles to Jebba on the
Niger and took until 1909 to complete. All these lines were built by
the colonial governments concerned and remained state controlled.
They were chiefly intended to open up the areas which the natural
waterways left untouched, and they were successful in expanding
existing trades as well as creating new ones. All this extension of
business was of great value to Jones as it meant more cargoes for his
ships and in addition he was almost entirely responsible for the shipment of the railway equipment to the colonies. This did not necessarily
mean large profits. In fact, in the case of the Southern Nigerian
Railway, Jones charged a very low rate. When he was challenged
about this he pointed out that if he had not been prepared to accept a
nominal figure for the delivery of this cargo the railway may not have
been built for many years.[26]

---

[26] Royal Niger Company Papers (RNCP), vol. XII, p. 353, letter from Jones to
Lord Scarborough, 13 September 1907.

The provision of these railways plus a cheap and regular steamship service assisted the produce of West Africa to reach the outside world at a competitive price. This was particularly valuable in the case of palm oil, the major export, the world price of which fell continuously from 1860 to 1900. In the case of cotton, Jones did more than just provide cheap transport. He undertook to carry without cost all the crop produced in West Africa during the first two years it was produced on a commercial scale. Later he became president of the British Cotton Growing Association and did much work to promote its growth in many areas of the empire and especially in West Africa. Apart from these direct activities, Jones was an active investor in many colonial mines, plantations and forests, and he was so prosperous a businessman and so successful a publicity expert that many followed where he pioneered. He also financed the Bank of British West Africa, and this was an essential institution for the numerous credit transactions necessary in modern trade. Any schemes designed to further the cause of West Africa and its trade were automatically assured of his support.

Alfred Jones never held political office, but his influence on successive governments was great. For most of the time he was the senior partner of Messrs. Elder Dempster and Company, Jones made weekly visits to London. These frequently included calls at the Foreign Office, the Colonial Office and the Board of Trade, so he could press forward his projects. In the House of Commons he could rely on the support of the members representing the Merseyside constituencies. In addition, he had the ear of Thomas Sutherland, MP, who besides being chairman of the Peninsular and Oriental Steamship Company was the leader of the shipping lobby in Parliament.[27]

These connections gave Jones the opportunity to put some pressure on the Government, but more important still was his ability to influence public opinion. The public pronouncements of so eminent a figure were always news and were well reported. His views were thus constantly before the members of the Cabinet as well as the general public, and as few criticisms of himself or his policies were ever published, a picture favourable to his interests was always created.[28] Jones was thus able to secure the support of the population for many of

[27] Letter from Thomas Sutherland to the Under Secretary of State for Foreign Affairs (Paunceforte), FO 84/1917, 23 March 1888.
[28] E. D. Morel Collection, reference F.8, letter from L. V. Vasz to E. D. Morel on 21 May 1905, in the London School of Economics.

his schemes, and in this way he influenced official policy and modified the attitude of the Government.

It was against this background that Jones made his way as cabin boy, clerk, manager and director. In succeeding chapters we will see how he gained control of Elder Dempster and Company and then used this firm to obtain a monopoly of the West African carrying trade. This, in turn, gave him great wealth and power, and enabled him to have an overwhelming influence on the trade and development of West Africa.

CHAPTER TWO

His Early Life

I

ALFRED LEWIS JONES WAS BORN IN CARMARTHEN, South Wales, on
24 February 1845, of what might best be described as respectable,
middle-class, Welsh parents. His birthplace has been variously given
as in Picton Place or in Lammas Street but, although the area appears
to have changed little over the years, there is considerable local
controversy as to the exact house in which he was born.[1] Alfred's father
was Daniel Jones, a currier or leather worker who at one time had been
the reputed owner of the Carmarthen newspaper, *The Welshman*.
Alfred's paternal grandfather was Charles Jones, a local alderman and
also a currier, and one of his great-grandfathers was the John Lewis
who had kept the Half Moon Hotel in Carmarthen at the beginning of
the nineteenth century.[2] Mary Jean Jones, Alfred's mother, was the
eldest daughter of the Rev. Henry Williams, the rector of Llanedi, and
amongst his near relatives were numerous clergy, many doctors, a
barrister and a wine merchant.[3]

It would not be true to suggest, therefore, that Alfred Jones came
from a very poor background although this has been stated on many
occasions. While his parents were not affluent they were highly
regarded in the district, and many of his uncles and cousins were
pursuing successful careers in the church, in the professions and in
business. It is unlikely that Alfred would ever experience poverty, but
there is little doubt that Daniel and Mary Jones did have serious
problems to overcome. Daniel appears to have suffered from inter-
mittent ill-health which effectively reduced his earning power. This

[1] *South Wales Daily News*, 14 December 1909, obituary. *The Times*, 14 December
1909, obituary, erroneously states that Jones was born in Llanelly.
[2] This was demolished during the 1950s.
[3] See family tree, table 19, p. 146.

was particularly unfortunate as the task of providing for nine children must have been a heavy burden even though only Alfred and one girl, Mary Isobel, were to survive to maturity. It seems certain, therefore, that financial pressures played a significant part in Daniel Jones's decision to leave Carmarthen and the opportunity probably presented itself as a result of the sale of *The Welshman* to a Mr. Morgan.[4] At all events, in 1848 when Alfred was three, the family moved to Merseyside and from then onwards their home was to be in Liverpool.

Little is known of Daniel Jones's financial affairs after his move from Carmarthen, but apparently his change of venue was not especially beneficial. His ill-health continued and, although he was able to pursue his career as a currier, he was able to earn only a modest income. Nevertheless, there is no evidence to suggest that his children were ever deprived in any real sense, and Alfred's description of his childhood was that it was 'happy and uneventful'.[5] Daniel, in fact, appears only as a shadowy figure in the memories of both Alfred and Mary Isobel, for however great was their respect and love for their father, it was their mother who was the dominant figure in the Jones's household.

Mary Jean Jones, born in 1809, brought up her family as befitted the daughter of a clergyman. She had a religious nature and was careful to give comprehensive spiritual guidance to Alfred and her other children. Each Sunday saw the whole family at church but, although a firm believer in the value of discipline, she was able to instil her principles and attitudes into her offspring without causing any rancour and both Alfred and Mary Isobel were devoted to her in later life. She felt herself to be of gentle origins and, as a lady, bore the loss of her children and her other misfortunes with patience and composure. Her major consolation lay in her close bond with Alfred and she took the greatest possible interest in his progress. By the time of her husband's death she was already heavily dependent on Alfred and, thereafter, their friendship became even closer. The success of his career during her lifetime and the promise of further achievements in the future were vital factors which enabled her to be more easily reconciled to her disappointments.

Alfred fully reciprocated his mother's feelings and it was, perhaps, the wish to please her that first fired his restless ambition. An early

---

[4] Letter to the author from Hugh Jones of Carmarthen, 7 December 1962.

[5] Alfred Jones's autobiography, first published in the magazine *MAP* on 28 December 1901, and reprinted in *Trading in West Africa*, P. N. Davies (ed.) (Croom Helm, London, 1976), pp. 183–6.

demonstration of his regard for his mother is provided in his sister's biography.[6] As a junior clerk he earned such low wages that he could not afford any tram fare so walked some four miles to work each day. Nevertheless, when he saw an old china teapot in a pawnbroker's shop in Brunswick Road he decided to buy it for his mother. The price was too much for his slender resources but by repeated calls at the shop he eventually secured it on more reasonable terms. The gift was greatly appreciated and later, in more affluent times, retained its attraction in spite of the competition of Crown Derby and Dresden.

During his childhood in Liverpool Jones attended local schools where he was regarded as rather a studious boy.[7] He was particularly fond of arithmetic and as he had a good head for figures was usually to be found near the top of his class. Jones always maintained that part of the reason for his success in business was his good health, and this was also true of his school days for he seldom, if ever, lost time through accident or sickness. As far back as he could remember Jones was ambitious and anxious to succeed.[8] With the advantage of a strong constitution and the ability of working long hours without ill-effect he was well equipped to seize any opportunities which came his way. In addition, although he was fond of swimming and had developed a genuine affection for dogs, his real interest, even at this early stage, was in his work and in his desire to 'ascend the ladder' for both his own and his family's sake. Family, to Jones, really meant his mother, but it was during his schooldays that a lasting affection started between Alfred and his sister, Mary Isobel. She became his constant companion and her friendship was to prove a major influence on him for the remainder of his life.

At the age of fourteen Alfred Jones decided that the time had come for him to strike out for himself. He then found that in the Liverpool of 1859 prospects of employment for a youth without influence and only a simple education were strictly limited. After due consideration, therefore, he decided that the sea offered him his best opportunity for a worthwhile career and he began to make frequent visits to the local docks. Alfred spoke to the masters of numerous ships and received many rebuffs due to his youth and inexperience. Yet he refused to be discouraged and finally persuaded the master of a vessel of the African

---

[6] Biographical notes on Jones by his sister, Mary Isobel Pinnock. Reproduced in *Trading in West Africa*, op. cit., pp. 187–8.

[7] Jones's autobiography, op. cit.

[8] Ibid.

Steam Ship Company to give him a job as a cabin boy. It speaks well for his powers of persuasion that he secured this appointment. West Africa's reputation as the white man's grave no doubt reduced the number of applicants for the position but it would also have made the captain extremely reluctant to take so young a boy to such a terrible region.

Jones was only to make one journey to West Africa and no records of his voyage have survived. However, it must have been typical of many such trips made by the steamers of the African Steam Ship Company at that time. In 1859, the company owned seven vessels ranging from the *Cleopatra* of only 1,280 tons down to the *Retriever* of 329 tons; Jones must have travelled in a very small ship.[9] The vessel undoubtedly followed the usual route from Liverpool via St. Georges's Channel and across the Bay of Biscay. Then, while coal was loaded at Lisbon or Dakar, Jones would have obtained his first glimpse of a foreign port. His first introduction to British West Africa would have come a little later, perhaps at Freetown in Sierra Leone or Bathurst at the mouth of the River Gambia. The next stage of the voyage was along the coastline of West Africa where every little river and creek had its own small port or stopping place so the routine of loading and unloading a few pieces of cargo would have quickly become familiar to Jones. He would also have witnessed the difficulties in getting the ship away from each tiny port as the local boatmen, in spite of frequent warnings, would hang on until the last possible moment.[10] At every stop Jones would have seen something new to interest him so that by the time his ship arrived at Fernando Po he would certainly have gained a useful knowledge of West Africa and its inhabitants.

At this date the Spanish island of Fernando Po was the southernmost point of the services offered by the African Steam Ship Company. It would take only a few days, perhaps a week, for the ship to discharge its cargo, to load local products and take on coal and water. The journey home would have taken less than the five or six weeks of the outward voyage as fewer minor calls would be necessary: as soon as the vessel was fully laden she would have headed straight for England. Judging by other sailings undertaken by the company's vessels it is probable that the ship averaged about nine knots for the 10,000 mile trip, so Jones would have been away from Liverpool for less than

[9] *African S.S. Company MSS* in the author's possession. Hereinafter referred to as ASP.

[10] *E. D. Morel Papers*, letter from Jones to Morel, 9 September 1901.

three months.[11] Short as it was, this brief period was to shape his future life, for Jones had made a very favourable impression on his captain during the voyage. Consequently, when the vessel returned to the Mersey he made a point of recommending the boy to the ship's agents and, as a result, they offered him a position as a junior clerk.

II

The African Steam Ship Company had been established in 1852 by Macgregor Laird, a member of the Birkenhead shipbuilding family.[12] Laird had earlier, in 1832, joined with Richard Lander to organize an expedition to explore the River Niger, but trading had been poor and the venture had not been a financial success. Furthermore, of the forty-eight Europeans who had taken part in the expedition, thirty-nine had died of disease.[13] Laird himself had nearly died and so had decided not to repeat the experiment, but nevertheless he continued to watch West African affairs very closely. He noted in particular the steady growth of trade between the United Kingdom and the West African coast and by 1850 this had developed into quite substantial proportions.[14] In Laird's opinion that meant that great scope must exist for a regular steamship service, so he approached the Government and after long negotiations obtained a ten-year mail contract, together with a substantial subsidy.[15] Armed with this contract, Laird sought and received the support of a body of influential men who were prepared to join with him in organizing and financing the new concern and thus the African Steam Ship Company came into existence.[16]

The early sailings of the new company were from London with a call at Plymouth, but in 1856 it was decided to make Liverpool the

[11] ASP, voyage of the *Faith*.

[12] DNB, vol. XXXI, 1892, p. 407 (Macgregor Laird).

[13] Macgregor Laird and R. A. K. Oldfield, *Narrative of an Expedition into the Interior of Africa by the River Niger in the Steam Vessels* Quorra and Alburkah *in 1832, 1833 and 1834* (Richard Bentley, London).

[14] ASP, *Statement of the Trade between England and the West Coast of Africa*. This forms part of the company's prospectus.

[15] C. W. Newbury, *British Policy towards West Africa, Select Documents, 1786–1874* (Oxford University Press, London, 1965), p. 114, letter from Macgregor Laird to Earl Grey, 'Steam Communication with Africa', 25 March 1851. See also ASP prospectus, p. 4.

[16] The capital structure of the African Steam Ship Company is given in the appendix, table 3, p. 128.

UK terminal. To do this it was necessary to appoint agents, and the task was given to Messrs. William and Hamilton Laird, brothers of the founder of the African Steam Ship Company. Hamilton Laird died in 1860 so a member of his staff, J. T. Fletcher, was taken into partnership and it was this new style firm of Laird and Fletcher with which Alfred Jones found employment after his one trip to West Africa.

The office in which Jones found himself was extremely small, with never more than thirteen employees, but it always managed to fulfil its two main functions quite efficiently. Its prime task was to ensure a rapid turnround of the company's seven vessels and see to their crewing, victualling, bunkering and repair. In addition, when the sailings were transferred to the Mersey in 1856 the Liverpool agents were placed in effective control of all the company's activities and all decisions were made by them. The deaths of Hamilton and Macgregor Laird did not affect this arrangement, but when William Laird retired in 1863 (he was succeeded by L. H. Parr),[17] the control of the African Steam Ship Company was again centred in London. For a while this made little practical difference to the day-to-day operations carried out by Messrs. Fletcher and Parr and their employees were kept fully occupied.

For such a tiny office the firm possessed a veritable galaxy of talent. Apart from the partners, Fletcher and Parr, who were to prove themselves capable and successful businessmen, the agency included John Holt, Alexander Elder and John Dempster. The first of these had been apprenticed to William Laird in 1857 to learn the coal trade.[18] Laird's increasing interest in West African shipping meant that most of Holt's time was concerned with that particular trade so it is not surprising that when he had completed his apprenticeship he determined to seek his fortune on the Coast. He sailed from Liverpool in *Cleopatra* in June 1862, severing his connection with Fletcher and Parr.[19] It also ended the friendship which had been developing over the previous two years with Alfred Jones, but the two men were to meet again when Holt was building up his business as a major West African merchant and Jones was endeavouring to control the West African shipping trade.

[17] See his obituary in the *Liverpool Courier*, 9 November 1885.
[18] *Merchant Adventure* (John Holt & Co., Liverpool, 1948). The indenture between John Holt and William Laird is reproduced on p. 12.
[19] C. R. Holt (ed.), *The Diary of John Holt* (Henry Young, Liverpool, 1948). An extensive account of the outward voyage is given in pp. 3–22.

Alexander Elder, born in Glasgow in 1834, was the son of David Elder who for many years was manager of Robert Napier and Sons, engine and shipbuilders.[20] One of his older brothers, John Elder, served an apprenticeship with Napier and subsequently founded the firm of Randolph, Elder and Company. Later this concern took the name of John Elder and Company and eventually became known as the Fairfield Shipbuilding and Engineering Company.[21] Alexander Elder served his time as a marine engineer with them and then sailed as chief engineer on the s.s. *Brandon*, the first ship fitted with compound engines to cross the Atlantic. He then obtained a similar situation on board the s.s. *Columbian* and saw service in the Crimean War, spending some hours in Sebastopol on the day of its fall.[22]

The other employee of note was John Dempster who had been born in 1837 at Penport, Thornhill, Dumfriesshire where his father, William Dempster, was builder to the Duke of Buccleuch. When the Duke began to develop his interests in Birkenhead the Dempster family moved there and in 1851 John, then aged fourteen, joined William and Hamilton Laird as a junior clerk. In 1856, Alexander Elder also became a member of Laird's staff to act as superintendent engineer for the African Steam Ship Company which, as previously noted, had transferred its sailings to the Mersey at that date. Elder's position in the firm was very much superior to that of Dempster who was still a minor clerk of little consequence but the smallness of the office and the nearness of their ages, Elder being then twenty-two and Dempster nineteen, helped to ensure a growing friendship. The fact that both originated in Scotland provided a further bond, but there is no evidence to suggest that in the early years of their acquaintanceship they ever envisaged the common future which fate had ordained for them.

Macgregor Laird was still alive when Alfred Jones joined the Liverpool Agents and they apparently met on numerous occasions:

... Mr. (Macgregor) Laird had a great idea of the future of West Africa and I have taken my ideas from him. When I was a very small boy I used to carry the tea to Mr. Laird and Mr. Laird used very often to give me half-a-

[20] C. Wilson and W. Reader, *Men and Machines, a History of D. Napier and Son, Enginers, Limited* (Weidenfeld and Nicolson, London, 1958). This is not an account of the marine engineering firm but it contains many references to it as the principals were related.

[21] E. C. Smith, *A Short History of Naval and Marine Engineering* (Cambridge University Press, 1937), p. 178.

[22] *Journal of Commerce*, 26 January 1915, obituary of Alexander Elder.

crown. That half crown was put away and I have it still. I did not lose it and it has yielded me very good interest.[23]

Just how great an influence Macgregor Laird exerted on the youthful office boy who served his tea is open to question: it may have been an ex post rationalization on Jones's part, but there can be no doubt that Parr did provide help and encouragement at a critical time of his life. Not only did he pay for Jones to attend night school but he also invited him to his home quite frequently and this was an invaluable help in strengthening the boy's social background. At this early stage in his career Jones lived in Freehold Street in the West Derby area of Liverpool.[24] To save money he usually walked to work and carried his lunch with him for his pay was very poor: he started at half-a-crown a week and even by the age of twenty he was earning only a pound. This meant that he had to leave home very early in the morning and that he would arrive home extremely late at night, particularly on those occasions when he went straight from work to an evening class at the Liverpool College in Shaw Street.

Alfred Jones remained with Fletcher and Parr throughout the 1860s, gradually gaining in status and salary. The departure of Holt in 1862 had had little effect on his prospects but subsequent resignations were a different matter. It is not certain why Alexander Elder decided to leave Fletcher and Parr in 1866 for his annual salary had been raised from £300 to £400 the previous year,[25] and there is nothing to suggest that he ever had any serious disagreements with the two partners. It may be that the failure of the African Steam Ship Company to expand its fleet in accordance with the needs of the trade led him to believe that the agency's prospects were not particularly bright.[26] A more likely explanation is that his position as superintendent engineer brought him into frequent contact with the company secretary, Duncan Campbell, and he may have wished to end what, to his mind, was a potentially dangerous situation.[27] The deciding factor, however, was probably the offer of a responsible post as engineer and shipwright surveyor to the Liverpool branch of the Board of Trade. The security

[23] *The Times*, 20 August 1902; speech by A. L. Jones at a banquet given in his honour by the inhabitants of West Africa.
[24] The house was destroyed by bombs in 1941 but the street is otherwise little changed.
[25] ASP, private journal of Fletcher and Parr, no. 1.
[26] P. N. Davies, *The African Steam Ship Company*, op. cit., p. 218.
[27] See below, p. 26.

of government service was, no doubt, a great inducement to a canny Scot!

The resignation of Elder brought to a temporary end the close association which he had developed with John Dempster, although there is no reason to suppose that the two young men did not keep in touch. Dempster remained with Fletcher and Parr and with the departure of Elder became the highest paid member of the staff, earning £297 in 1866 and £350 the following year. Had Dempster remained with Fletcher and Parr his salary would have continued to rise for as chief clerk he was a valuable asset to the firm, but his position and, in fact, the whole of the trade was to be dramatically altered by the advent of a new steamship company which was to compete on the West African route.

III

The new line was the British and African Steam Navigation Company, registered in Edinburgh in 1868 with an issued capital of £68,400.[28] It was intended that its ships would operate from Glasgow via Liverpool to the West Coast of Africa so an agent to handle the Liverpool side of the business was obviously a necessity. The only experienced firm was Messrs. Fletcher and Parr but they already represented the African Steam Ship Company. In view of this, John Dempster was asked if he would consent to act as Liverpool agent for the new line. He was clearly a good choice for he had spent his entire career in the West African trade and when he decided to seek a partner he chose Alexander Elder who was still employed by the Board of Trade, bringing into being the firm of Elder Dempster and Company.

The appointment of an efficient Liverpool agency was crucial to the success of the British and African Steam Navigation Company. The trade between Glasgow and West Africa was growing[29] and it was to suit the convenience of this traffic that the line was to be established, but Liverpool was at the centre of the trade and it was there that the shortage of cargo space was most apparent. Without Dempster's help, therefore, it is quite possible that the projected shipping line would not

---

[28] The capital structure of the British and African Steam Navigation Company is given in the appendix, table 4, p. 129.

[29] See: *Glasgow and Africa, Connexions and Attitudes, 1870–1900*, an unpublished Ph.D. thesis presented to the University of Strathclyde by W. Thompson in 1970.

have been viable. In the event, of course, both Dempster and Elder were quite convinced of the potential of the West African trade and of their ability to obtain cargoes and were well content to associate their future prosperity with that of the British and African. Proof of their wholehearted confidence in the venture is the fact that they invested in the company at its inception and took every opportunity of increasing their shareholdings.[30]

The loss of Elder in 1866 and of Dempster in 1868 significantly enhanced Alfred Jones's prospects and by 1870, then aged twenty-five, he was in a relatively senior position and earning £125 a year.[31] By that time he was making a name for himself by his shrewd decisions and smart business acumen but his pleasure in this progress was marred by the death of his father in February 1869. This blow made his relationship with his mother even closer and he continued to live with her and his sister, Mary Isobel, at the family home in West Derby. The following year Isobel married John Pinnock but, as he was a merchant engaged in the West African trade and spent much time abroad, she continued to live with her mother and brother.

The British and African Steam Navigation Company began its monthly service from Glasgow via Liverpool to the West Coast of Africa in January 1869, the first sailing being by the s.s. *Bonny* which had been built for the new line by John Elder and Company at Glasgow.[32] The African Steam Ship Company and its agents, Messrs. Fletcher and Parr, did all they could to restrict the progress of the rival line and appealed to their customers to support them. They quickly adopted a more amenable policy towards their shippers and raised fresh capital by issuing new shares. This enabled additional tonnage to be constructed and chartered but in spite of all efforts revenue began to fall:

> Owing to competition which has existed since January last, your Directors have deemed it necessary to make important reductions in the Rates of Freight and Passage Money, and also to increase the number of sailings; the profits of the Half-year just ended have consequently been diminished.[33]

[30] For details of the share distribution in the British and African Steam Navigation Company see *The Trade Makers*, op. cit., pp. 427-32.

[31] ASP, Fletcher & Parr, private journal no. 1.

[32] Just as all the early vessels of the African Steam Ship Company were built by the family of Lairds (the Birkenhead Iron Works) so all the early steamers of the British and African were built by the brother of Alexander Elder (John Elder and Company).

[33] ASP, directors' report for the half-year ending 31 October 1869, p. 5.

In fact, the competition with the British and African Steam Navigation Company lasted for only a twelve month period and then the two lines came together and agreed to share their sailings.[34] The new agreement was at first in the nature of an uneasy truce and the directors of the African Steam Ship Company called up more capital and issued debentures on a substantial scale. The fleet was then gradually increased and modernized but the steady progress of the company was impaired by two events in 1872. The first concerned the secretary, Duncan Campbell, for it was discovered that he had embezzled a sum which 'approached £20,000'.[35] The second was the termination of the mail contract, ending the subsidizing of the route as originally negotiated by Macgregor Laird. It was not, however, an unmitigated disaster for the company still received the sea postage for whatever mail it carried and it was relieved of the responsibility and expense of running unprofitable services.

A new agreement between the African and British and African companies was made in 1873, providing that a steamer of each line should sail every alternate week and illustrating the increasing harmony between them. The basic reason for the success of these arrangements was fear of competition from outside firms: both concerns accepted the principle that co-operation with a friendly rival was preferable to unrestricted competition with innumerable interlopers. Under these circumstances, the African Steam Ship Company paid small but regular dividends and came under heavy criticism from Fletcher and Parr for not building up their fleet more quickly. The Liverpool agents, dependent on commission for their income, were naturally eager to expand trade while the London office was mainly concerned with reducing risks and cutting costs. With two such divergent points of view, it is not surprising that antagonism developed between Liverpool and London, and this reached a head in 1875 when the agency agreement came up for renewal. The Liverpool agents were then asked if they would be prepared to accept a reduced commission. Fletcher and Parr replied that they were prepared to discuss a reduction, but they 'hoped the proposed economy was not to be limited to the Liverpool Agency'. The chairman of the African Steam Ship Company seems to have taken this as a personal slur on himself and his fellow directors, and the atmosphere worsened. In February 1875 the Liverpool agents

[34] ASP, directors' report for the half-year ending 30 April 1870.
[35] ASP, pamphlet issued by Messrs. Fletcher and Parr who, in fact, recovered most of the stolen money.

were again asked if they were prepared to accept the reduced rate of commission. They answered that it was the 'indisposition of the directors to replace the *Soudan* wrecked at Madeira that was affecting the profits of the Company, and it would, therefore, be unfair to expect them to pay for the omissions of others'. They further offered to take over the sailings which this ship should have made if the company continued to feel unable to replace her by purchase or charter. In this way, they felt that they would be able to prevent the British and African, or any interlopers, from getting the benefit of the African Steam Ship Company's reduced sailings. A reply from the London office came by return of post to say:

> . . . the directors had unanimously decided to open an office of their own in Liverpool with a manager who would be under the more immediate control of the board.[36]

IV

Alfred Jones continued to make progress in the employ of Messrs. Fletcher and Parr throughout the early 1870s. The extent to which he was responsible for the growing co-operation between the African and British and African lines is not certain, nor is it possible to do more than guess at his role in the dispute between Liverpool and London. What is clear is that his salary increased to £137 in 1871, £150 in 1872 and £175 in both 1873 and 1874, and it is to be expected that his authority rose accordingly.[37] It was at this time that he is said to have made many suggestions for extending the business, but 'his colossal charter-schemes, as they were then thought, fairly appalled his old-fashioned employers. . . .'[38] As a result of their attitude, Jones was unable to institute any major changes in agency policy but he did obtain permission to organize a small amount of chartering on his own account and for this he received a commission which, in 1875, amounted to £26 15s. 3d. Thus his total remuneration for that year was just over £201, the most he had ever earned, but any satisfaction he may have felt was rapidly dissipated by news of the loss of the agency of the African Steam Ship Company.

It was obvious to Alfred Jones that the loss of their key agency would mean substantially less work for Fletcher and Parr and, consequently,

---

[36] ASP, pamphlet issued by Messrs. Fletcher and Parr, p. 9.
[37] ASP, Fletcher and Parr's private journals, nos. 1 and 2.
[38] *Shipping World*, 22 December 1909, obituary of Alfred Jones.

considerably less scope for him within the firm. He was, of course, well aware of Elder and Dempster's successful venture and knew of John Holt's return from West Africa after having laid the foundations of a profitable and lasting concern. It seemed to him, therefore, that in spite of his achievements within Fletcher and Parr's he was in danger of being left behind by his more progressive and adventurous former associates. The loss of the African Steam Ship Company's agency appears to have been the final straw to this ambitious man and he decided to leave his employment and establish his own business.

Alfred Jones remained with Fletcher and Parr for a further two years while he finalized his plans and accumulated more capital. In 1876, he received £175 in salary which, with his commission on chartering of £57 9s. 7d., gave him an income of £232 and in 1877 he earned a total of just over £247.[39] The achievement of these figures is a great tribute to Fletcher and Parr's resilience in very trying circumstances, for until 1875 the vast majority of their work had been related to the African Steam Ship Company. The loss of this agency meant that they had virtually to rebuild their firm by moving on to different trades and developing the firm's other interests which included the agencies for the Liverpool and Antwerp Steamers Company and the Peninsular and Oriental Steam Navigation Company.[40] Thus Alfred Jones was able to maintain his income at a crucial stage in his business career but this favourable consideration was more than counterbalanced by a shock which destroyed much of his contentment with life. This was the death of his mother in January 1877, and it was probably this event more than any other single factor which encouraged him to concentrate all of his considerable energies on his commercial activities. Following the death of their mother, Alfred's sister, Mary Isobel Pinnock, continued to live with him together with her two young daughters, Florence Mary and Blanche Elizabeth, as her husband spent much of his time abroad on business.[41] Then in May 1878 John Pinnock died from a tropical disease at the age of only thirty-two. It occurred on board the s.s. *Benin*, a vessel of the British and African Steam Navigation Company, when off Madeira while returning from a

[39] ASP, Fletcher & Parr's private journal, no. 2.
[40] Fletcher and Parr subsequently changed their name to J. T. Fletcher and Company. They currently (1977) operate under the title of J. T. Fletcher (Shipping) Limited.
[41] Details of Jones's family tree are given in the appendix, table 19, p. 146.

trading venture in West Africa. Tropical disease had gained another victim and Alfred Jones had gained a permanent housekeeper for his sister and her children were to make their home with him for the rest of his life.

The deaths of Jones's mother and brother-in-law did not affect his determination to build his own business, and on 1 January 1878 the firm of Alfred L. Jones and Company came into being and acquired offices at the North Western Bank Building, 6 Dale Street, Liverpool.[42] Messrs. Fletcher and Parr's offices were also in this building, evidence, perhaps, that Jones maintained friendly relations with his former employers. This would not be surprising for he had spent about eighteen years with them and had always been on the very best of terms with Parr. In addition, Jones's presence in the same building would have facilitated the continuation of business contacts which had been developed while he was employed with Fletcher and Parr and, no doubt, the convenience of this arrangement would have been beneficial if they had wished to pass on any unwanted trade.

At first Jones was concerned only with shipping and insurance broking although his firm was also described as general commission agents.[43] His experience with Fletcher and Parr stood him in good stead and he was able to do some work for them, receiving commission to the extent of £115 during 1878.[44] This was a useful start and by working long hours, paying great attention to detail and taking only short holidays he was gradually able to increase the number of his clients and the firm prospered. Jones quickly found that working for himself suited him well:

Any anxiety experienced at the start was more than compensated for by the independence of my new position, and the knowledge that success depended upon my own exertions.[45]

As he gained confidence and support Jones was able to diversify his activities and he chartered a number of small sailing-vessels to carry goods to West Africa. He later claimed that he made more money in his first year on his own than during the whole time he was with Fletcher and Parr. As this amounted to only just over £2,000 during

[42] *Gores Directory*, 1880.
[43] Ibid.
[44] ASP, Fletcher and Parr's private journal, no. 2.
[45] A. L. Jones's autobiography, op. cit.

the entire period,[46] his statement may well be true and this cash, together with his previous savings and credit, enabled him to undertake a new facet of his enterprise in his second year.

Early in 1879 he bought some of the ships he had chartered the previous year and then operated them in his own right on West African routes. The success of these voyages was a key factor in his progress but he did not allow this to alter his long held opinion that the future of the carrying trade to the Coast, as elsewhere, lay with the steamship. When, therefore, an advantageous moment arrived he disposed of his little fleet and made arrangements to charter a small steamer. This had immediate repercussions. The established lines, the African Steam Ship Company and the British and African Steam Navigation Company, appear to have taken fright at the prospect of a new rival. The agents for the latter firm were particularly concerned for Elder and Dempster knew Jones very well and their former association in Fletcher and Parr's office enabled them to make an accurate assessment of his potential. With this in mind and, probably encouraged by their friendly rival the African Steam Ship Company, they decided to avert future difficulties by offering him a junior partnership.

Jones's personal knowledge of Alexander Elder and John Dempster was also an important factor which he had to consider when making his decision, but perhaps the most significant single consideration was that after trading on his own account for eighteen months he was in an excellent position to judge the possibilities of his own business. In comparing the advantages of a small but independent position with a partnership in a larger and more established firm, Jones decided that he could not afford to ignore the scope and challenge that a senior position with Elder Dempster would offer him. He therefore terminated his steamship charter and dissolved the firm of Alfred L. Jones and Company. Then in October 1879 he joined his former colleagues in Messrs. Elder Dempster and Company.

[46] ASP, Fletcher and Parr's private journals, nos. 1 and 2.

CHAPTER THREE

The Achievement of Power

I

ALFRED JONES WAS TO BE A JUNIOR PARTNER with Elder Dempster until 1884, and at first he did little but learn thoroughly every aspect of the business:

> Until one has made himself practically acquainted with every detail of the business which he is called upon to direct, it is impossible to gauge its possibilities or properly carry out the duties of a director, therefore, my first object was to become thoroughly acquainted with each branch of the work the firm was engaged in, a thing not to be done in a moment.[1]

The decisions made by Elder Dempster at this time cannot be traced to any single partner, but there is little doubt that Jones played an increasingly important role. The strengthening of ties between the two British lines, the smashing of rival companies and the early agreements with German shipping interests all bear his stamp. It is also significant that it was following Jones's appointment as a junior partner that a major change occurred in the relationship between Elder Dempster and their principals, the British and African Steam Navigation Company. For many years Elder Dempster had acted as Liverpool agents for the Glasgow line but soon after the advent of Jones they were invited to act in a managerial capacity. This meant that Elder Dempster henceforth controlled all their vessels and organized many aspects of the British and African which then became, in effect, only a financial body. It may be unfair to ascribe this change solely to Jones's influence but, on the other hand, until this time there had been little basic change in the agreements between the shipping line and their agents since they had started in business together in 1868.

[1] A. L. Jones's autobiography, op. cit.

Alfred Jones's influence may also have been a decisive factor in the financial reconstruction of the British and African which began in 1881 and which was to pay for the expansion of its fleet. The effect of this was to raise the nominal capital from £200,000 to £250,000 and the issued capital from £200,000 to £210,960.[2] Then, on 23 April 1883, the British and African changed its status and became a limited company. At the same time the nominal capital was increased to £750,000 and the issued capital was more than doubled to £492,240.[3] The issued capital was further increased in 1884 and 1885 and by the latter year it had reached £546,000 which, in fact, proved to be its highest point.[4]

It could be argued, of course, that as a junior partner, Jones had little real authority. This is true in a legal sense for Elder and Dempster could always out-vote him but, on the other hand, they would have had to give him some scope or risk provoking his resignation. Jones was also assisted by the sustained support provided by W. J. Davey who had also been made a junior partner in 1879. Like Jones he was not a native of Liverpool, having been born in Cornwall in 1853, and it was not until 1871 that he moved to Merseyside and obtained employment in Elder Dempster's office.[5] His progress thereafter was steady, if unspectacular, and culminated in the offer of a partnership. But although his advancement was entirely due to the favourable opinion of Alexander Elder and John Dempster he appears to have fallen quickly and completely under the new partner's personality, and he was to remain Jones's right-hand man for the rest of his life.

While Elder Dempster and Company were progressing into management and persuading their principals to expand, their rival, the African Steam Ship Company, was developing on different lines. The sacking of Fletcher and Parr in 1875 was followed by the opening of a company office in Liverpool and Alexander Sinclair was appointed as branch manager. The change was regarded by the directors as a satisfactory one:

[2] In 1881, the issued capital was altered from 320 shares of £625 to 2,500 (less 156 unissued) shares of £100 (£90 called).

[3] 15,000 shares of £50 = £750,000:
11,720 shares taken up (£42 called) = £492,240.

[4] In 1884 1,280 new shares were issued on which £25 was called up. In 1885 these 'new' shares had a further £17 called, making them equal to the 'old' shares. The total share issue was then £13,000 of £42 = £546,000. See appendix, table 4, p. 129.

[5] *Journal of Commerce*, 2 November 1900.

The Directors are happy to state that the change in the Liverpool management has worked to their satisfaction and their expectations as to the economy likely to arise therefrom are being fully realised.[6]

The sinking of the s.s. *Soudan* in February 1875, which had been partially responsible for the break between Fletcher and Parr and the African Steam Ship Company, was not a disaster in itself, for all but £3,000 (the amount carried by the shipping line) was covered by outside insurance. When, however, this was combined with a poorness of trade which resulted in losses of £4,606 and £2,769 for the half years ending in April and October 1875, the directors were justifiably concerned. Their reaction, unlike that of the British and African which continued to expand under the guidance of Elder and Dempster, was one of retrenchment. Head office was moved to less expensive quarters and they reduced their own remuneration from £1,200 to £600 per annum. In 1876 the loss of *Monrovia* cost the company £3,000 but as there had been some improvement in trade it was possible to absorb this item. This increase in trade was maintained the following year and was assisted by an agreement made with the British and African in respect of sailings to the south-west coast of Africa.[7]

During the next few years the African Steam Ship Company made only slow progress. The emphasis remained on retrenchment and the debenture issue which amounted to £82,000 in 1875 was reduced to £58,000 in 1876 and progressively to £30,000 in 1880.[8] Behind this conservative policy lay the fluctuations which characterized the trade and also the opposition of rival lines, including that of the West African Steam Navigation Company, which ensured that freight rates were kept to a very low level.[9] On the other hand, a joint service from Hamburg to West Africa was begun in March 1879, in co-operation with the British and African, and this proved to be an immediate success. Partly owing to the demands for additional tonnage on this route and perhaps influenced by the example of the British and African, the African Steam Ship Company then began to expand its fleet.[10]

To finance this expansion the debenture issue was raised by £25,000 to £55,000 but even so its capital and fleet remained much smaller

[6] ASP, directors' report for the half year ending 31 October 1875.
[7] ASP, directors' report for the half year ending 30 April 1875, p. 5.
[8] ASP, see directors' reports for the relevant years.
[9] ASP, directors' reports for the half years ending 30 April and 31 October 1879.
[10] See *The Trade Makers*, op. cit., p. 82.

than that of the British and African. Furthermore, the results achieved by the African during this period continued to be poor although the enlarged fleet was almost fully employed, largely owing to the activities of yet another competitor, the Anglo-African Steam Ship Company. This line began to operate early in 1883 so freight rates had to be reduced and further losses were incurred in chartering vessels in conjunction with the British and African to make special voyages against the new competitor. These measures proved successful: the Anglo-African was wound up by order of the Court of Chancery in 1884, but the cost to both the established lines was heavy.[11]

This was a typical example of the increasing co-operation between the African Steam Ship Company and the British and African and, incidentally, of the growing importance of Elder Dempster and Company. The British and African had its head office in Glasgow while the African was controlled from London, so the close liaison between the two firms really rested on the proximity of Elder Dempster and Alexander Sinclair in Liverpool. In fact, most of the working arrangements and agreements were the result of their consultations and together the two lines were able to resist the opposition of the many companies and tramp steamers that attempted to enter the trade. In this connection, it should be appreciated that even when no rival line was seeking to enter the trade, many single ships were continuously seeking to find an opening. The scale of this attempted intervention may be judged by the fact that from June 1884 to June 1885 no fewer than fifteen extraneous vessels sailed from Hamburg and Liverpool to West Africa. The reaction of the directors to this particular onslaught was to reduce their tariff rates still further:

> Owing to the extremely depressed state of the Steam Shipping Trade there are a large number of steamers of a similar class seeking employment, many of the owners of which would rather face loss than have their vessels laid up. At the rates now charged by our (African Steam Ship) Company and the British and African Company it is not possible for outside steamers to compete successfully with our vessels.[12]

II

From the foregoing it will be apparent that although the two established lines were able to maintain their position in the West African

[11] ASP, directors' report for the half year ending 30 April 1884, p. 6.
[12] ASP, directors' report for the half year ending April 1885, p. 7.

shipping trade this was frequently achieved only by utilizing un-remunerative freight rates. It is also clear that by 1884 the two British companies were being forced to co-operate more and more if they wished to survive and it seems highly probable that Elder Dempster played a key role in arranging mutually beneficial policies.

As noted earlier, it is not possible to define Alfred Jones's influence in these matters but it is to be expected that he took ever increasing interest. By 1884 he was ready, indeed, to run Elder Dempster and Company and he put proposals to this effect to the two senior partners. It was not to be expected that they would give him the control he desired and yet, surprisingly, they did so and ended their association with the firm they had created. The secrecy which surrounded the departure of Alexander Elder and John Dempster has never been dispelled and in his autobiography Jones merely stated that:

> My opportunity came soon after when on the retirement of Mr. Elder and Mr. Dempster, I rose to be the senior partner of Elder Dempster and Company.[13]

This somewhat simple explanation is repeated by A. H. Milne in his biography of Jones:

> A few years after this, Mr. Elder and Mr. Dempster retired from the business. It was then carried on by Mr. Jones and Mr. Davey. . . .[14]

But it is unlikely that the two senior partners just retired. Both were comparatively young – Elder fifty and Dempster forty-seven – and both were not only to outlive Alfred Jones but were to remain actively in business in Liverpool for another sixteen years. The *Dundee Advertiser* of 14 December 1909, in its obituary of Jones, when writing of the time he agreed to join Elder Dempster, states:

> On condition of receiving a certain proportion of the Company's shares he agreed to join the firm. He then gradually bought up the shares till he controlled the concern.

This view of the events leading to the change in control is probably based on an interview given by Jones to Rudolph de Cordova and published in 1903.[15] Unfortunately the conversation was not specific

---

[13] A. L. Jones's autobiography, op. cit.
[14] A. H. Milne, *Sir Alfred Lewis Jones, K.C.M.G.* (Henry Young, Liverpool, 1914).
[15] 'The New Gospel of Wealth', *The Sunday Strand*, November 1903.

enough to be of much assistance and it would seem that Jones was merely glossing over the affair. Another version of these events of 1884 is given in other obituary notices, and *The Times* of 13 December 1909 is typical of these:

> The story was that when a young man he had risen to a responsible position in the office of Elder Dempster and Company, he went to the heads of the concern and told them he saw his way to an immense development of their business if they would put the control of it in his hands, and that he was prepared to buy them out on terms to be agreed upon if they were not prepared to carry out his views. They replied that the purchase of the concern was far beyond his resources at the time and that they were not prepared to entertain his proposals. He then asked for six months to obtain the money required and, at the end of that time, so good was his credit in Liverpool, and so high was his reputation for business capacity and enterprise, that he returned to the partners and told them he had raised the amount required and was prepared to advance it on terms which would give him complete control of the business.

John Holt, in a letter to James Knott dated 13 May 1891, put the matter in a nutshell:

> Fletcher and Parr were the trainers of the West African (Steam) trade. Elder and Dempster started the British and African S.S. Co. in opposition to Fletcher and Parr, and later Jones came on the scene with a couple of tramps which he took off in order to get into a partnership with E.D. & Co. which ended in Elder and Dempster leaving Jones and their Correspondent Clerk Davey as their successors.[16]

In a letter to Elder dated June 1895, John Holt also wrote:

> . . . as a ship's agent pure and simple as you and Mr. Dempster used to be in bygone days in Liverpool – when nobody had a thought of your giving up the interest of your shipping and against whom, rates being equal, no opposition would have had ever started.[17]

Thus Elder and Dempster were, apparently, well thought of, their business was prospering and yet they handed it over to Alfred Jones. As an unlimited company (Elder Dempster was legally a partnership) it was under no obligation to forward returns under the Company Acts of 1856 and 1862. Consequently, there is a lack of solid information

---

[16] John Holt Papers (JHP), letter from John Holt to James Knott, 13 May 1891.
[17] JHP, letter from John Holt to Alexander Elder, June 1895.

so any attempted explanation of this remarkable action must be quite tentative. Thus it is not possible, for example, to verify the suggestion that Jones gradually acquired sufficient shares to gain a controlling interest and then pushed out the senior partners. In any case, the shares of a private company such as this were customarily held by the principals, their families and close friends, so it would have been difficult for Jones to buy enough shares, even assuming he had sufficient money to pay for them.

The story put forward by *The Times* seems improbable and would need documentary evidence before it could be accepted, but it does appear to possess a germ of truth. If we consider that it would have been impossible for Jones to have gradually secured a controlling number of shares, the only reasonable assumption for a small private company, then we are left with the alternative that he offered Elder and Dempster such a large sum of money for their interest that they found it convenient to accept. But it is almost certain that this is only half the story. Jones undoubtedly received some shares when he joined the firm, and he was probably able to buy a few more in his five years as a junior partner. His fellow junior partner W. J. Davey could be relied on to support him, but in comparison with the shares held by Elder and Dempster and their friends their combined holdings were very small. To counteract this unfavourable distribution of shares Jones had two possible courses of action and it is to be expected that he carried these out simultaneously. Thus he ingratiated himself with any shareholder he could by holding out the promise of higher dividends if he were in control. In this task his tremendous reputation in Liverpool stood him in good stead so he was able to threaten Elder and Dempster with the possibility of his persuading an adequate number of shareholders to change their allegiance. Jones could also suggest, both to the shareholders and to the senior partners, that if he were not allowed to buy control of the company he would leave it, and that the rival concern that he would start must certainly reduce the profitability of Elder Dempster, if it did not end its existence altogether.

In these ways Jones could have maintained a heavy pressure on Elder and Dempster. By making their personal positions appear to be slightly insecure within their own firm and by threatening to start a rival company Jones would have been able to make his offer to buy them out the more attractive. Apart from the pressure to sell and the substantial financial inducements offered, Elder and Dempster had also to contend with the man himself. Alfred Jones's forceful personality, large capacity for work, enormous knowledge of the trade and his drive and initiative all made him a very formidable character. The necessarily close daily contact of the partners must have resulted in friction at times and on these occasions Jones's strength of purpose and single-mindedness must have been of immense value in wearing down the opposition of his seniors. In due course, it seemed to Elder and Dempster that they had to decide either to accept their subordinate's generous terms or be prepared to fight him. Realizing that a struggle might be financially disastrous for their interests and having such a rewarding alternative, they therefore allowed Jones to buy them out.

III

When Alfred Jones obtained control of Elder Dempster and Company in 1884 it was only the first step towards his domination of the West African shipping business. Elder Dempster at this date was still only a relatively tiny firm of shipping agents with a precarious hold on the trade, and if this was to be maintained and subsequently expanded many serious problems had to be overcome. Perhaps the two most important of these were the continuation of friendly relations between the two established lines, and the elimination of extraneous competitors. Individually, these were quite substantial difficulties but, fortunately for Jones, they tended to cancel one another out. By keeping on the closest possible terms the regular lines were able to put up an effective barrier against any outside interest and both realized not only how much could be gained by co-operation but also how disastrous rivalry would be. Thus Jones's task was made easier in both ways: the possibility of a rift was lessened, competing steamers got short shrift and the two companies were enabled to maintain their place in the trade. It was, therefore, of paramount importance to Jones that he continued the friendly connection between the two firms, and his success in achieving this objective was to be the basis for his entire strategy in implementing his plans for the future.

Another factor of prime importance to Jones was the relationship between Elder Dempster and the two British lines sailing to West Africa. It was, of course, essential that he retained the goodwill and co-operation of both these companies but the way in which this was achieved differed in each case. Jones did not feel it was necessary for him to invest in the shares of the British and African Steam Navigation Company at this stage for Elder Dempster already possessed a virtually exclusive say in the running of this line: 'Practically they have no accounts with anyone except through their Liverpool Agents.'[18]

On the other hand, Jones had absolutely no say in the policies of the African Steam Ship Company so he made it his business to buy its shares whenever they came on to the market. Details of the share distribution of this line are not available[19] but as Jones had gained a controlling interest by 1900, it seems likely that he had collected their shares from an early date. In the short term every share meant a vote in his favour at annual general meetings, and as his holdings increased so did his ability to block any moves by potential opponents. Jones, in fact, continued to expand his interests in the African Steam Ship Company until his death in 1909 when he owned 26,328 shares of £20 each, fully paid.[20] By that date, the issued capital of the company amounted to 33,732 shares,[21] so Jones held over 75 per cent of the total.

A final, crucial, problem which faced Jones throughout his period as senior partner of Elder Dempster was that of retaining the goodwill of the trading firms who provided the bulk of his cargoes. As late as the mid-1880s it was still quite customary for many merchants to own sailing-vessels although, by then, most of their goods were carried by the regular lines. In addition, a few of these traders would sometimes join together to charter sailing (and occasionally steam) ships, but this rather depended on the level of freight rates. Some of the larger merchants also thought it would be of advantage to establish their own independent line, but as this would necessarily involve co-operation with other trading firms (frequently deadly rivals) these ideas seldom got very far. Nevertheless, the possibility that merchants might acquire or charter vessels, might utilize the services of an outside line or a tramp steamer, or even start their own line, was a tremendous source of worry to Jones and required constant effort to be overcome.

---

[18] Petition of the British and African Steam Navigation Company Limited to the Rt. Hon. the Lords of Council and Sessions, section 8, 26 February 1891.

[19] The African Steam Ship Company being established by Royal Charter did not come within the provisions of the Company Acts of the 1850s and was not required to submit returns of shareholders to the Registrar of Companies.

[20] Agreements relating to the formation of Elder Dempster and Company, Limited, in 1910. Third Schedule, p. 13. See *The Trade Makers*, op. cit., p. 455.

[21] ASP, directors' report for the twelve months ending 31 December 1909, p. 7.

IV

The period from 1884 to 1895 was a particularly difficult one for Alfred Jones, yet he succeeded in achieving all his main objectives. Under his guidance Elder Dempster remained on friendly terms with the two British lines and the two firms maintained cordial relations between themselves. Indeed, after 1891, the relationship linking the three concerns became even closer, for in that year Elder Dempster became the managing agents for the African Steam Ship Company as well as retaining that position for the British and African Steam Navigation Company. It was fortunate for the established lines that this close co-operation existed as several other shipping companies made attempts to enter the West African shipping trade. All of these attempts were defeated with one exception: the Woermann Line of Hamburg. This German firm could not be easily disposed of because it had certain advantages, so an arrangement was made whereby it agreed to restrict itself to particular areas on the Coast and not to enter the United Kingdom trade to West Africa. Jones and the two established lines were also attacked during this period by the Royal Niger Company (the largest firm of West African merchants) and by the African Association Limited, an amalgamation created by a number of merchants to work in specific areas on the Coast. It took all Jones's skill to defend his position in the short run but, ultimately, he was able to make satisfactory arrangements with both these opponents.

Before 1887 Elder Dempster had been ships' agents and ships' managers but never shipowners. This situation was rectified in that year when Jones bought the s.s. *Clare*. In the next few years the Elder Dempster fleet grew rapidly and by 1890 it owned eleven vessels totalling 28,373 gross tons. This fleet was transferred to the African Steam Ship Company the following year as part of the arrangement whereby Elder Dempster became the company's managing agents, and it marked yet another important milestone in Jones's career. Ever since he had become associated with Elder Dempster, Jones had worked for the best possible understanding with the African Steam Ship Company and had constantly worried in case any disagreement would upset what he regarded as the foundation of his position in the West African carrying trade. Accordingly he had taken every opportunity to ingratiate himself with the company and he felt that his efforts had borne fruit when he was able to secure the management of the line for his own firm.

Jones's own holdings in the African Steam Ship Company must have been relatively small at this time so the decision to make Elder Dempster managing agents must have been made purely on grounds of increased efficiency. In his dealings with the Royal Niger Company and the African Association, Jones had demonstrated quite conclusively to the directors of the African Steam Ship Company that their interests, like those of the British and African, were safe in his hands. They therefore placed the running of their line in his keeping with the sole proviso that Alexander Sinclair, former manager of their Liverpool office which was not closed, should be appointed a partner in Elder Dempster and Company.

The result of this activity was that for the first time Jones could really control and integrate the fleets of both the regular British shipping lines. These had both made considerable progress in the years which followed Jones's achievement of power in 1884, but the transfer of the Elder Dempster fleet had meant that whereas in 1885 the African's tonnage had been considerably less than the British and African's, by 1891 the position had been reversed.[22] The changes in the relative sizes of the two fleets was reflected in alterations in the capital structure of the two companies. Thus the British and African reduced its issued capital from a peak of £546,000 in 1885 to £390,000 in 1888, at which it remained throughout the 1890s.[23] During the same period the African Steam Ship Company increased its issued capital and debentures from £256,152 in 1885 to £747,182 in 1900.[24]

The largest increase in the capital of the African Steam Ship Company was in 1891 when it was necessary to finance the purchase of the Elder Dempster tonnage[25] but even without this type of investment, the company consistently pursued a policy of steady expansion. This is not surprising when it is realized that trade between British West Africa and the United Kingdom more than doubled in monetary terms between 1884 and 1900[26] and, as this was a period of falling prices, in real terms the increase was very much greater.[27]

Why, then, should the British and African, formerly the more progressive of the two lines, fail to keep pace with the African Steam

[22] See *The Trade Makers*, op. cit., p. 89.
[23] See appendix, table 4, p. 129.
[24] ASP, directors' reports for the relevant years.
[25] ASP, directors' report for the year ending 31 December 1891, p. 5.
[26] See appendix, table 1, p. 126.
[27] See above, Chapter 1, p. 6.

Ship Company? Both had the benefit of Elder Dempster's advice but while the London-based firm expanded, the Glasgow-financed company allowed its interests to suffer a relative decline. It may have been just Scottish caution! In general, world trade in this period was developing more slowly than had been predicted[28] and consequently there was much surplus tonnage. This depressed freight rates and the few buoyant routes attracted much attention from shipowners anxious to at least earn their depreciation. The West African trade was subjected to many attacks of this nature and it is possible that these persuaded the directors of the British and African that it would be unwise to increase an already large investment in what might not be a virtual duopoly for much longer.

From the time Alfred Jones achieved control of Elder Dempster in 1884 all his energies were directed to making his firm supreme in the West African shipping trade. The close co-operation of the two regular British lines, aided by the agreement with the Woermann Line of Hamburg, enabled Jones to prevent the merchants from taking up shipowning or chartering on a significant scale. Great as these victories were, however, they did not satisfy Jones for he was well aware that his seemingly strong position was based on very insecure footings. The reasons for his disquiet were threefold: growth in the number of attacks by organized lines; the increase in tramp steamers attempting to obtain cargoes, and nagging doubt about the attitude of the larger firms of merchants. Average world freight rates declined by 40 per cent between 1889 and 1895[29] and this forced more and more shipping companies to look enviously at the comparatively busy trade organized by Elder Dempster. Simultaneously, the low rates made chartering a very attractive proposition and stimulated the Royal Niger Company, the African Association and other large firms to press for preferential rates.

Alfred Jones had been successful in preventing an amalgamation between the Royal Niger Company and the African Association in 1888 and, thereafter, had favoured first one and then the other, but it was unlikely that he could continue to satisfy both concerns. In fact, it appeared to be only a question of time before demands were made on him that he could not meet. It was also quite conceivable that these two concerns, the largest in the West African trade, would one day

[28] William Ashworth, *An Economic History of England* (Methuen, London, 1960), p. 148.
[29] A. W. Kirkaldy, *British Shipping* (Kegan Paul, London, 1914), p. 630.

end their disagreements, in which case they would be able to combine their cargoes and be in a position either to dictate freight rates or establish their own line. With these possibilities in mind and, no doubt, seeking an end to the unremunerative levels to which unrestricted competition was forcing freight rates, Jones consulted the Woermann Line and with their agreement decided to create a conference system to regulate the West African shipping business.

V

A shipping conference is a combination of shipping companies formed to restrict competition in the carrying trade of a particular route. It has two main aims: the first to regulate rivalry between the regular companies themselves so as to obtain and maintain reasonable rates of freight. To this end unified rates are charged and the trade is then divided either by fixing the number of sailings for each line during a specific period, by allocating certain ports to each company, or by pooling an agreed proportion of the freight receipts. The second aim is to restrict, or prevent, the entry of outside interests into the trade and this is normally achieved by the use of a deferred rebate system.[30]

It is not suggested that Alfred Jones pioneered the conference system in any way. The first deep sea conference had been established in the Calcutta trade in 1877 and by 1895 similar institutions were common on routes throughout the world.[31] In these circumstances, it is not surprising that Jones should wish to follow what was becoming the common practice so in 1895 he inaugurated the new arrangements. According to George Miller, when giving evidence before the Royal Commission on Shipping Rings,[32] his first knowledge of the event was when he was informed through the post. He then had only a month in which to agree to give all of his cargoes to the conference lines and in the absence of a viable alternative he decided to consent. If he had wished he could have provided his own ships but this would have been both expensive and troublesome.

Miller was typical of the West African merchants. None wished to join the scheme, yet all did so, and once having shipped with the

---

[30] A. W. Kirkaldy, op. cit., pp. 183–4, and Daniel Marx Jr., *International Shipping Cartels* (Princeton University Press, New Jersey, 1953), p. 3.
[31] S. Marriner and F. E. Hyde, *The Senior, John Samuel Swire* (Liverpool University Press, 1967), pp. 61–73, and F. E. Hyde, *Shipping Enterprise and Management – Harrisons of Liverpool* (Liverpool University Press, 1967), pp. 69–74.
[32] RCSR, evidence of George Miller, Q.4311–4314.

conference the deferred rebate ensured their continued support. In practice the conference operated as the original circular had laid down. All freights were increased by 10 per cent and this increase became known as primage. Freight was accepted only from merchants who signed a declaration that all their shipments would be made via the conference lines for the succeeding six months. Once the six month period had elapsed the rebate due could be claimed by the shipper for all outward cargo and for palm oil and kernels for the homeward journey. This claim would not, however, be paid until after a further six months' exclusive shipment. Thus Elder Dempster and Company always had in their possession a sum equal to 10 per cent of nine months' freight receipts. This gave the firm an interest-free loan which was a valuable addition to their working capital and although it was continually being repaid it was simultaneously being replaced by fresh payments of primage.

When Jones came to terms with Woermann and established the conference certain rules were laid down which were to guide the future activities of the member firms. The Woermann Line, for example, was prohibited from calling at British ports, but the two British lines were allowed to load and discharge at all continental ports including Hamburg, the home base of the German firm. It was also agreed at this time that the through rate of freight from New York to West Africa should be the same as that charged from Liverpool to West Africa. This meant that cargo from the United States would be carried across the Atlantic, trans-shipped at Liverpool and then delivered to its destination on the Coast for the same cost as freight that was merely delivered from the Mersey to West Africa. The results of these arrangements were twofold: firstly the conference lines were insulated against the competition of any rival American shipping line and, secondly, American goods were marketed in West Africa at a very cheap rate. This naturally provoked the hostility of many British manufacturers who found American products more highly competitive than would otherwise have been the case. The British merchants who used ports other than Liverpool had a further grievance. The conference system prevented these firms from sending their goods direct to the Coast. They were, therefore, forced to ship to Liverpool and trans-ship at that port and, unlike their American competitors, they had to pay the full costs of their carriage and handling.

All the merchants and shippers concerned agreed to accept the conference terms because there was little time for alternative arrangements to be made. Having once begun the deferred rebate made it difficult to break away and this was as true for the Government as for ordinary traders. The Crown Agents for the Colonies were treated as principals right from the start of the new system. This meant that they were entitled to rebate but would lose it if they chartered or shipped by an outside line. Alfred Jones interpreted this to mean that if the Crown Agents broke the rules of the conference on a single item then they would forfeit the entire rebate for all their shipments. The Crown Agents undoubtedly objected to this arrangement but, probably in return for some concessions and, perhaps, to suit their own convenience, they continued to give their support to the established lines. While the larger firms of merchants were strongly against the deferred-rebate system from its inception many smaller traders, like Paterson, Zochonis,[33] praised the conference for providing speedy and regular services. These welcomed the more equal treatment of large and small merchants, as this suited their interests, so they were quite content to support the shipping ring. The commission houses which sent goods to West Africa against specific orders were also keen upholders of the conference as they did not generally find it necessary to refund the rebate to their clients. They were thus able to pocket the primage when it was returned and this gave them every incentive to hope for the perpetuation of the system.

As a result of the conference, private chartering came to an end and those merchants who still possessed ocean-going sailing vessels found it best to dispose of them. The Royal Niger Company and the African Association then remained as the sole owners of non-conference tonnage on the route and, in course of time, Alfred Jones was able to remove both of these obstacles to his duopoly. In addition, other shipping companies became wary of entering the West African trade and, in fact, only one British firm attempted to operate a rival service between the establishment of the conference in 1895 and the death of Jones in December 1909.

In retrospect, therefore, it can be seen that Alfred Jones achieved power by a number of distinct steps. By posing a threat to the regular lines he was able to secure a partnership with Alexander Elder and John Dempster. Then by removing Elder and Dempster from their own company he became senior partner and henceforth was to be its sole policy maker. Elder Dempster was still, at that time, a relatively

[33] RCSR, op. cit., evidence of Hutton and Zochonis on behalf of the Manchester Chamber of Commerce, Q.13260.

small shipping agency and it required very favourable circumstances if it was to reach its full potential. By obtaining the agency of the African Steam Ship Company to add to that of the British and African Steam Navigation Company, Jones went a long way to ensuring the necessary conditions for survival and expansion. The basis of his progress lay in the continuing co-operation between the two lines and even this satisfactory position was improved at a later stage when Elder Dempster effectively managed and organized both the British firms, for Jones could then operate their combined fleets as a single, economic, entity. The setting up of the shipping conference was, thus, only the final phase in a saga and, thereafter, Alfred Jones had an almost complete authority in the British-West African carrying trade. Furthermore, in conjunction with the Woermann Line of Hamburg, he enjoyed virtually total control of the Continental-West African shipping route as well. The power of his position was such that Alfred Jones, as head of Elder Dempster, was able to resist all external competitors, enlarge his fleets, strengthen his position in West Africa and diversify into many other activities and trades.

CHAPTER FOUR

The Exercise of Power

I

FROM 1895 TO THE END OF 1909 Alfred Jones effectively controlled the West African shipping trade and, thus, played a significant role in the economic development of the four British territories on the Coast. The basis of his personal authority lay in his position as senior partner of Elder Dempster and Company, a situation which was to remain unchanged and unchallenged until his death. In turn, Elder Dempster's power lay in its arrangements with the two British operating lines and their German rival, for their co-operation in the conference system presented any potential competitor with a unified front that could not be easily broken. Nevertheless, it is not to be thought that the establishment of the conference solved all Jones's problems: a more correct view would be that it provided a basic weapon which could be utilized to create favourable opportunities for further advances.

Jones was a great realist and he appreciated that he must take every chance to consolidate his authority and then extend it. In spite of the strength conferred by the regulation of the trade, Jones was particularly concerned with the activities of the Royal Niger Company and the African Association for these two firms controlled large quantities of cargo. The imposition of the deferred rebate meant that these concerns, like all other merchants, could not utilize the services offered by any non-conference line or any itinerant tramp steamers. This did not mean, however, that the regular lines immediately carried all cargoes on West African routes. A few merchants still owned individual vessels which they used to ship their own goods and it took some time for these to be eradicated from the trade. Some merchants sold their ships for use in other regions and some failed to renew ageing tonnage; the remainder were gradually bought or acquired in some way by Alfred Jones. A typical case of this occurred in June 1897, when the *Koningin*

Wilhelmina was bought from Messrs. De Nieue Afrikaansche Handels of Rotterdam.[1]

Single ships were only a minor irritation: Jones's basic worry was with the two largest firms for both the African Association and the Royal Niger Company already carried part of their own shipments in vessels they either owned or chartered. If one of these groups had decided to expand their shipping activities the other would have certainly followed their example, but Jones knew that this was un-economic unless the two could come together to form a joint service. His main protection against such an eventuality lay in the bitter rivalry on the Coast so he was greatly alarmed when he was asked by John Holt, then chairman of the African Association, to attend a meeting with Sir George Goldie who represented the Royal Niger Company.

Jones travelled to London for the meeting on 8 November 1895, and first visited the Foreign Office. In an interview with C. M. MacDonald[2] Jones expressed his opinion that he would be asked to support an application of the Royal Niger Company which wished to extend its charter to include the coastal regions:

> Mr. Jones told me that the interview was to take place that afternoon and that he had reason to believe that Mr. Holt had been for some time past in communication with Sir George Goldie respecting a possible amalgamation of the interests of the African Association of merchants (of which Mr. Holt is the Chairman) with the Royal Niger Company, with a view to the extension of the Company's charter in some form or other over the Niger Coast Protectorate.[3]

Jones explained that in the past he had always worked against any extension of Royal Niger Company's charter[4] and he wished to inform the Foreign Office that although he was attending the meeting it did not mean he had changed his views. He was still, in fact, convinced that only the Crown could provide a proper government in the coastal regions.

When the meeting was over Jones returned to the Foreign Office and again met MacDonald. He stated that Goldie had wanted his company to extend its charter so as to take over the administration of the areas between the Niger basin and the sea. The Royal Niger

[1] *Journal of Commerce*, 18 June 1897.
[2] J. E. Flint, op. cit., p. 129, gives details of MacDonald's career.
[3] FO 2/85, confidential memorandum, MacDonald to FO, 8 November 1859.
[4] See above, chapter 1, p. 11.

Company proposed to leave all trading in this region to the African Association and all shipping was to be placed in the hands of Elder Dempster. Jones, no doubt mindful of the strength that this arrangements would confer on the trading firms, told Goldie that this plan was not acceptable to the shipping interests he represented and he would report, to this effect, to his directors. Goldie then replied:

> If you do you will spoil the whole thing and, remember, there are rumours of an opposition line of steamers and it is for the Niger Company to decide which course they will take.

Jones then said:

> That will not weigh with me at all – if you are in it I shall be glad to oppose you.[5]

This potential struggle never took place. Goldie's plan could have gone forward only if all parties had accepted it without reservation. Jones's opposition effectively prevented any immediate response by the Government and gave time for the new Colonial Secretary, Joseph Chamberlain, to decide his own policy. In January 1896 Goldie learned officially that not only was the Royal Niger Company to be prevented from expanding but that its existing charter was to be revoked. In these circumstances there was no incentive to continue the fight with Jones so he came to an agreement whereby he retained the right to charter four ships a year, and sent the remainder of his cargoes via the conference lines without loss of rebate.[6]

II

The agreement with the Royal Niger Company left the African Association as the only large firm with its own ships on the West African route. Jones was, therefore, very anxious to come to terms with John Holt, the chairman of the Association, and by June 1896 a provisional agreement had been reached. According to Holt, this provided for all its goods and passengers to be carried by the conference lines at rates that were to be no higher than those charged to other shippers and, in addition, a sliding scale of rebates was to be given. This was to vary between 6 and 20 per cent depending on the annual

[5] FO 2/85, op. cit.
[6] J. E. Flint, op. cit., pp. 214–5.

quantities carried. Elder Dempster agreed to buy the African Association's fleet for £70,000 (the cost to be offset against freight shipped over the ensuing four years) and also undertook not to indulge in trade themselves.[7]

Negotiations continued until November 1896, and then final agreement was achieved. Holt wrote to Elder Dempster confirming his verbal arrangements with Jones and stating that he would write again after he had informed his Board of his intentions.[8] His second letter duly arrived to say:

> As already verbally intimated to you since my letter of 23rd November, I have met my Board and have informed them that I have come to an agreement with you for the sale of the Company's fleet for a specific sum of money and made freight arrangements with you for five years – details bearing on these main points definitely fixed with you ought to be settled in a legal form and I should be glad if you would make an appointment with your solicitor and Mr. John Dickinson so that the necessary instructions may be given. In the meanwhile please note that the *Erasmus* is due here tomorrow and if you will let me know at once I will give instructions to have her placed at your disposal and handed over to you on arrival, you making the necessary arrangements for forwarding at once the cargo that she has on board from Rotterdam, and the cargo that is now prepared for completing her loading here.[9]

What followed can only be described as a disaster for John Holt. The *Erasmus* and her sister ships[10] were duly handed over to Elder Dempster and their cargoes were forwarded as requested. But once Alfred Jones had these vessels in his possession he was under no compulsion to keep to the terms of the verbal agreement he had made with John Holt. This was because he had neglected to arrange for his solicitor to meet with Holt's legal representative! Thus, while Jones had the ships, Holt had only promises. The effect of this will be realized by reference to a

[7] JHP 6/6, rough memo made by John Holt, 10 June 1896.
[8] JHP 6/6, letter from John Holt to Elder Dempster and Company, 23 November 1896.
[9] JHP 6/6, letter from John Holt to Elder Dempster and Company, 3 December 1896.
[10] The vessels included in the deal were the steamships *Ebani* (1,093 net tons) and *Erasmus* (713 net tons) and the sailing ships *Eboe* (305 net tons), *Luke Bruce* (310 net tons), *Charlotte Young* (302 net tons) and *Montezuma* (326 net tons). The s.s. *Christopher Thomas* (91 net tons) was returned by the African Association for further service.

letter written by Holt to the African Association resigning from his position as Chairman:

> I feel keenly the position Messrs. Elder Dempster and Company have put me into with the Board of the African Association, and equally so the utter want of confidence in me as shown by the discussion of yesterday, and proved by the adverse vote which can be construed in no other sense, unless it be also more want of confidence – a vote of censure.[11]

John Holt subsequently wrote a personal letter to Alfred Jones complaining of the breaking of their understanding:

> If you want to keep faith with me carry out the terms of the agreement you made with me. Your not having done so has already done me very serious injury. Pinning my faith to your honour I announced (with your full knowledge) to my Board, that I had made an agreement with you. A fortnight later I had no written document to produce as evidence, and my word was discredited. Your action has had the effect of driving me from the Chair and the Board. At the time of making the agreement, not a word was mentioned about any guaranteed minimum freight. That was not mooted by you until a much later date. You undertook to pay £70,000 for the Company's named fleet and in return you were to have its entire carrying for a limited term at rates, terms and conditions neither better nor worse than the best given to any other person or persons. The conditions you now seek to impose with a minimum freight annually and a penalty clause which seems anything but clear is one which it is not competent for me now to deal with.[12]

The frustration experienced by Holt was worsened by the knowledge that the Board at the African Association had failed to support him by one vote. This vote, in fact, would have been forthcoming but his friend Cookson was forced to leave after a four-hour discussion as he had previously arranged to chair a meeting of the City's Health Committee.[13] It is not possible to detail here the many differences between the members of the Board but the picture which has survived is one of constant friction between the 'war' party led by Holt who wished to fight the Royal Niger Company and the 'peace' party led by Cotterell who wanted to come to terms.[14] What is certain is that if Holt had been backed by a united Board he would have stood a far

[11] JHP 6/3, letter from John Holt to the African Association, 11 December 1896.
[12] JHP 6/6, letter from John Holt to Alfred Jones, 5 January 1897.
[13] JHP 6/3, letter from Cookson to the African Association, 14 December 1896.
[14] P. N. Davies (ed.), *Trading in West Africa*, op. cit.; Harry Cotterell, *Reminiscences of one connected with the West African Trade from 1863 to 1910*, pp. 40–1.

better chance of repudiating Jones's action. Once they had failed to support him he felt obliged to resign.

With Holt out of the way Jones proceeded to deal directly with the African Association and the original terms were adhered to with the addition of a clause about guaranteed minimum freight.[15] When Holt heard of this he wrote and gave the Association full details of the negotiations.[16] He also issued a pamphlet which gave his side of the dispute and this was sent to the shareholders with a letter which asked for their support at the forthcoming annual general meeting. This took place on 4 March 1897, and was to prove a rather stormy affair.

Holt began by giving a detailed analysis of the progress made by the African Association while he was its chairman and pointed out that he had been successful even though the market had been falling. He then referred to policy which he had initiated which had resulted in the Association building its two steamers:

> It is not an easy matter to fight an uphill battle, and I appeal to you, Gentlemen, would the Steamship Companies have come to terms if those steamers had not been built? Would they have made the terms they have made with us if those boats had not been built, and are our competitors in Africa any more likely to come to terms when they feel the pinch of trade? What brought us together? Not good times, certainly. . . .
>
> *Chairman* (Mr. Rogerson): I am very glad to have heard Mr. Holt's remarks. I may say that we have recently concluded an agreement with the African Steamship Company and the British and African Steamship Company, through Elder Dempster and Company on favourable terms to our mutual benefit, both to us as merchants and to them as shipowners, and we have disposed of all our fleet.

Alfred Jones, also a shareholder in the African Association, attended the meeting and thought it desirable to say a few words:

> There is no doubt that our worthy friends Mr. Cookson and Mr. Holt are well versed in this trade but I think that the time has come, seeing that they have retired from the Board, when we can fairly ask to have the Board elected – reduced as it is – in a way that is likely to work harmoniously together for the future. There is no doubt that Mr. Holt's policy has done a great deal for the Company: he is a very shrewd, hardworking fellow and drives a hard bargain, but sometimes these people don't get the best of it. However, he has done well.[17]

[15] JHP 6/3, letter from Alfred Jones to the African Association, 11 January 1897.
[16] JHP 6/6, letter from John Holt to the African Association, 11 January 1897.
[17] JHP 6/6, notes on AGM of the African Association, 4 March 1897.

At the conclusion of the discussion the Board received 24,710 votes in support of their policy while Holt and Cookson obtained only 2,258 and 1,514 respectively. A resolution proposing that Holt and Cookson be re-elected to the Board was not acted upon as both men refused to stand. Thus, the agreement with Elder Dempster was confirmed and Jones's position in the West African shipping trade was further enhanced. However, it must be a sad reflection on Jones that he chose to use such devious tactics. It appears that his original, verbal, agreement with Holt would have given him control of the African Association's fleet and cargoes – the ensuing difficulties were only about specific terms.[18] Was Jones inherently greedy or was he just incapable of mercy when his opponent made a blunder? These are distinct possibilities when one takes into account Jones's single-mindedness but it may be that he was playing a far deeper game. By discrediting Holt, Jones's friends assumed power in the Association – a good thing in itself – and they quickly came to terms with the Royal Niger Company. This ultimately benefited both organizations enormously and both, perhaps, were a little thankful for the part he played in bringing them together. But if this hypothesis is correct and Jones was seeking to placate the Royal Niger Company, it was not very successful.[19] In any case it would have been a very risky project for once the African Association and the Royal Niger Company began to work in harmony there could be no way in which Jones could prevent their ultimate unity. In the event, this did not happen until 1929 when circumstances were entirely different.[20] Jones did remain on friendly terms with the African Association and was able, on the surface at least, to patch up his differences with John Holt. Whether Holt ever really forgave him is another matter![21]

III

The establishment of the conference, together with the arrangements made with the Royal Niger Company and the African Association, provided a very firm foundation for Jones's subsequent control of

[18] *Journal of Commerce*, 10 March 1897. The value of freight shipped by the Association in a good year amounted to £700,000 and it paid about £100,000 for it to be carried.

[19] See below, chapter 6, pp. 82–4.

[20] F. J. Pedler, op. cit., pp. 297–310.

[21] See below, chapter 6, p. 84.

West Africa's external communications. Very few attempts were made to enter the trade. The *Prestonian*, managed by Henry Tyrer of Liverpool, made a voyage to West Africa in 1903 and returned for a second trip in 1904. For several reasons, including pressure from Jones, the voyages were then discontinued,[22] and a similar fate befell the Sun Line when it was organized by a consortium of Gold Coast mining companies in 1906.[23] The competition of the Hamburg-Bremen Africa Line was a much more serious affair and ended in a complete reorganization of the German side of the West African shipping trade.[24] Even in this case, however, the structure of the conference remained unscathed and Jones retained a position of enormous authority.

With the benefit of a secure power base, duly consolidated, Jones was able to devote much of his time to activities other than the elimination of competition. The running of even one hundred ships[25] was only a routine procedure once the rivalry of outside firms was ended. Of course, Jones still had to lay down the broad lines of his policy but, although he continued to take an immense interest in the smallest detail of many operations, he was gradually able to delegate more and more of the less important tasks. This enabled him to continue with greater force a process that he had begun when he first took control of Elder Dempster for he felt that if he could acquire and own the ancillary services on the Coast it would be both prudent and profitable. He therefore made every effort to buy the boating companies belonging to the merchants, developed a series of coastal services to facilitate the movement of cargo to the better loading places, invested in numerous enterprises designed to provide essential facilities and created a credit and banking structure that encouraged the expansion of all types of trade.

The boating companies were a major objective. These had sprung up because of the difficulties experienced by deep-sea ships on the almost harbourless coast of West Africa. In many places cargo and passengers had to be carried through the surf by small boats manned by local Africans. Most merchants found it speeded up these operations if they bought and worked their own surf boats, but in some areas the shipping companies provided them from the start. Jones was quick to see the advantage in extending these services for it would provide a

[22] See below, chapter 6, pp. 88–9.
[23] See below, chapter 6, p. 89.
[24] See below, chapter 6, p. 89.
[25] See *The Trade Makers*, op. cit., p. 405.

certain method of preventing competitors from entering the trade. He made it his business to acquire as many expatriate concerns as he could and when, as sometimes happened, the owners were reluctant to sell he devised a scheme to ensure their co-operation. This involved the increase in freight rates so that they included an element to cover the cost of unloading in West Africa. The charge was made whether or not the shipping company's facilities were used, so there was little point in merchants retaining their own surf boats.[26] By this means, Jones was able to control the loading and discharging over much of the coastline, but it should be remembered that in some districts cargo was dealt with in the rivers and creeks without the need for specialized craft.

The existence of these waterways in certain parts of West Africa enabled ships to penetrate some way into the interior. Obviously the larger sea-going vessels were at a disadvantage in this respect so Jones established a number of branch line services which were intended to feed the main line steamers. Some of these smaller vessels collected and delivered cargo from inland river ports and trans-shipped to the larger craft at convenient places on or near the coast. Others were used to move goods coastwise so that the sea-going ships could not only be much larger and take advantage of considerable economies of scale, but could significantly reduce their number of calls per voyage. It should be noted that throughout this period Lagos was by far the largest port on the Coast. In 1906, for example, its inward and outward freight amounted to over 200,000 tons, more than ten times greater than any other West African port at this time, and all of it had to be carried over the bar by surf boats or moved from Forcados by branch line steamers.[27]

Jones also established a number of other subsidiary firms which provided steam tugs, lighters, barges and river craft. Facilities were built for the repair and maintenance of these vessels and, later, some assembly work and construction was undertaken. Minor work on both branch and main line ships was an additional service supplied by these workshops and they were also responsible for the preparation and laying of most, if not all, the buoys used to guide shipping in the rivers and port entrances. Other subsidiary companies provided hotels, cold storage and victualling facilities and, in time, Jones created a complete

[26] RCSR, op. cit., Q.6934, evidence of Mr. J. H. Batty.
[27] RCSR, op. cit., Q.5096 and Q.4876.

network of integrated concerns that channelled the produce of West Africa to his main line ships.[28]

IV

Another field in which Alfred Jones was to play a vital role was in banking. The limitations of barter and local currencies were such that by the 1870s they had largely given way to the use of British and foreign silver coins. The Africans valued new silver more highly than old so freshly minted coins were increasingly in demand. Thus, although the annual average of British sterling silver issued for West Africa was only about £24,000 in 1886, it had risen to £116,000 in 1891 and amounted to over £600,000 in 1906.[29] While silver was an improvement on earlier methods of exchange it was not really convenient for large transactions. Each £100, in whatever denomination, weighed 28 lb. and the cost of transporting and counting this money was both tiresome and expensive. This was particularly true for Elder Dempster:

> . . . this traffic needed much more care, more attention to security, larger strong rooms and more personal dealings with the people to whom the consignments were addressed than any other kind of trade.[30]

When George Neville, Elder Dempster's Lagos agent, returned to Liverpool in 1891, he spoke to Jones about the growing trade in silver and suggested the creation of a bank. Jones agreed at once and, accordingly, Neville approached the recently formed African Banking Corporation.[31] The consequence was that a branch of the bank was opened in Lagos, but early difficulties led to disillusionment and in 1892 it decided to withdraw. On learning of this decision, Alfred Jones intervened and agreed to pay the African Banking Corporation £1,000 so that he could take over and operate the branch himself. As Elder Dempster was a private company the Crown Agents for the Colonies were reluctant to transfer the privileges of its predecessor, in particular being concerned about the Government Account and the right to import new silver from the Mint at cost. Jones therefore

---

[28] In 1910 all these activities were vested in the West Africa Lighterage and Transport Co. Ltd.

[29] *Report of the West African Currency Committee*, 1912, Cd. 6426, p. 6.

[30] Richard Fry, op. cit., p. 12.

[31] This bank was primarily interested in South Africa.

established a limited company, the Bank of British West Africa and, with Neville's aid, was able to overcome all the initial problems.[32]

The new company was formed on 30 March 1894, and Jones owned 1,733 of the 3,000 shares.[33] Most of the remainder were taken up by his partners, Davey and Sinclair, so the bank was very much the preserve of Elder Dempster and Jones took the chair from the beginning. Neville became the first manager of the bank so he and Jones effectively controlled its activities during the early years of its existence. Under their guidance progress was steady but not dramatic, so although a profit was made no dividend was paid after the first year's working:

> The Bank has as much business as it cares to do at present, and the directors have no wish to extend it too rapidly, although there is an unlimited demand for money on the Coast with good security. In addition, the directors are very pleased at the success of the banking system in West Africa which has been the means of conferring a very great benefit on the people of that country. There is no doubt that the country which introduces its coinage and language into a new territory succeeds in a great measure in securing the trade of the place.[34]

A substantial profit was made during the second year and 8 per cent dividend was paid. Bills purchased were valued at £430,544 – an increase of £172,982 over the previous year – while £151,520 of new silver was shipped to West Africa as against £64,800.[35] The right to import this silver from the Mint was a major factor in the bank's advance and there was some criticism of this concession.[36] In spite of this the bank continued to progress and it established branch offices in many parts of West Africa. The very success of the Bank of British West Africa then encouraged a rival concern to challenge its monopoly. This was the Anglo-African Bank formed in 1899 by a group of West African merchants. By 1905, it had developed sufficiently to change its title to the Bank of Nigeria and there was some talk of an amalgamation with the Bank of British West Africa. When this failed, severe competition began and attempts were made to end the Bank of British West Africa's monopoly of silver importation. For reasons which

[32] Richard Fry, op. cit., pp. 23–6.
[33] See appendix, table 5, p. 130 and table 6, p. 121.
[34] *Journal of Commerce*, 17 July 1895, report on the First Annual General Meeting of the Bank of British West Africa Limited.
[35] *Liverpool Mercury*, 17 July 1896, report on the Second Annual General Meeting of the Bank of British West Africa Limited.
[36] See below, chapter 6, p. 92.

have never become clear, Alfred Jones was able to stave off these attacks and the privilege was retained until after his death.[37]

During the whole of the Alfred Jones era the Bank of British West Africa made only moderate profits. By 1910 the authorized capital was £1 million, the paid-up capital £200,000 and reserves amounted to £80,000. Deposits by then were just over £1 million and net profits amounted to 8 per cent on the capital employed.[38] By shipping company standards this was a reasonable return but, in comparison with banking expectations, it was rather poor. The explanation is that financial considerations were only part of Jones's motivation in seeing that an efficient banking system was established. He would, in fact, have been prepared to have accepted little or no direct return from the bank if this had been necessary for he appreciated that the removal of structural bottlenecks would enhance trade and thus the size of the cargoes carried by his ships. Jones was also influenced by other motives,[39] and wished to extend his interests still further by seeking permission to issue notes. This, however, was not permitted by the Colonial Office.[40]

V

The acquisition of the boating companies, the development of branch lines, the operation of workshops and the control of banking within West Africa did not satisfy Alfred Jones. Nothing was too small to be beneath his attention and nothing was too large to be tackled. The motivation for these peripheral activities is complex: the desire to make profits was always present but in many cases physical necessity was equally significant. West Africa's lack of a modern infrastructure meant that if individuals or companies wanted particular facilities they either provided them themselves or did without. In some instances, of course, action of this kind gave tangible fringe benefits. Thus the training of pilots was of positive advantage in that ships could be safely brought to anchorage – the fact that their knowledge was largely confined to Elder Dempster employees and not available to potential competitors was an additional bonus.

[37] Richard Fry, op. cit., pp. 42–51.
[38] Richard Fry, op. cit., p. 61. In comparison the African Steam Ship Company paid an average dividend of 4.3 per cent in the period 1890 to 1899 and an average of 4.8 per cent in the years from 1900 to 1909.
[39] See below, chapter 7, pp. 105–6.
[40] See below, chapter 6, p. 92.

In many parts of West Africa land (particularly outside the urban areas) was not supposed to be actually bought but, even so, speculation could and did happen. Jones acquired many sites for specific purposes such as the construction of workshops, offices, cold stores, hotels and slipways. These sites were always as large as possible to provide for future expansion and, no doubt, with the object of gaining from any appreciation in land values. A small amount of land was also acquired with the object of encouraging new crops and methods of cultivation. Here, again, the possibility of benefiting from a rise in the value of the real estate may well have played an important role in formulating policy.

The certainty of mineral wealth being found in West Africa also prompted Jones to take action. He was convinced that when internal communications improved they would ensure the profitability of many new industries and this was a major factor in his constant support for the construction of railways. In 1901, therefore, he established the Liverpool West Africa Syndicate Limited, which was to acquire and hold concessions of many kinds together with rights and properties. In time, its activities increased to include mines, quarries, mills, timber, factories, railways and tramways. It was frequently used to hold properties and options which did not conveniently fit anywhere else in the huge Elder Dempster organization and it was through this company that Jones shared, to a small extent, in the gold discoveries of 1904. Had he lived he would also have profited, via this interest, in the tin boom of 1909, but his real gain (and perhaps motivation) lay in the increased demand for shipping space that these new industries eventually generated.

VI

Apart from creating an integrated network in West Africa, Alfred Jones was also busy in the United Kingdom. According to John Holt, Jones's business interests in Liverpool in 1897 were as follows:

> A. L. Jones is Master Porter for the two (shipping) Companies – also steve-dore for ditto. As the Liverpool Cartage Company he does the cartage of the two Companies and of as many of their shippers and consignees as by his influence he can obtain. In the Sefton Street stores he or his firm store (palm) oil which has the privilege of extended transit by the two lines – said stores are open spaces belonging to Mr. Elder, Mr. Dempster and Mr. Jones. The charge for carting and one month's rent is 1s. 6d. per ton. A yard at Coburg

59

Dock quay is also utilised as an Oil Store at the same rate although there is no cartage whatever on this oil it having only to be rolled across the street a few yards. The two Companies rent the remaining spaces in Coburg Dock quay where they charge $\frac{3}{4}d$. per cask per day and so force the oil into Mr. Jones' yard. The charge was $\frac{1}{2}d$. per cask each day until Mr. Jones became Master Porter.[41]

As indicated above, any cartage that was required was performed by the Liverpool Cartage Company in which Jones had large holdings, and it is interesting to note that he was one of the first on Merseyside to see the possibilities of mechanical road transport. Consequently, he was associated with the trials organized to test hill climbing ability in 1898, 1899 and 1901, and later he was active in the Liverpool Self Propelled Traffic Association and also invested in the Road Carrying Company.[42] Jones's other interests on Merseyside included a ships' chandlers and a share in the African Oil Mills Company. Before the First World War most of West Africa's palm kernels were crushed in Europe but Jones encouraged the establishment of facilities in Liverpool to try to divert some of this traffic. The new works were opened in 1894 but, although it was well equipped and organized, it did little to dent German supremacy in this field.[43] Jones was sometimes criticized for the activities of the mill but he does not seem to have taken a direct part in its management.[44]

The need for coal to provide power for Jones's ships encouraged a further diversification. Cheap and reliable sources of suitable coal were found at Garth and Maesteg, in Glamorgan, and the collieries were bought. They were then operated by Elders Navigation Collieries Limited, a firm almost entirely owned by Jones until his death.[45] Bunkers were subsequently supplied to Elder Dempster vessels, via Port Talbot, at the main UK ports and at Las Palmas, Tenerife and Freetown. Supplies at these latter places were in the hands of wholly-owned subsidiary firms. These were the Grand Canary Coaling Company, the Tenerife Coaling Company and the Sierra Leone Coaling Company, and they not only provided fuel for Elder Demp-

---

[41] JHP 6/6, rough memo., written by John Holt in 1897.
[42] The Motor Trader, 22 December 1909, obituary of Jones.
[43] Committee on Edible and Oil Producing Nuts & Seeds, 1916, Cd. 8248.
[44] Journal of Commerce, 1 December 1904.
[45] The collieries employed about 1,000 men on average and produced approx. 5,000 tons of coal per week. Ocean Highways, an illustrated souvenir of Elder Dempster and Company, 1902, p. 61. See appendix, tables 7 and 8, pp. 132–3.

ster's own vessels but catered for a very wide market. Bunkers for the Admiralty, for many foreign navies and for over 200 different shipping lines meant the sale of a quarter of a million tons annually from Las Palmas.[46] Most of this coal was bought from South Wales and not produced by Elder's own collieries. Nevertheless, it made a useful contribution to overall profitability and by bringing Jones to the Canaries in the first instance was to have major consequences on the economy of the islands and ultimately on the Jamaican fruit industry.[47]

[46] *Ocean Highways*, op. cit., p. 28.
[47] See below, chapter 5, pp. 66–70.

CHAPTER FIVE

The Rewards of Power

I

THE MOST DIRECT AND OBVIOUS CONSEQUENCE of Jones's success in regulating the West African shipping trade was the growth in the size of the fleets which he controlled. The following table shows how the number of ships, and their total tonnage, rose during the time he was the senior partner of Elder Dempster and Company:

Year	Number of ships	Total gross tonnage[1]
1884	35	53,310
1890	50	95,251
1895	61	147,153
1900	87	269,232
1905	95	265,405
1909	101	301,361

Alfred Jones also consistently strengthened his personal control as and when the opportunity could be created. Having achieved power in Elder Dempster in 1884 he then ensured that what had been a relatively minor firm of shipping agents became an indispensable part of the West African shipping trade. By 1890, when the agency and management of the African Steam Ship Company was added to that of the British and African Steam Navigation Company, Jones could be said to have effective control of the trade. But he appreciated that he needed to achieve power within the two shipping companies if he was to make absolutely certain that this position did not change. As noted above,[2] Jones put this policy into effect by buying the shares of the African Steam Ship Company whenever they became available and by 1900 he owned sufficient to be able to direct its affairs.[3]

---

[1] Note that these figures include some vessels that were managed by Jones and his companies and that all were employed on West African routes. See P. N. Davies, M.A. thesis, op. cit., pp. 251–5.

[2] See above, chapter 3, p. 39.

[3] *Committee on the Currency of the West African Colonies*, 1899, Q.1071.

The long and close association between Elder Dempster and the British and African Steam Navigation Company, dating back to the establishment of both firms in 1868, obviated the need for Jones to acquire its shares. His holdings in the company were quite nominal,[4] therefore, until 1900, when he bought the entire firm complete with all its assets for £800,000. This was accomplished by forming a new concern, the British and African Steam Navigation Company (1900) Limited, and issuing $4\frac{1}{2}$ per cent debentures to the extent of £800,000. As the book value of the fleet had been certified at nearly £$1\frac{1}{2}$ million the issue was quickly taken up, and this money provided the capital to buy out the original shareholders.[5]

Jones subsequently sold a number of ships owned by Elder Dempster to the new concern. On 26 November 1900 *Monmouth*, *Priam*, *Lake Megantic* and *Sangara* were transferred, followed three weeks later by *Montezuma*, *Montreal*, *Lake Erie*, *Lake Champlain* and *Montauk*. In exchange Elder Dempster received 63,000 ordinary £10 shares, all but a few hundred of the total issue. From then until his death at the end of 1909 Jones was always able to guide the policies of the British and African and so, together with his influence with the African Steam Ship Company, he was able to consolidate his grip on the West African carrying trade.

Apart from acquiring shares and eventually obtaining a controlling interest in the two British shipping lines engaged on the route, Jones also operated a number of vessels on behalf of Elder Dempster and Company. As noted earlier,[6] the company bought its first steamer in 1887 and from then on one or two new or secondhand ships were secured each year. This tonnage was usually transferred to the regular lines fairly quickly but a small number appear to have been permanently run by Elder Dempster on their own account.[7] This arrangement was placed on a more formal footing in 1899 when Elder Dempster Shipping Limited was established with a nominal capital of £1 million made up of 100,000 ordinary shares of £10 each.[8] Jones then offered £600,000 of $4\frac{1}{2}$ per cent debenture stock to the public and

[4] See *The Trade Makers*, op. cit., pp. 429–32.
[5] *Journal of Commerce*, 23 October 1900.
[6] See above, chapter 3, p. 40.
[7] According to Elder Dempster's fleet list some 88 ships were acquired by Elder Dempster in the period 1887 to 1909 but only 14 were retained. See P. N. Davies, M.A. thesis, op. cit., pp. 251 or 5.
[8] See appendix, tables 13 and 14, pp. 139–41.

this was quickly taken up. Jones did not, however, release any of the ordinary stock for sale. Instead he transferred seventeen ships, the property of Elder Dempster, to the new firm and received in exchange the cash provided by the debenture holders plus 50,000 of the ordinary shares. Thus Alfred Jones, acting as Elder Dempster, obtained the whole of the ordinary share issue together with the loan of £600,000 on extremely satisfactory terms.[9]

Jones's financial manoeuvrings did not affect the ships themselves and they continued to work for Elder Dempster as before. Many of these particular vessels were, in fact, used on North Atlantic routes but, like the other ships under Jones's control, they went where he directed. There was considerable flexibility between the lines managed by him so that while the great majority of his tonnage was perpetually engaged on West African routes, individual ships could quickly be diverted to take advantage of whatever cargoes were offered. It was in this way that Jones first became interested in the New Orleans cotton trade. Single cargoes multiplied and although he began by using surplus tonnage, purpose-built vessels were soon constructed. In this trade it was not considered necessary to establish a separate line, but vessels belonging to Elder Dempster Shipping Limited were frequently to be found.

II

Jones's interest in Canadian routes began in a similar way but had a very different ending. The shipment of occasional cargoes from Liverpool led to a familiarity with the trade and this was extended in 1894 when Elder Dempster took over a service, formerly undertaken by the Dominion Line, from Bristol. A further development came in 1898 when Jones bought the Beaver Line operated by the Canada Shipping Company Limited.[10] This then continued to operate a service from Liverpool and, after defeating the competition of the Beaver Line Associated Steamers Limited (which had not been taken over by Jones), the line made steady progress. The rise in shipping freights engendered by the Boer War further enhanced profitability but when Jones heard that the Canadian Pacific Railway Company intended to

[9] Until 1904 all the ordinary shares of the company were held jointly by Jones and Davey. Their distribution was then widened but Jones retained his controlling interest until his death. See appendix, table 14, p. 141.

[10] F. C. Bowen, *History of the Canadian Pacific Line* (Sampson Low, London, 1928).

begin its own service he decided it would be wise to let it acquire the Beaver Line.[11]

In Jones's opinion there could be no future in competing with an indigenous company, particularly one that could offer through rates on ship and rail. So in 1903 he made the best bargain he could and received £1,417,500 from the Canadian Pacific Railway Company. In return, the name and goodwill of the Beaver Line was transferred to the new operator together with fifteen ships – strangely enough, none of these vessels had ever been registered with the Beaver Line.[12] Elder Dempster's service from Capetown to Canada, begun in 1901, was not affected by this arrangement and its sailings were maintained. Thus Alfred Jones had finalized an extremely satisfactory venture. He had bought the Beaver Line at a modest cost and then, after securing a good return on his capital, sold at a handsome profit. By concluding the deal with the CPR he had avoided what might have been a disastrous fight with a substantial concern that had many natural advantages on this route and, in addition, had been able to dispose of tonnage he no longer required.

Another rewarding diversification for Alfred Jones was the joint service organized by Elder Dempster and the Woermann Line to the Congo Free State. This began on a casual basis but as trade developed better arrangements had to be devised. Accordingly, in 1891, with the full approval of King Leopold II, a syndicate was formed by Jones and Woermann and monthly sailings began from Antwerp to Matadi. As tonnages increased still further it was decided to put the trade on a more formal basis and to make some provision for Belgian participation. In 1895, therefore, Elder Dempster formed the Compagnie Belge Maritime du Congo and the Woermann Line set up the Société Maritime du Congo. Both of these firms represented a partnership: the shipping line providing the carrying capacity and the King (the Congo at this time was really his personal estate) supplying the cargoes.

The consequence of this arrangement was that throughout the period from 1895 to 1911[13] Elder Dempster and Woermann carried all the imports and exports of what was to become the Belgian Congo.

[11] H. A. Innis, *A History of the Canadian Pacific Railway* (P. S. King, London, 1923), pp. 169–70.
[12] See appendix, table 16, p. 143.
[13] The agreement was terminated by mutual consent after the deaths of Jones and the King.

A further consequence was that because the level of trade could be accurately forecast the load factors of the vessels concerned could be kept at a very high level. This did not mean, however, that Jones (and Woermann) received enormous profits – Leopold was too good a businessman for that – but it did mean that three or four vessels were constantly in service at rates which represented a satisfactory return on the capital employed.

III

The need to provide bunkering facilities for his ships engaged on West African routes led Alfred Jones to diversify into the coal business. As noted above,[14] Jones had bought two collieries in Glamorgan and used their output to supply fuel for his vessels both at home and abroad. In time this trade developed to such an extent that large quantities of coal had to be bought from additional mines in South Wales, and much of this fuel was resold to other shipowners, particularly in the Canary Islands.

One consequence of this activity was to make Las Palmas a major bunkering centre, another was to bring the islands more into the mainstream of world commerce. In 1884, when Jones first established a coal dump at Puerto de la Luz, the Canaries were at a very low ebb economically as their former staple, cochineal, had been replaced by other types of dye.[15] Jones decided, therefore, that he would assist the inhabitants in any way he could and, in addition to extending the bunkering business, he established a marine engineering workshop complete with a patent slip. He also formed the Interinsular Steam Ship Company to provide communications between the islands and he built and operated a cold storage plant and two hotels, but it was in the development of the fruit industry that Alfred Jones really made an impact.

It will be seen from the following table that as the sale of cochineal declined, the expansion in exports of fruit more than compensated. A few bananas had frequently been taken to Britain by individual captains, but the difficulty of keeping the fruit from ripening had prevented a large-scale trade from developing. However, in 1878, Messrs. Fyffe, Hudson and Company successfully shipped bananas in

[14] See above, chapter 4, p. 60.
[15] See below, chapter 7, p. 105.

Imports from the Canary Islands to the United Kingdom[16]

Average for	Cochineal	Bananas	Tomatoes	Total
	£	£	£	£
1885–89	64,579	—	—	99,179
1890–94	36,184	—	—	255,757
1895–99	29,805	—	—	612,307
1900–04	14,186	785,559	312,849	1,246,361
1905–09	19,147	863,120	440,675	1,542,217
1910–14	13,388	727,396	546,254	1,494,108
1915–16	85,248	1,077,596	729,660	2,068,928
1917–18	(No figures available)			
1919–20	33,223	2,529,420	1,339,525	4,048,975

crates lined with cotton wool and carried on deck.[17] By 1884 the trade was growing to substantial proportions and Alfred Jones was taking an active interest. Thereafter Elder Dempster vessels carried bananas whenever space was available: topping up with this cargo after bunkering became a regular and profitable activity on the homeward voyage from West Africa.

Although the new trade prospered many difficulties were experienced in carrying the fruit and arranging for it to arrive in Britain at the correct stage of ripeness.[18] There were also major problems, especially in the north of the country, in introducing a new food for mass consumption:

When Jones first began to import Canary bananas in his African ships he encountered great difficulties in obtaining a market for them – difficulties of transport and difficulties of retail sale. But he was not to be beaten. Finding that the retailers would not help him, and that even the carters put difficulties in his way, he engaged a number of coster-mongers, bringing some of them, it is said, from London and loading up their barrows from one of his ships, he told the carters to go and sell them in the streets of Liverpool for what they would fetch, and that he did not want to be paid for them. By this means he popularised the consumption of the banana first in Liverpool and afterwards throughout Lancashire and the North of England.[19]

The growth of this new aspect of Jones's enterprise placed some stress on Elder Dempster's staff in the Canary Islands for they had been

[16] Compiled from the *Annual Statements of the Trade of the UK*, HMSO.
[17] Patrick Beaver, *Yes! We have some. The story of Fyffes* (Publications for Companies, Stevenage, Herts., 1976), p. 16.
[18] Ibid., p. 8.
[19] *The Times*, 13 December 1909, obituary of Alfred Jones.

primarily trained in maritime rather than agricultural affairs. Consequently, Jones was anxious to find someone who would accept responsibility for buying and loading the correct quantities of bananas at the right price and in the appropriate condition. In 1888, therefore, he sent A. H. Stockly out to Las Palmas and within a year, although he was still only twenty-four, placed him in charge of that aspect of Elder Dempster's banana trade. By 1892, Stockley[20] was back in London and with his friend, A. R. Ackerley, the chief salesman, was effectively running the whole business. In accordance with his agreement with Jones, Stockley received a third of the profits on the sale of the bananas as his remuneration, and in 1898 his share came to over £3,000.[21] By that time, therefore, Elder Dempster were finding the Canary banana trade an extremely attractive proposition for in addition to the direct profit made from selling the fruit they also gained from its carriage on their vessels.

Alfred Jones was not, of course, the only importer of bananas from the Canaries, and Fyffe, Hudson always retained a substantial share of the market. But it was to Jones that the Colonial Secretary, Joseph Chamberlain, turned when he was informed that the United Fruit Company, the largest buyer of Jamaican bananas, was proposing to establish its own plantations in Cuba. Chamberlain knew Jones well from their mutual interest in West Africa and he was also aware of his existing links with Canary bananas. Jones, careful not to turn a powerful friend into a dangerous enemy, listened to Chamberlain's request and then sent Stockley to the West Indies to make a full enquiry.

Stockley's report was far from encouraging. He noted the long distance, the need to provide specialized ships and the problems of marketing enormous quantities of bananas in England and came to the conclusion that it was not a viable proposition. Jones agreed[22] but Chamberlain persisted and entered into an arrangement with a Captain Lamont. This provided for the construction and operation of three steamers which were to undertake a fortnightly service to Jamaica carrying a minimum of 20,000 stems of bananas per voyage. An annual subsidy of £20,000 was to be paid and Lamont used this as collateral to get the ships laid down but then failed to attract further

---

[20] A. H. Stockley, *Consciousness of Effort. The Romance of the Banana*. Printed for private circulation, 1937, p. 24.

[21] Patrick Beaver, op. cit., p. 20.

[22] Letter from A. L. Jones to A. H. Stockley, 24 April 1899, reproduced in A. H. Stockley, op. cit., p. 30.

capital.[23] This placed the Colonial Secretary in a difficult position so he again contacted Jones and asked for his help.

The interview took place at Highbury on 26 December 1899 and Jones subsequently informed Stockley of what had occurred:

> *Chamberlain:* Oh, Mr. Jones, I want to see if you can help me out of a somewhat disagreeable business. The man I trusted to take on my Jamaica contract has let me down. Now you have done so much for West Africa and the Empire that I feel sure you will reconsider your decision of a year ago and come to my help. I will see that you shall be met in every possible way as regards the contract, and the only condition which I must make is that you take the two ships now in frame off the builders' hands.
>
> *Jones:* It is a matter I shall have to think over and consider very carefully; what subsidy were you to pay for the fortnightly service?
>
> *Chamberlain:* £20,000 per annum.
>
> *Jones:* I certainly could not think of accepting that amount, and I should say off hand that £60,000 would be the very least the service could be run for; you must remember the great risk that the proposed market for the fruit might not materialise, and in that case the whole thing would mean heavy loss.
>
> *Chamberlain:* I certainly must ask you to go further into the figures, as £60,000 is far more than I can ask to be granted. I can, however, promise you that should this service be started early in 1901, I could then see that your patriotic action was rewarded, and I hope that will be some inducement to you.[24]

The promise of some official recognition if he took up the contract appears to have revitalized Jones's interest and he decided to reopen negotiations. An annual subsidy of £40,000 for a ten-year period was eventually agreed and, in return, Jones took over the unfinished vessels and undertook to provide a fortnightly mail, passenger and fruit service to Jamaica. Jones then established the Imperial Direct West India Mail Service Company Limited,[25] and its first voyage was successfully completed in March 1901, when the *Port Morant* landed 23,000 bunches of bananas at Avonmouth.[26]

The consequences of Chamberlain's policy and Jones's enterprise were that the Jamaican growers received an alternative market for their

[23] A. H. Stockley, op. cit., p. 31.
[24] Ibid., pp. 32–3.
[25] See appendix, tables 11 and 12, pp. 137–8.
[26] Patrick Beaver, op. cit., pp. 26–7.

fruit and the shipowner was granted a knighthood. It seems certain, however, that the distinction of becoming a Knight Commander of the Order of St. Michael and St. George was not awarded solely on account of his work for the West Indies.[27] Alfred Jones's service in promoting the interests of Empire in West Africa were widely known and his work in establishing the Liverpool School of Tropical Medicine had been particularly well publicized.[28] It is probable, therefore, that Chamberlain was already well disposed towards Jones and that their collaboration over the Jamaican fruit contract was but the final act which provided the precise timing and nature of the honour that was bestowed.

IV

The monopoly which Jones had created in the West African trade gave him enormous power and enabled him and his associated companies to expand and diversify into many other activities. It did not, however, guarantee large profits and the tariff freight rates that he charged were neither excessive nor oppressive. On the other hand, substantial profits were made on the carriage of non-tariff or unclassified items, particularly 'lumpy' objects, and in addition to being the sole importer of new silver[29] Jones established a monopoly for the supply of coal and cement to the British West African territories.

Coal was always regarded by shipowners as a topping up cargo which could be utilized to fill what would otherwise have been empty spaces. It was far better to carry coal at very low rates than to carry nothing and it formed a useful ballast if the ship was light. There was little demand for coal in West Africa from the local inhabitants but stocks were needed by the Government for their railways and the mining companies also used large amounts. When the conference system was introduced the Crown Agents for the Colonies asked Elder Dempster if they could import coal in chartered vessels without losing their rebate. Jones refused to allow this so the Crown Agents suggested that the Colonial Government should tender locally for their coal requirements. When this was done Elder Dempster secured the contract.[30]

---

[27] A. H. Milne, op. cit., p. 103.
[28] See below, chapter 7, pp. 107–8.
[29] See above, chapter 4, pp. 56–7.
[30] RCSR, evidence of Sir Ernest Blake, Q.10793.

From 1895 to 1905 Elder Dempster supplied most of the coal required in British West Africa. This situation was aided by the high freight rates charged for the carriage of coal and which had to be included in any tender. When the shipping companies provided the coal they could always reduce the freight element in their charge to themselves, so ordinary merchants could not compete even if one had been prepared to lose his rebate. The consequence was that the price of coal in Lagos remained very high and led to the Governor, Sir William Macgregor, asking for a tender to be published in England.[31] This asked for 15,000 tons of coal to be delivered in Lagos where the current price was 45s. per ton. A firm of merchants, Miller Brothers, tendered at 35s. per ton and intended to get round the rebate problem by getting the colliery owners to supply directly to West Africa with the aid of chartered steamers. Unfortunately for Miller Brothers their bid became known to Elder Dempster, who then bid 32s. 6d. per ton and obtained the contract.

An officer was later discharged from the telegraph office in connection with this deal,[32] but the fact that Elder Dempster could still find it worth their while to supply coal at 12s. 6d. per ton below the existing level indicates the tremendous profits which they had enjoyed for some ten years. In this particular case their profit was reduced by £8,000 (15,000×12s. 6d.) yet they were still able to complete what was apparently a worthwhile agreement.

Cement was another item which Jones supplied in bulk to the Colonial Government on the Coast. It was illegal for government departments to buy cement locally[33] but, before the rebate system was introduced, merchants like John Holt were able to conduct a profitable trade in this commodity:

> We used ourselves to buy from that Company (the Burham Cement Company) and we shipped several cargoes out before this rebate system was on, until one fine day we found out that we could get it no longer from them. We made enquiries why, and they said, 'because we have given Elder Dempster and Company the monopoly of this brand.' So we are in this position, that we could not offer any other brand, because the Burham Company's brand is the only one allowed by the Crown Agents and Elder Dempster and Company had the monopoly of that one brand; therefore we were out of it.[34]

[31] RCSR, evidence of John Holt, Q.5541, and *Journal of Commerce*, 3 June 1907.
[32] RCSR, evidence of George Miller, Q.4328.
[33] *Colonial Office Papers*, CO 147-136.
[34] RCSR, evidence of John Holt, Q.5043.

A copy of Holt's evidence was sent to the Crown Agents who then stated that they had no official knowledge of the business arrangements between Elder Dempster and the Burham Cement Company. They continued:

> The Crown Agents have never in their contracts for cement specified any particular brand but have always required the supply to conform to the requirements of their standard specification.[35]

It later became clear that Jones had secured the whole supply of this particular type of Burham cement. The exact nature of his agreement with the company has never been revealed but it appears to have given him the exclusive right to the brand in West Africa and, in return, he seems to have guaranteed that only this product would be carried in his ships to the Coast.

The net results of this activity were that for over a ten-year period only the Burham brand was available in West Africa and that it all came via Elder Dempster who, no doubt, received a return on each transaction in addition to their normal profit on its carriage. However, as a consequence of the publicity which the Royal Commission of Shipping Rings brought to this matter, the system was changed. This ended Elder Dempster's practice of supplying cement to Lagos at a price which included cost, freight and insurance and merchants were once again able to ship it themselves at the normal freight rate. The shipping firms continued to insist that only the Burham Brand be carried so it would appear that Jones was able to retain at least some of his commission from the cement firm.[36]

A further allegation by John Holt was that in addition to carrying cement and coal 'on ship's account' Sir Alfred Jones:

> . . . carried at special rates for the Sierra Leone Coaling Company, the Grand Canary Company and other trading firms which he controlled or in which he was interested. Both of these companies, he said, sell coal, cement, petroleum in cases and other commodities at c.i.f. prices which merchants who have to pay tariff rates, cannot touch. The shipowners, for example, or a trading firm in which they are interested, can sell cement at 9s. a barrel, whereas the ordinary merchant could not charge less than 10s. 6d. The Sierra Leone (Coaling) Trading Company, he said, can undersell merchants in all cheap goods such as iron pots or rice, on which the tariff rate is high in

---

[35] RCSR, statement by Sir Ernest Blake, p. 380, Question C.
[36] RCSR, evidence of John Holt, Q.5041.

relation to the value of the goods. They cannot, however, do so in cases where, as in the case of cotton goods, the freight bears a very small proportion of the value. He regarded this as proof that this Company received differential rates of freight from the Shipping Companies. Sir Alfred Jones, however, denied that these suppositions were correct.[37]

The Royal Commission did not accept Holt's views on this matter but neither did it completely absolve Alfred Jones. The situation was such that it would have been easy for Jones to have arranged for internal transfers and preferential treatment to cover those cargoes in which he had an interest. It seems, however, that while Jones undoubtedly manipulated rates to his own advantage on occasion he was too clever to make this a regular practice as he knew it would upset the merchants and may have encouraged them to band together.

V

The ordinary tariff rates charged by Elder Dempster also came in for much criticism. A specially vociferous opponent was E. D. Morel and, as he had worked for Jones from 1890 to 1900, he could speak with a certain degree of authority. Many of his comments about Jones's association with the Congo were well founded[38] but his series of articles written during 1906 concerning the 'Effects of a Monopolist System in Ocean Carriage'[39] appear to be less objective and were, perhaps, primarily designed to stimulate the activities of the then, sitting, Royal Commission.

Thus, although it was true that many rates could not be compared with those on other routes, neither could the circumstances: i.e. Elder Dempster charged 20s. per ton for carrying salt to Lagos whereas it cost only 4s. 6d. to Calcutta. The explanation in this case is that on many routes salt was carried as a ballast cargo on the outward voyage, the ship returning with a good paying cargo. Other commodities where rates were queried could frequently be excused on the grounds that while on some routes they formed a single, homogeneous cargo, in the West African trade they were carried in small quantities as part of a general cargo. This, of course, is an argument frequently put

[37] RCSR, complaints as to non-observance of conference usages in certain matters. Vol. 1, p. 70.
[38] See below, chapter 7, pp. 121–3.
[39] Morel published seven articles in the West African Mail (of which he was editor) on this subject on 16 November, 7, 14 and 21 December 1906, and 4 and 18 January and 1 February 1907.

forward by shipping companies in defence of their rate structures. In the present case, however, some of the force of the argument is lost when the high cost of transporting rubber at 70s. per ton and cocoa at 50s. per ton is considered. These may have been very reasonable rates when the quantities were small, but they were clearly greatly overpriced when these commodities developed into major items of trade.

In spite of these criticisms, the Royal Commission took the view that the ordinary tariff rates were, by and large, not unreasonable. This was partly due to evidence given as to the difficulties of the trade,[40] but no satisfactory explanations were ever given about freight charges for unclassified items. Such goods as petrol and dynamite were charged at an extremely high level and could be arbitrarily increased at any time. 'Lumpy' items like boats and engineering equipment were also rated at far above the amount charged for smaller units of the same material. To quote just one example: the cost of transporting two boilers of twenty tons each out to Lagos cost no less than £15 per ton[41] whereas the rate for iron was only £1 12s. 6d. per ton.[42] It must be agreed that bulky cargoes cause delay and extra expense but there can be no doubt that Alfred Jones extracted the last penny when special items had to be carried, and there was no redress, even for the Crown Agents. They either paid the freight that was assessed or did without the goods on the Coast.

Whatever complaints were made, or felt, about the rates fixed or assessed for the West African trade there were no suggestions that the profits that were made were not ploughed back. Many of those travelling to West Africa had cause to praise the shipping lines for the greatly improved standard of their vessels and their facilities. The Crown Agents noticed this particularly because the number of complaints from their passengers dropped considerably after the deferred rebate system had been adopted.[43] In fact, both the Crown Agents and John Holt thought the ships might be too good for their purpose, the latter considering that this was a direct result of the monopoly profits enjoyed by the shipowners.[44] But Sir Walter Egerton, in a letter to the Colonial Office dated 31 March 1907, wrote:

[40] RCSR, evidence of Sir Walter Egerton (Governor of Southern Nigeria), Q.11647–11650.
[41] Ibid, Q.11430 and 11515.
[42] RCSR, evidence of John Holt, Q.4823, p. 3.
[43] RCSR, evidence of Sir Ernest Blake, Q.10952.
[44] RCSR, evidence of John Holt, Q.5109.

It is only right to add that the class of vessels of the passenger service have been immensely improved within the last five years, but this would probably have taken place in any case owing to the large development of the passenger service, the increased amount of freight offering and the competition of the German Woermann Line.[45]

VI

The achievement and exercise of power in the West African shipping trade provided Alfred Jones with a firm foundation for the further expansion and diversification of his interests. Inevitably it also enhanced his personal status so that in addition to holding a large number of commercial positions he was asked to undertake numerous philanthropic and semi-official activities. In return he was rewarded with much approbation and many decorations, including his knighthood, and was made an Honorary Fellow of Jesus College, Oxford.

An almost incidental consequence of Jones's success was in the transformation of his financial affairs. Jones never appears to have pursued money for its own sake, or even for what it might buy him: he seems to have regarded it simply as a sinew in the never-ending fight to achieve or maintain his business aspirations. Nevertheless an important yardstick in estimating the achievements of a firm or an individual must necessarily be a monetary one and there is no reason why Jones should not be subjected to this test.

It is difficult, in retrospect, to ascertain the real income of an individual at particular times in his life. However, it is relatively easy to establish an overall pattern by using the family background as a starting point and to fix a finishing line by examining the net assets at retirement or death. In addition, various pieces of information may be gleaned from statements or documents issued on special occasions such as the beginning or end of an enterprise or on the celebration of an anniversary. Statutory returns may also provide a good guide to individual or company progress but information of this type is less plentiful for the nineteenth century than it may be for today.

In the case of Alfred Jones, who began to earn his own living at the age of fourteen,[46] it is certain that he received little financial support from his family. It seems likely, in fact, that any small contribution he could make to the family budget would have been gratefully received

---

[45] This letter was reproduced in the Minutes of the RCSR, Section 7, p. 199.
[46] See above, chapter 2, pp. 18–9.

but it probably took until he was twenty and earning £50 a year before he was fully self-supporting. Thereafter, his income rose steadily and in his last year as an employee of Messrs. Fletcher and Parr reached a peak of £247.[47] In 1878 Jones established his own firm and later claimed to have made more money during that year than he had earned during his whole career with Fletcher and Parr. An analysis of their accounts shows that Jones received £2,016 in the period from 1860 to 1877,[48] so it may be supposed that his net assets at this time did not exceed £2,000. Assuming an equally profitable second year and some compensation from Elder Dempster, it is a reasonable assumption that when they made him a junior partner in 1879 he was worth £5,000 at most.

Jones was a junior partner for five years at an unknown salary but it seems improbable that he would have earned much less than when he was on his own. Assuming a salary of approximately £2,000 per year, and even allowing for a very simple life style, there seems no way in which Jones's net position could have exceeded £10,000 when he became senior partner of Elder Dempster in 1884.

An examination of Alfred Jones's will shows that his estate was originally valued at £674,000 but was later resworn to £583,461.[49] Thus if his original capital, estimated at £10,000 is deducted from this latter amount it indicates that in the twenty-six-year period from 1884 to 1910 Jones added over £22,000 net to his capital each year! Of course this is an average figure which is a gross simplification as it omits any consideration of the earnings of interest and dividends which would automatically grow as the stock of capital increased. Nevertheless, it does give a clear impression of the scale of Jones's earnings for as well as accumulating capital at a prodigious rate he was also living at a very comfortable, although not extravagant, level.

In order to place Jones's achievements into a true perspective it should be remembered that the incidence of taxation was extremely light at this time so capital formation was considerably easier then than now. On the other hand, the value placed on Jones's estate was undoubtedly too low. Two of his executors had predeceased him[50] and the sole survivor found his task an enormous responsibility for which

[47] See above, chapter 2, pp. 27–8.
[48] See appendix, table 2, p. 127.
[49] See appendix, table 19, p. 146.
[50] These were his solicitor, Augustus Frederick Warr and his partner, William John Davey.

he was not adequately prepared. He was O. H. Williams, who owed his appointment to the fact that he had married Jones's eldest niece, and although he was a trained solicitor and a director of several companies he did not take an active part in the affairs of Elder Dempster.

Williams was faced with a difficult decision almost immediately for within a few days he was asked to grant an option for all Jones's commercial interests. The offer was made jointly by Sir Owen Philipps[51] and Lord Pirrie[52] and they must have acted extremely quickly for other potential purchasers soon found that they were too late.[53] There can be no doubt whatever that Williams lessened his burden by agreeing to sell the estate as a whole but had he waited, or sold the assets piecemeal, he would certainly have obtained a substantially better price. In the event, Jones's business interests were vested in a new firm, Elder Dempster and Company Limited, which was controlled by Philipps and Pirrie.[54] This had the effect of reducing any hardship and confusion to employees and public alike and may have been a major consideration that had helped to influence the executor's decision to sell. At the same time it must be appreciated that the purchase of these businesses, 'at cost price without any additions whatsoever'[55] (i.e. nothing for goodwill), represented a tremendous bargain for the buyers and, hence, tends to undervalue the extent of Alfred Jones's success as an entrepreneur.

---

[51] Sir Owen Philipps, later Lord Kylsant, was chairman of the Royal Mail Steam Packet Company and the driving force behind a number of shipping companies known as the Royal Mail Group. P. N. Davies and A. M. Bourn, 'Lord Kylsant and the Royal Mail', *Business History*, vol. XIV, No. 2, July 1972, pp. 103–23.

[52] Lord Pirrie was the chairman of Harland and Wolff, the Belfast firm of shipbuilders. He was already a substantial shareholder in some of Jones's companies.

[53] The African Association Limited made an approach to Williams in January 1910, but were told that an option had already been granted. RNCP, S.95, vol. VII, Transport, p. 363 et seq.

[54] See appendix, table 15, p. 142.

[55] Royal Mail Steam Packet Company, minutes, vol. XVI, 23 February 1910, p. 63.

CHAPTER SIX

The Limitations of Power

I

ALFRED JONES ENJOYED TREMENDOUS POWER AND AUTHORITY once he had regulated the West African shipping trade but it must not be thought that his control was absolute. His apparently secure position rested basically on the fact that the three really substantial merchanting firms who traded with West Africa could not agree among themselves. These concerns were the Royal Niger Company, Messrs. Alexander Miller, Brother and Company, and the African Association Limited, and as they were continuously engaged in a tremendous struggle for trade on the Coast it was not an easy matter for them to overcome their differences and join together to oppose the shipping lines.

John Holt, whose business was expanding rapidly during the 1890s, was convinced that the merchants would go to great lengths to avoid having to combine together to run their own shipping line:

Cohen: Do you say it would be impossible to form a combination of shippers and merchants for the purpose of resisting what you consider the exorbitant demands of shipowners?

Holt: Yes.

Cohen: Could they not combine for that purpose?

Holt: Yes they could if they could reconcile their differences but the merchants of West Africa (I know them) are all competitors. We are all big fighters one against another.

Cohen: But you are all anxious to have the freights lowered; you have one common object?

Holt: We have one common object, I quite agree, and the West African merchants are big and powerful enough, if they could only be combined to put an end to the rebate system and the shipping monopoly. But you cannot get these men to unite; they are competitors one against another.

Cohen: Do you not think they would combine if they felt strongly on the matter?

Holt: If they felt that they were going out of existence altogether unless they did combine, I suppose they would, but so long as there are so many of them, and their interests are so divergent, they are at the mercy of a line of steamers or of conference liners such as Woermann and Sir Alfred Jones together, and so the steamship people can do quite what they like with them.[1]

There was also a personal aspect that tended to prevent merchants from joining together to become shipowners. In spite of the many hard things said about Alfred Jones, most of the traders had a grudging admiration for him, and they did not wish to harm his interests so long as he did not press them unduly. This is obvious from the following evidence given by George Miller to the Royal Commission on Shipping Rings:

Sir Hugh Bell: Am I right in saying that it is not so long ago that Sir Alfred Jones was an employee of Elder Dempster and Co. and then bought them out and established his house?

Miller: It is a good many years ago; it would be quite twenty years ago. That in one's lifetime is a good bit.

Bell: Would not that have been your opportunity to have founded a line, and made these large profits, and had the remedy, which you now suggest to us as a possibility, in your own hands?

Miller: We have it in our own hands and I confess we could start a line if we thought it desirable to do so.

Bell: But you do not think it desirable?

Miller: Well we do not. There is a personal element in it. I do not want to do anything that would bring harm to anyone, especially to an old friend; personally, I do not want to do that, unless obliged to do it by other people. But it cannot go on indefinitely.[2]

II

It is clear from the foregoing extracts that Alfred Jones had to tread a wary path if he was to avoid a complete alienation of the merchant body. He regarded the rebate system as the bedrock of his authority and would not accept any criticism of the conference structure. He was also unwilling to end his monopoly of cement and coal as these

[1] RCSR, evidence of John Holt, Q.4913–4916.
[2] RCSR, evidence of George Miller, Q.4473–4475.

provided substantial profits but, on the other hand, he was anxious to be amenable in most other respects. Thus, as noted above,[3] Jones restricted trading on ship's account to very small proportions and he undertook to prevent the petty trading that was carried on by his vessels' officers and crews.

The practice of trading on one's own account was of long standing in the West African shipping service and it was always regarded as a compensation for the arduous conditions that usually prevailed. Until the conference was set up in 1895, fear of the merchants' reaction had kept this activity within modest limits but, then, the apparent power of the deferred rebate system appears to have infected crew members who considerably increased their personal shipments.

George Miller and John Holt made many complaints about this business and when, in spite of various promises made by Jones, it still continued they arranged for a meeting with other West African traders. This took place on 27 January 1897, and shippers were present from Rotterdam, Hamburg, France, Bristol, London, Glasgow, Manchester and Liverpool. George Miller spoke to the assembly and mentioned that he had written to Elder Dempster to inform them of the proposed gathering of merchants. He went on:

> In reply to this letter Mr. Jones called upon me in Glasgow last Wednesday and expressed his regret that this step was being taken, but said he was to a certain extent willing to help us. I pressed him to give me a letter in those terms which I might read to this meeting but he did not see his way to do it. According to my promise I called yesterday on Elder Dempster and Company and talked the matter over with Mr. Jones. I again asked him to give me something I might read to this meeting which would indicate the position he proposed to take up. In reply to that, however, he said he did not see his way to add anything to the correspondence which is in your hands, and that in that correspondence he had said all that he felt inclined to say. Each of us can form our opinion as to what spirit animates Elder Dempster and Company, and whether they are in earnest or not in earnest in any desire to put a stop to the trading of which we complain. I do not mean to assert that the Directors of the steamship companies themselves know the extent – the full extent of the trading that goes on. I have no doubt, however, that it is well known by Elder Dempster and Company, the Agents. They profess to make light of it and do not admit that it assumes the extent or proportions which we believe it has done.[4]

[3] See above, chapter 5, pp. 73–3.
[4] JHP, 6/4, report of meeting held 27 January 1897.

After many speeches in support of Miller's denunciation of the trading carried out by the ships' crew members the meeting approved a memorial that was to be sent to Elder Dempster and a committee was formed to deal with the matter. Both Holt and Miller were elected to this body and both took an active part in persuading Alfred Jones to act more decisively. Their efforts were eventually successful and Jones prohibited trading by members of his seagoing staffs: it seems that the protests of such a large combination of West African merchants could not be ignored so easily as earlier, individual, complaints had been.

The success of this activity led Miller to decide to put the *ad hoc* committee on a more solid basis and, with Holt's support, he called for a second meeting of all shippers engaged in the West African trade.[5] This gathering was also, like the first, held in Liverpool and it was agreed that a permanent organization was desirable. The West African Traders Association then came into being with, as its object:

> . . . the redress of existing and the prevention of future grievances as may effect the West African Trade, and generally to protect and further the interests of trade. To act on behalf of any member of the Association in such matters as may be more conveniently dealt with by the Association than by the isolated or independent action of a member.[6]

During this meeting it was stated that the trading activity of the ships' crews had been almost entirely stopped.[7] A constitution was subsequently approved and, thereafter, the West African Traders Association continually harassed the shipping companies when the interests of its members were threatened. It could not, of course, exert pressures on the major issues such as the rebate system and the cement and coal monopoly on which Jones was not prepared to co-operate, but it could and did rectify many smaller matters that irritated the merchants.

The importance of the association lay, not so much in what it actually achieved, but in its potential. If Jones had allowed his relations with the merchants to deteriorate the association would have been a ready-made vehicle for magnifying any discontent. In fact Jones was always very careful not to push the larger traders too far and was able, therefore, to prevent the natural leaders of the group from having many real grievances.

[5] JHP, 6/4, printed letter addressed to all West African merchants and signed by George Miller, 6 November 1897.
[6] JHP, 6/4, report of meeting held on 1 December 1897.
[7] Ibid.

III

Alfred Jones's dispute with the African Association was ended in 1897[8] when John Holt lost control and, thereafter, relations remained on an even keel until his death. Jones's disagreement with the Royal Niger Company was resolved in 1896[9] but, although an uneasy truce was maintained, their links were never very cordial. Jones was well aware that the Niger Company (it lost its Royal prefix in 1900[10]) controlled sufficient cargo to be able to justify its own ships and he was careful not to antagonize it, but controversies did arise from time to time.

A major area of disagreement between Jones and the Niger Company concerned the use of conference vessels on the River Niger. Ocean-going ships could ascend the river towards the end of the rainy season and the smaller branch line craft could operate along many of the larger tributaries. As the price for the continued support of the Niger Company for the conference, Jones had verbally agreed to keep his ships off the river but, in spite of this, his vessels were occasionally discovered. This will be seen by the following extracts from a letter sent by Lord Scarbrough to Jones on 25 October 1905:

> Note on Sir Alfred Jones' interview with Lord Scarbrough at 19 Artinger Street, July 13th, 1904.
>
> 'Sir Alfred Jones undertakes on behalf of the Steamship Companies not to interfere on the Niger in any way in future. He has already informed the Colonial Office that he cannot undertake transport on the river.'
>
> Extract from Niger Company's representative dated 29th of September, 1905:
>
> 'The *Ekuru* of Messrs. Elder Dempster took 255 tons from Ajekuta and 44 tons kernels from Lakoja.'[11]

As a retaliation the Niger Company occasionally chartered an additional outside vessel. An example of this took place in 1906 when the *Vlug* carried produce to the United Kingdom. Jones was quick to point out this breach of his understanding with Scarbrough, and the incident was not repeated.[12] Freight rates were another source of

[8] See above, chapter 4, pp. 52–3.
[9] See above, chapter 4, p. 49.
[10] See J. Flint, op. cit., chapters 12 and 13.
[11] RNCP, misc. papers 1904–05, vol. II, MSS Afr. S.95, p. 517, letter from Scarbrough to Jones, 25 October 1905.
[12] RNCP, vol. 12, p. 116, letter from Jones to Scarbrough, 9 July 1906.

conflict and Scarbrough frequently asked for concessions. Jones, however, always refused until, in 1907, the building of the Southern Nigerian Railway involved the carriage of massive quantities of equipment and special arrangements had to be made.

Jones and Scarbrough met to discuss these plans and took the opportunity to place their relationship on a proper businesslike footing. The result of this meeting, held in August 1907, was the following agreement:

1. Sir Alfred L. Jones agrees on behalf of the Steamship Companies to keep out of the Niger and to hand over all the river carrying entirely to the Niger Company. . . .

2. The Niger Company agree to ship entirely by the Steamship Companies' steamers reserving, however, the right to charter two steamers (instead of four as heretofore) each year for the purpose of their own trade only.

3. Lord Scarbrough will be willing to advise his Board to arrange with the Steamship Companies for the supply of coal to the Company on the basis that they supply all the Niger Company's requirements of Double Screened Large Steam Coal from Approved Admiralty Colliery at actual cost price plus 12s. 6d. freight in return for their exclusive shipments through Elders.

4. The above arrangements to continue for two years; then to be terminable by either party giving six months notice from any time.[13]

Unfortunately this agreement was not the end of the difficulties between the two men. Although future freight rates were to be fixed by consultation, no decision was made about the rates which Jones had already negotiated for the carriage of the Southern Nigerian Railway material. These were very low, but as Jones pointed out, if he had not quoted a minimal figure for delivering the cargo the railway would not have been built.[14]

Jones's policy towards the Niger Company had thus resulted in a compromise. He kept the ocean carriage and the Niger Company retained the river transport. At times Jones threatened to re-enter the trade on the Niger but this was believed by Scarbrough to be only a bluff.[15] At the same time, however, he was determined not to be caught napping:

[13] RNCP, vol. 7, p. 160, memorandum of interview between Sir Alfred Jones and Lord Scarbrough on 21 August 1907.
[14] RNCP, vol. 12, p. 353, letter from Jones to Scarbrough, 13 September 1907.
[15] JHP, 17-3, letter from Scarbrough to John Holt, 10 June 1909.

I agree with you that Sir Alfred is the centre of a whirl of ideas re Nigeria – an incubator in fact – but I doubt very much whether he will hatch out anything beyond ideas. At the same time, we will not go to sleep.[16]

From the foregoing it is clear that while Jones and Scarbrough might bicker over various points it was in their mutual self-interest to maintain their understanding. Jones always believed that attack is the best form of defence but he also realized that if he pushed Scarbrough too far he might easily destroy the balance he was so anxious to retain.

IV

It was equally necessary for Jones to keep George Miller and John Holt reasonably content with the services and conditions he provided. His relationship with Miller (in spite of their disagreements over the rebate system and the West African Traders' Association) was serene, and the two were usually on a friendly, if businesslike, footing. This was probably not unconnected with the arrangements between Elder Dempster and Messrs. Alexander Miller, Brother and Company by which the latter enjoyed certain agencies from the shipping lines.

John Holt had, of course, known Alfred Jones for many years and it was Holt who was instrumental in organizing a testimonial and banquet for Jones on his fiftieth birthday in 1895.[17] Jones reciprocated by taking Holt's son into his Hamburg office and providing him with a sound training.[18] The dispute over the African Association's fleet and Holt's disapproval over Jones's attitude to affairs in the Congo ended any real friendship but Holt appears to have been genuinely sorry when Jones died.[19]

In spite of his personal relations with Miller and Holt, Jones obviously could not rely on their support unless their interests were safeguarded. Fortunately for him they were usually in conflict on the Coast so they seldom found it practicable to join together even though it would have been to their mutual advantage. This was a major reason for the failure of the many attempts made by Henry Tyrer to provide alternative shipping facilities on West African routes.

[16] JHP, 17-3, letter from Scarbrough to John Holt, 15 July 1909.
[17] JHP, 6-7, note that both Alexander Elder and John Dempster refused to contribute to this.
[18] JHP, 6-5, letter from Jones to Holt, 16 September 1895.
[19] Morel Papers, F.8-2, letter from Holt to Morel, 14 December 1909.

Henry Tyrer had established himself as a shipping and commission agent in Liverpool in 1879 and, as an ex-employee of a West African merchants, Grant, Murdock and Company, had attempted to take an interest in that trade. Jones's links with the two British shipping lines prevented Tyrer from making the progress he would have wished so he decided to see if he could bring another company on to the route hoping, no doubt, that he would be able to act as its representative. Tyrer's first success came in 1891 when he succeeded in persuading the Prince Line to inaugurate a service to West Africa.[20] Unfortunately for Henry Tyrer, Alfred Jones was able to make the sailings of the Prince Line unprofitable and in 1892 it withdrew from the trade:

> . . . while writing you I would wish to name the detention suffered at the (Oil) Rivers, and the Rivers only, part of this is explained by the African Association's Agents systematically giving the preference to what they call the Mail Boats, even when our ships had been there some time, immediately the others arrived work was either stopped on ours altogether or practically and all the energy and interest centred on the others to get them away – consequently our ships with their present appliances on board could easily discharge and load in twelve days, then why should they be there regularly six and eight weeks. . . .[21]

The ending of the Prince Line's services to West Africa was a great blow to Henry Tyrer and so, after a great deal of effort, he arranged for the General Steam Navigation Company to begin a new operation to the coast.[22] Again Alfred Jones was able to make the intruder's activities unprofitable[23] and, in consequence, the General Steam withdrew its ships in 1895.[24]

Henry Tyrer's West African business was substantially reduced by these events. Yet he knew the trade and was still convinced that if a new firm could be organized on a proper scale it would be able to provide an effective challenge to Jones's monopoly. But Tyrer was a shrewd businessman and he appreciated that without the assistance of at least some proportion of the shippers a new company would have only a limited chance of success. When, therefore, he had gained the interest of Sir Christopher Furness he approached John Holt who

[20] JHP, 26–3A, correspondence between John Holt, Henry Tyrer and James Knott (of the Prince Line) in 1891.
[21] JHP, 26–3A, letter from James Knott to John Holt.
[22] *Journal of Commerce*, 10 October 1894.
[23] *Financial News*, 19 February 1895.
[24] *Journal of Commerce*, 11 June 1895.

welcomed the prospect of a new line and urged George Miller to back it. Furness, Withy then discussed the financial structure of what was to be called the West African Traders Company with Holt and Miller, but when they realized the extent of the capital that was required from them they decided not to invest and the project fell through.[25]

John Holt was always a more enthusiastic proponent to an independent shipping line than George Miller due to the latter's concern for this competitive position on the Coast.[26] Nevertheless on at least one occasion it was Miller who approached Holt with a view to their setting up their own carrying company. Holt's reply shows that he needed little urging:

> I have thought over our conversation at the Club and now write you as promised. The first essential to be agreed upon is the principle of being interested in freight earnings on our merchandise, in which we do not at present participate, although we know that on the average there is more profit on capital used in providing the means of carrying our goods and produce than there is in the sale of these goods – along with the alienation of our freight there are numerous conditions which I need not detail, all of which are detrimental (to a greater or less degree, but in the aggregate to a very considerable amount) to our interests.
>
> Having decided that we will carry our own freight the next thing is to decide when to begin and who will be our allies. From your point of view you may not wish to begin before 1902 and many things may happen before then to influence your views – but to begin in 1902 a decision should be come to at once (October 1900) and acted upon. Plans should be got out and orders given for the steamers to be ready then. Builders would probably quote much below current prices for the date so far ahead. If you and the Niger Company will go into this proposition, I am willing to join you. I would say first that you find the capital necessary to build two steamers, the Niger Company the same and I will find capital for one. Make a company of these five steamers and issue debentures of equal value to build another five and pay for them, and could get the next five on credit until built when we could get out more debentures.[27]

Holt did not really want to take the smaller firms into the proposed line though he would have been glad to have carried their cargo. He

[25] JHP, 22-5, letter from Henry Tyrer to John Holt, 24 July 1895, and JHP, 26-3A, correspondence between John Holt, George Miller and Furness, Withy during 1895.

[26] JHP, 26-3A, letter from John Holt to Furness, Withy, 2 December 1895.

[27] JHP, 26-3A, letter from John Holt to George Miller, 3 October 1900.

THE LIMITATIONS OF POWER

did not think that either the African Association or the West African Traders Association would back them as Jones would use his influence with particular merchants to vote against any such proposal. This did not deter Holt, however, because he really wanted to keep the scheme to a small number of strong firms:

> I should have no hesitation in going with you and the Niger Company with our steam carrying without any fear whatever as to results. The (African) Association being out of it would not at all deter me – they will be influenced if not governed by Jones.
> The (African) Association people are living idiots if they suppose that Jones is seeking their interests in what he is doing. He wants monopolies himself, but he will do his utmost to dis-unite those whose unity may seem to him the creation of something on an equal footing with himself. He is trying to get the government on his side, against the merchants, whose strength he fears.[28]

These grand plans for an independent shipping line came to nothing. Jones succeeded in placating both Miller and the Niger Company by removing the more serious of their outstanding grievances and Holt could not continue by himself. Jones also made it very clear that he was prepared to fight very hard to uphold his position and this combination of concession and firmness, in just the right proportions, effectively prevented the merchants from taking any positive action.

Tact may not have been Jones's strongest feature but he knew when to look the other way. The rebate system specifically included the French ports in West Africa but, in practice, merchants shipping produce to Marseilles and Le Havre were not penalized if they used non-conference vessels.[29] Jones is also thought to have used preferential rates to influence the more important firms of merchants. If this was the case, and no evidence of it has survived, the extent and effects cannot be calculated. One authority thought that differential freights were a significant factor in Jones's hold on the trade[30] but only one fact is indisputable. While Jones was alive the merchants did not form their own shipping line and neither did they give their support to any outside company. The reason for Jones's success in this respect cannot be accurately apportioned but must certainly include his own under-

---

[28] Ibid.
[29] RCSR, evidence of John Holt, Q.4922–4924.
[30] C. Leubuscher, *The West African Shipping Trade, 1909–1959* (A. W. Sythoff, Holland, 1963), p. 27.

standing that no system, however, powerful, could operate effectively without some considerable degree of co-operation from the shippers.

V

Alfred Jones's regulation of the West African shipping trade was challenged only three times between the establishment of the conference in 1895 and his death at the end of 1909. One attempt was organized by Henry Tyrer who, by 1903, had built up a highly successful business based on the importation of Scandinavian wood-pulp. The *Prestonian*, a small steamer of 1,152 gross tons, was normally operated by Tyrer between Denmark and Preston but in February 1903 she was sent to West Africa carrying salt, stock fish and general groceries outward and returning with mahogany for the account of W. B. MacIver and Company. *Prestonian*'s shallow draft enabled her to go up river and she used her own gear to discharge and load her cargo. The voyage was a viable one so was repeated the following year, but then Tyrer decided not to continue with this venture.

To some extent Jones was responsible for Tyrer's change of heart. After *Prestonian*'s first voyage he had discussed the situation with W. K. Findlay[31] and threatened to withdraw the £3,000 he had invested with MacIver's and also withhold the deferred rebate due from previous shipments. These threats were not, apparently, implemented[32] but would certainly have been put into effect after the second voyage unless a definite undertaking had been given. Thus Tyrer would have had a difficult job persuading MacIvers to continue their shipments but, in the event, a personal factor ended his interest. This related to his nephew, John E. Wilson, who had gone out as supercargo on *Prestonian*'s second voyage.[33] Unfortunately this young man was seized by an alligator when swimming at Capstown, near Benin,[34] and the shock of this tragedy so sickened Henry Tyrer that

[31] W. K. Findlay joined Lever Brothers when MacIvers was bought by them in 1910. He subsequently became chairman of the Niger Company and before his death in 1966, at the age of 99, gave the author of this work considerable help in his research. See P. N. Davies, *Trading in West Africa*, op. cit.; W. J. Reader, *Interview with Mr. W. K. Findlay, Liverpool, 4 March 1964*, pp. 140–54.

[32] Ibid.

[33] HTP, *Instructions to Mr. John E. Wilson, Supercargo, s.s. Prestonian*, 2nd voyage.

[34] HTP, letter from William Kerr, Master of *Prestonian*, to Henry Tyrer, 10 April 1904.

he returned his ship to its usual route and took no further part in the West African trade until 1916.[35]

A second attempt to enter the West African shipping trade came as a result of the initiative of the Gold Coast mining companies. These firms felt that the rates charged for the delivery of coal and machinery were excessive and when Jones refused to consider a reduction they decided to operate their own firm. This concern became known as the Sun Line and it started monthly sailings in October 1906. The home port of the new company was Glasgow but it also took outward cargo from Liverpool, Newport and Rotterdam. All its ships were chartered vessels and they were anxious to carry produce on their return voyages from the Coast. Regrettably, for the Sun Line, the deferred rebate system was too strong to permit any merchants to take advantage of this service and practically the only return freight was the gold produced by the mining companies themselves. In these circumstances the Sun Line was not viable and was dissolved after running at a loss for two years.[36]

The third and most serious attempt to challenge the conference came from the Hamburg-Bremen Africa Line. This German firm began a service to West Africa early in 1907 and severe rivalry developed between it and the Woermann Line. The conference then reduced its rates by no less than 40 per cent (on the relevant routes) to all merchants who would bind themselves for a five-year period.[37] This had the desired effect and an agreement was made between the Woermann Line and the Hamburg-Bremen Africa Line. Under this arrangement the rival firm bought eight steamships from Woermann who, in turn, recommended that it be admitted to the conference.[38] Jones agreed as its share of the trade came from Woermann and he regarded the situation as only a reorganization of the German side of the West African shipping trade. But the need to accept the Hamburg-Bremen Line into the conference shows that its position was not so strong that it could ignore a really powerful competitor.

Once the German competitor had been accommodated Jones rescinded most of his previous concessions and restored parity by

---

[35] The author of this present work is expecting to publish a similar book on Henry Tyrer in the near future.
[36] RCSR, appendices, part II, p. 196, letter to the Colonial Office from John Rodger, Governor of the Gold Coast, 21 June 1907.
[37] RCSR, evidence of George Miller, Q.4374.
[38] RCSR, evidence of J. H. Batty, Q.6834.

raising handling charges.[39] He was able to do this because of the lack of competition and the power of the deferred rebate system. It seems to have been a poor reward for the loyalty of his shippers, who had ensured his victory by continuing their support, but it was all part of Jones's flexibility and no more than the merchants expected. Jones fully appreciated the strengths and weaknesses of his position so when he could secure an advantage he did so, being ready at all times to retreat and accommodate if it proved absolutely necessary.

VI

An additional factor which tended to limit the power of Jones's monopoly was the fact that any excesses inevitably provoked public criticism. Jones, therefore, always made it his business to be on friendly terms with the government of the day, so he was particularly sensitive to parliamentary criticism. Typical of many such questions was that asked by C. Watson in May 1907, when attention was drawn to the conference freight rates.[40] Fortunately for Jones he had his admirers as well as his detractors in the Commons, so that when Wedgwood queried the rebate system, Jones was defended by Winston Churchill.[41]

Jones also feared adverse press criticism and would go to great lengths to prevent hostile comment. He was, in fact, remarkably successful in presenting himself to the nation as a shrewd, but honest, shipowner whose chief desire and pleasure was to help to spread the flag and trade in West Africa. Few personal criticisms of Jones were ever printed and those that were seem to have been largely discounted by their readers. In part, this was due to his genuine efforts to meet complaints, especially when they did not conflict with what he regarded as his essential interests! As he wrote in a letter to E. D. Morel: 'It is not in our interest to treat people badly.'[42]

Jones, however, did have a major weak spot in his public relations, for his position as Honorary Consul for the Congo in Liverpool brought him into conflict with the Congo Reform Association. This body, led by Morel, received enormous public sympathy and support

[39] RCSR, evidence of J. H. Batty, Q.4959.
[40] *Daily Post*, 24 May 1907. *West African Freights.*
[41] *Houses of Parliament:* Notices of Motions and Orders of the Day, Thursday, 19 July 1906, Question 57.
[42] Morel Papers, box F.8, letter from Jones to Morel, 7 September 1901.

so its quarrel with Jones caused him much bad publicity. Jones made great efforts to prove to Morel that conditions in the Congo were not as bad as had been suggested and when this failed he attempted to minimize the hardships being experienced by the natives in the public mind.

To this end Jones sought to influence the judgement of missionaries returning from duty in the Congo. These normally obtained much publicity for their exposures of Belgian atrocities and Jones was determined to reduce their impact as much as possible. A letter written by Holt to Morel describes one such effort:

> . . . Jones is badly alarmed by Berney's exposures in the press. Has telegraphed him and written him to come and see him. At last got him to lunch at the Club and after lunch kept him for an hour and a half explaining to him how much he had done for Africa, how much he had spent on philanthropy, how little importance money was to him, how he spent freely over natives and others in the Congo, Tropical School, Cotton, etc. etc. How his steamers were losing £150,000 per year (?) – would show him the accounts if he liked. Would send him out to the Congo and give him £5,000 to publish a book on what he saw there. . . .[43]

Jones did, in fact, send two people to the Congo to investigate Morel's charges. These were John Henderson and Mrs. French Sheldon and they were to '. . . write about the Congo from the Congo State part . . .'[44] and '. . . see everything which is to the credit of the Congo'.[45] It was when Morel refused to accept their reports that he and Jones finally fell out and, thereafter, he remained Jones's most knowledgeable and vociferous critic.

VII

The monopoly established by Jones was also limited to some degree by the two official inquiries held while his power was at its peak. The first, but less important of the two, was that held by the Committee on the Currency of the West African Colonies in 1899. Jones gave his evidence in public and he presented a strong case for retaining the

---

[43] Morel Papers, box F.8-1, letter from Holt to Morel, 29 November 1906.
[44] Morel Papers, box F.8, letter from Jones to Captain Tubbs, his Marine Superintendent at Banana, 10 June 1903.
[45] Morel Papers, box F.8, letter from Jones to Captain Tubbs, 3 October 1903.

existing system. The hearing was really concerned only with the banking and financial aspects of West African development but many of Jones's other interests were inevitably mentioned.[46]

Jones was naturally concerned with protecting the interests of the Bank of British West Africa. In 1895 he had attempted to secure permission to issue notes to the value of £20,000 but this had been refused by the Colonial Office.[47] This made him even more keen to retain his monopoly of the silver currency so he wrote to the Colonial Office urging that the existing system be left unchanged.[48] Jones pressed this point still further while giving evidence to the Currency Committee and his view undoubtedly carried some weight. However, the deciding factor was the attitude of the Treasury which disliked the possibility of sharing its profit from minting the coins with the colonial governments concerned. (This was the customary practice.) Accordingly the Treasury supported Jones and no change was made until 1912. It was, nevertheless, a close decision![49]

The second official inquiry which restricted Alfred Jones's freedom of action was the Royal Commission on Shipping Rings. The terms of reference of this body were very wide so all Jones's activities, both in and out of West Africa, came under careful scrutiny. The evidence was heard mainly in 1907, towards the end of Jones's life, so it provides a superb commentary on the development of his vast commercial empire. The witnesses covered all shades of opinion and included John Holt, J. H. Batty and George Miller on behalf of the larger merchants; J. H. Hutton and G. B. Zochonus on behalf of the Manchester Chamber of Commerce and the smaller merchants; Sir Walter Couper for the Bank of British West Africa; Clifford Edgar for the Bank of Nigeria, and Sir Ralph Moore, a former High Commissioner of Southern Nigeria, but currently a director of the African Steam Ship Company.

Alfred Jones and John Holt gave their evidence in private. Holt later agreed that his contribution could be published but Jones insisted that

---

[46] *Committee on the Currency of the West African Colonies*, minutes of evidence given by Alfred Jones, Q.1067-1229, 1 December 1899.

[47] CO 147/102 CO 15343, letter from the Bank of British West Africa to the Colonial Office, 30 August 1895, together with the comments of the permanent staff.

[48] Africa West, No. 616, appendix VI, letter from the Bank of British West Africa to the Colonial Office, 16 November 1899.

[49] Richard Fry, op. cit., pp. 44-51.

his was kept secret and it does not seem to have survived.[50] The effect of Jones's testimony can be judged, to some extent, by the majority and minority reports issued by the Commission. A number of important recommendations were made but neither of the two reports suggested that the deferred rebate system be ended and both were apparently content to see the conference structure continue without basic change.[51] This seeming vindication of Jones's activities was not achieved without a price and even while the commission was sitting Jones completely altered the arrangements for the supply of cement to West Africa.[52] This was a decision which he would certainly not have wished to have taken but he had to face the realities of a very difficult situation and without flexibility of this kind the whole of his carefully erected structure may well have been condemned.

It is impossible, of course, to say to what extent Jones was able to influence the Royal Commission on Shipping Rings. It would seem, however, that he was able to show that the formation of the conference had enabled him to maintain regular services at a moderate cost. The commission may then have come to the conclusion that as these facilities were of such vital importance to the development of the British Colonies in West Africa[53] it was advisable to leave the system intact in spite of its manifold imperfections. It says much for Jones's powers of persuasion that the commission took such a sanguine view of his policies, but it should not be forgotten that the efforts made to ensure their good opinion constituted yet another factor which restricted his freedom of manoeuvre.

VIII

Thus the power and authority enjoyed by Alfred Jones, though great, was in no sense absolute. He could not afford to upset the merchants in case they combined against him and formed their own shipping line. Even the fixing of the tariff freight was dictated, to some degree, by external forces for if they were put too high it would have encouraged the shippers to have sacrificed their deferred rebates and have taken

[50] The author has contacted the libraries of the House of Commons, the House of Lords, the Board of Trade, the Public Record Office and the Colonial Office without success.
[51] RCSR, vol. I, *The Report*.
[52] See above, chapter 5, p. 72.
[53] See below, chapter 7, pp. 99–100.

advantage of the new services that would have been quickly offered by the fresh competitors attracted into the trade. It must also be remembered that even within the conference itself Jones did not have a completely free hand. As the senior partner, Elder Dempster enjoyed better shares and conditions than those possessed by the Woermann Line,[54] but this did not mean that Jones was able to act without consultation. Every decision, in fact, was the result of a compromise worked out between the two principals and this necessarily involved a great deal of 'give and take'.

Jones's actions were equally constrained by the need to keep the tacit approval of the British and Colonial Governments. This meant that he always had to act in what could be considered a reasonable manner and to preserve his links with those in authority he would frequently go to a great deal of trouble.[55] In the case of the Jamaican fruit trade it also cost Elder Dempster a large sum of money for it has been estimated that Elder Dempster lost more than £400,000 more than it received in subsidies.[56] The truth of this may be confirmed by the fact that Jones's successors, Philipps and Pirrie, wound up the Imperial Direct Line and sold their interest in Elder and Fyffes at their earliest opportunity.[57]

To Alfred Jones, of course, this was money well spent and he never asked the Colonial Office to renegotiate the terms of their agreement.[58] Jones understood that in the final analysis his policies had to be acceptable to the Government of the day and so he took good care to remain on amicable terms with those in power.[59] Jones also appreciated that politicians are highly influenced by public opinion so he made it his business to see that his affairs were always portrayed in the best possible light. This was sometimes difficult, as in the case of the Congo, for Jones's desire for Leopold's cargoes conflicted sharply with the image

[54] See above, chapter 3, p. 44.
[55] See below, chapter 7, p. 109.
[56] A. H. Stockley, op. cit., p. 57.
[57] P. N. Davies, *The Trade Makers* (Allen & Unwin, London, 1973), pp. 184–5.
[58] A. H. Stockley, op. cit., p. 57.
[59] Another example of the way Jones tried to aid the Government came in 1902 when he arranged for a meeting of British shipowners to discuss the activities of the International Mercantile Marine Company. When it became clear that the Government were not prepared to support a scheme for an amalgamation of Elder Dempster, Cunard and the Allen Line, Jones took the matter no further. F. E. Hyde, *Cunard and the North Atlantic, 1840–1973* (Macmillan, London, 1975), p. 143.

he wished to project. By and large, however, his public relations were excellent and backed up by the respect and support of the community at large he could usually rely on at least the tolerance of the politicians in Parliament. Nevertheless, Jones knew that in this, as with all other aspects of his business career, that he was walking a dangerous tightrope and that a relatively small error could well have brought to an end his monopoly of the West African carrying trade.

CHAPTER SEVEN

The Motivation and Character of Alfred Jones

I

ALFRED JONES'S PERSONALITY AND ACHIEVEMENTS were inextricably woven together for it was largely his strength of purpose that enabled him to dominate the West African carrying trade. In turn, it was this control of communications that enabled him to develop his full potential as an entrepreneur, and thus ensured that his activities were to have a significant and lasting effect on the economic growth of the British colonies on the West African coast.

Any consideration of Jones's achievements must necessarily be examined against the background in which he worked and he was particularly fortunate in operating within an environment which provided a constantly increasing demand for the products of West Africa.[1] Thus the ever rising need for traditional exports such as palm oil, palm kernels and timber was reinforced throughout his business career by the additional calls for the newer commodities which included cocoa, rubber and tin. It was also beneficial to Jones that the existing organization in West Africa was not capable of increasing exports at more than a modest rate. This was not just a matter of production for the most important items, i.e. palm oil, kernels and rubber, were merely collected. The real problem lay in moving these items, together with those that had to be produced, from the interior to places from where they could be shipped to Europe or America. This was primarily a transport problem but the lack of credit facilities and the uncertain political atmosphere were almost as important. It was the need to overcome these constraints on trade that was to provide

[1] See appendix, table 1, p. 126.

Alfred Jones with immense opportunities for expansion and diversification.

Overcoming the bottlenecks that were preventing the growth of West African exports obviously required large amounts of capital. The merchant firms were relatively small and were engaged in intense competition with one another so were in no position to make significant investments in the region. Even if these firms had possessed large financial resources it is unlikely that they could have agreed how to employ them. In later years when there were only four substantial trading concerns, the Niger Company, the African Association, Millers and Holts, mutual suspicions and jealousies continuously prevented co-operative action even when it would have been mutually beneficial to all concerned.

Like the trading firms, the British Government was in no position to proceed with large-scale investment in its West African possessions. The local colonial governments had originally been established to provide a framework to regulate the activities of the merchants. This meant, in practice, that a nominal control was exercised over the seaboard and rivers but the interior was scarcely touched. Successive British Governments regarded these responsibilities as an embarrassment and considered them to be more trouble than they were worth. Then in the nineteenth century came the beginning of a slow expansion of legitimate trade and this speeded up when steamship services began in 1852. The interest of the Government did not keep pace with even this moderate development of the economy and, in 1865, a Parliamentary Committee had advised almost complete withdrawal from West Africa.[2]

This was never a real possibility but, in spite of the gradual growth of commerce, funds for West African projects became even more difficult to obtain. At the Congress of Berlin in 1884, however, the British Government came to realize that if it took no action, France and Germany would reap a considerable benefit. A policy was then designed to prevent these foreign powers from cutting off the coastal settlements from the interior. But the British Government believed that the public would not support the undertaking of new expenses and responsibilities in West Africa and so it adopted the expedient of creating a chartered company, the Royal Niger Company, to rule the enormous area of the Niger basin. In this way imperial considerations

[2] *Parliamentary Papers*, 1865, V. (412), p. iii.

were satisfied without the taxpayer in Britain being asked to provide any financial support and it was not until 1900 that the state took full responsibility for what was to become Nigeria.

The local population was equally unable or unwilling to finance serious development in West Africa. The few native commercial firms tended to be small and usually enjoyed only a short life. Some leaders, such as Ja Ja, organized trade on a large scale, but even their resources were tiny compared with what was required and they were, in any case, constantly being eroded by petty wars and unnecessary expenses. In these circumstances, the only other possible source of capital to develop the resources of West Africa lay in the steamship companies, but when Alfred Jones was appointed a junior partner in Elder Dempster in 1879 they were quite unsuited for such a task. At that time they were still comparatively small and divided and although able to make moderate profits were more concerned with survival than expansion on a grand scale.

II

Alfred Jones understood at once that if he was to make a success of his new position he would have to preserve the tentative agreements between the African Steam Ship Company and the British and African Steam Navigation Company. He believed from the start that it was only by this means that he could hope to eliminate outside competitors and thus secure a lasting place in the trade for Elder Dempster and Company. Fortunately for Jones the threat posed by interlopers helped to draw the two shipping lines closer together and with a united front they were better able to defeat their rivals. As a result, under Jones's guidance competition was virtually ended and in due course the two British firms joined with the Woermann Line of Hamburg to establish the West African Shipping Conference.

Once the conference had been created Jones was in a position to control the West African shipping trade on a permanent basis. The only ships which then visited the Coast which were not owned or managed by him were a few sailing vessels and the four (later two) steamers per year which the Niger Company was permitted to charter. Apart from these very minor exceptions, Jones was responsible for the carriage of practically every shipload of goods to and from British West Africa. The use of the deferred rebate system then ensured that the structure could not be easily challenged and it proved to be so strong that it survived Jones's death and was not abolished until the outbreak of the First World War in 1914.[3]

Jones's ambitious nature dictated that he must not only organize the regulation of West African shipping but that he, personally must take direct control. To this end he removed Alexander Elder and John Dempster from their own firm and then used Elder Dempster as a kind of holding company for his own interests. He subsequently bought or inveigled himself into positions of power within the two British lines and ended up by technically owning, as well as operating, both firms and their subsidiary companies. Thus it can be seen that Alfred Jones must alone[4] take responsibility for the policies adopted by the shipping companies and the conference: a burden he was always quite ready to accept.

The setting up of the conference placed the shipping lines on a permanently profitable basis. This enabled them to borrow large sums on extremely favourable terms and much of this money was ultimately invested in one or other of Jones's companies and hence in West Africa where it could be used to help eliminate the many bottlenecks which were limiting the expansion of trade. In turn, this meant that Jones could always fill his ships with profitable cargo and it also ensured that the great expansion that was necessary to supply these commodities provided fresh opportunities for lucrative investment.

Not everyone, of course, was happy at the way in which this additional investment was obtained:

> The combination of shipping companies in West Africa has not, as far as I am aware, been productive of any beneficial results to British or Colonial trade, and the only stability of rates secured is by the ship owners concerned, who have established an irreducible minimum, below which rates cannot fall during the existence of the agreement in question. In my opinion, the present shipping monopoly is an unmitigated evil; and such improvements as have been made, in the way of better steamers, have been in spite, not in consequence, of the combination.[5]

Another point of view was that held by Sir Ralph Moor:

[3] The conference was subsequently re-activated in 1924 and continues, in a modified form, to the present day (1977).

[4] William John Davey was Jones's partner for most of his business life but his total interest in the Group's assets amounted only to a tenth of Jones's share. When Davey died, in 1908, he left £80,427.

[5] RCSR, letter from John Rodger to the Colonial Office, 24 July 1907. Appendices, Part II, pp. 195–6.

Personally I think the rebate system has been of immense service to the development of West Africa; without it I do not see how it would have been possible for us to have a steamship company and the service that has been essential to those administrating there, in order that they could develop the country.[6]

However obtained, there can be no doubt that the investments prompted by Jones in his own self-interest had a vital effect on the economic development of British West Africa. By 'priming the pump' he increased the tempo of change and thereby accelerated a process which, since the ending of the slave trade, had seen the gradual expansion of legitimate exports. In addition to these commercial side-effects, Jones's activities also played an important role when the political future of West Africa was being decided, for without the stimulus of his investments resistance to foreign governments may have been considerably lowered.

This hypothesis may be rejected on two counts. In the first place, although steamship services began in 1852, it was not until after 1879 when Jones became associated with Elder Dempster that the companies became large and prosperous enough to have any really significant impact on the growth of the economy. This was only five years before the British Government had to make its decision at the Congress of Berlin and it may be considered doubtful that Jones had, by then, achieved sufficient to influence its policy. On the other hand, it could be argued that the potential was clear for all to see and the way in which Elder Dempster were organizing the trade indicated a promising future. The second criticism of Jones's influence on political developments is that the British Government frequently acted without economic justification and it is likely that this would have occurred in the case of West Africa.

An impartial observer of these events was Emile Baillaud, who was commissioned by the French authorities to visit the British colonies in West Africa and study their administration. He thought that both Alfred Jones and Sir George Goldie had achieved many important things on the Coast but felt that unless Joseph Chamberlain had added his support when he came to power in 1895, then these territories would have been lost to France and Germany.[7] Baillaud also stressed

---

[6] RCSR, evidence of Sir Ralph Moor, Q.6997.

[7] For details of Baillaud's publications and a discussion of his views, see: Stephen Gwynn, *The Life of Mary Kingsley* (Macmillan, London, 1932), p. 260.

that the writings of Mary Kingsley did a great deal to mobilize public opinion and thus made the political task, undertaken by Chamberlain, considerably easier. Yet, even if Baillaud is correct, it in no way invalidates the proposition that without the services and investment provided by Alfred Jones, serious economic development in the British West African territories would have begun much later and would have been far slower in gathering momentum. If this had been the case, and investment had been markedly lower, the shipowners, the merchants, the state and the indigenous inhabitants of West Africa would all have been significantly worse off.

III

Alfred Jones possessed no special advantages of wealth, social background, connection or education. His only assets were his native intelligence and physical strength, and those traits of character that enabled him to maintain a sustained determination to succeed. For Jones to raise himself from modest surroundings to great power and wealth was a tremendous achievement on any terms; that he did so without any external assistance is some slight indication of his superb intellect, his enormous capacity for work and his ambitious nature.

As the surviving son of somewhat impoverished parents it is to be expected that Alfred Jones's first efforts in commerce were inspired largely by a desire to assist the family budget. This fairly normal reaction was reinforced in Jones's case by the early death of his father and by his particular affection for his mother. The gentle origins of this lady made her reluctant to accept help from her more affluent relatives and this diffidence would undoubtedly have been felt and understood by her young son. Jones also had the example of his well-to-do relations before him, but the most important factor in sharpening his ambition was his close family ties. The deaths of so many of his brothers and sisters and, later, of his father, left Alfred, his sister Mary Isobel and their mother as a tight little group, strongly linked by affection and respect. Isobel's marriage in 1870 disturbed this pattern only in minor ways for her husband was away on business a great deal and she continued to live in the family house. The death of their mother in 1877 and of Isobel's husband the following year brought Alfred and his sister even closer together and from then until his death Alfred, Isobel and her two young daughters were to share a comfortable and congenial home together.

By 1879, when Jones became junior partner with Elder Dempster, he was probably earning £2,000 per year[8] and was financially secure. The achievement of a responsible position and a degree of independence then enabled Jones to raise his sights and the accumulation of capital was seen more as a means to an end. The end which Jones was, by that date, seeing quite clearly was nothing less than the domination of the West African shipping trade and his progress, thereafter, was by a series of logical and well thought out steps and manoeuvres.

Having defined his objective, nothing was ever allowed to stand in his way. Thus Elder and Dempster were clinically removed from their own company,[9] and friendship with John Holt was not allowed to prevent Jones from taking advantage of their verbal agreement on the sale of the African Association's fleet.[10] But if Jones was hard on others he was equally hard on himself. Having worked his way up through the business he understood all aspects of the trade and maintained excellent public relations with his shippers and his employees. Just about everyone could consult him about their problems so long as they left when he offered them a banana! Jones always kept a bowl of this fruit on his table and when one was proffered to the visitor he knew that the interview was at an end. By adopting this policy Jones made certain that complaints could be dealt with before they developed and permitted him to keep a close watch on all possibilities, but it involved him in a great deal of work and thus necessitated a highly organized and strenuous way of life.

Jones's day began with a very early breakfast during which he received visitors and answered the morning mail with the aid of his many secretaries. These also accompanied him on his drive to his office so as to be able to take his dictation, as required, and some were always present at his working lunches and dinners. Jones believed that he should never waste a minute and this principle could be seen at its most extreme during his weekly visits to London. A number of his staff would travel with him and, at each stop, one would alight and return to Liverpool with his master's instructions. Urgent messages were telegraphed to him at these stations and replies were frequently dictated and sent before the train resumed its journey:

> Every moment of Sir Alfred's life has been filled and I venture to think every moment will be filled to the end. Sir Alfred is a man who travels about with

---

[8] See above, chapter 5, p. 76.

[9] See above, chapter 3, pp. 34–8.

[10] See above, chapter 4, pp. 50–3.

four shorthand writers and disposes smartly of his business letters on a railway station platform while the guard is making wild and frantic signs. Such a man who takes time by the forelock and holds on to it is sure to promote the trade of the world.[11]

Jones was a strong believer in 'early to bed and early to rise' and, although he never slept for more than seven hours, he made full use of his evenings. Apart from numerous official functions at which he was always ready to appear and say a few words he also entertained privately a great deal. His generosity was not, of course, without purpose and it would have been difficult to have found any social occasions which were completely divorced from his commercial interests. Practically every Governor and important official passed through Liverpool on his way to and from West Africa and Jones made sure that all were kept fully informed of his opinions and activities. The most convenient and conducive opportunities for the discussion of business of mutual concern was after normal working hours so Jones arranged many lavish evening meals at which his guests were treated with the utmost deference.

Jones was thus prepared to work from morning to night to promote what he had come to regard as his life's work. He expected, and seems to have received, the same degree of devotion from most of his employees, even though he always refused to pay more than the bare minimum in wages. This aspect of working for Jones might have been compensated for by the prospects of rapid promotion in an expanding organization but, nevertheless, it was a major source of irritation with some members of his senior staff. Thus when it was arranged to transfer Robert Miller from Elder Dempster to Elder and Fyffes, Jones asked him if his new salary had been fixed: 'No,' said Miller, 'but I am quite sure it will be more than I get here.'[12]

Jones undoubtedly expected complete loyalty and application from his employees and was given to sudden starts of anger when he thought that someone was not pulling his weight. It is reputed that he sacked a man for walking too slowly up the office stairs and dismissed another for standing in the hallway and looking through the window. The latter was subsequently retained when it was shown he was acting on Davey's instructions, but this took some time as Jones always found

[11] *Liverpool Echo*, 14 December 1909, reference to speech made by Lord Derby who presided at a banquet given to Jones when presented with his portrait on 17 December 1906.

[12] A. H. Stockley, op. cit., p. 151.

it difficult to admit he had made a mistake. But if Jones was too quick and harsh on some occasions he also had another side to his character, and once ordered his tailor to provide an overcoat for everyone in the office on learning, during a cold spell, that one of his clerks could not afford to buy one.

One alleged consequence of his pre-occupation with work was that Jones never married. He always said that he had been too busy to find the time. Whether this was strictly true or not cannot now be proved but those with an understanding of psychology might draw the conclusion from this that it was a 'sublimated urge' of some sort which gave Jones his intense dynamism and personal motivation.

IV

By 1884, when Alfred Jones became senior partner of Elder Dempster, he was financially independent.[13] He continued, however, to pursue profits as avidly as possible to further improve his competitive position and expand his interests. From this time onward he was also, ostensibly at least, motivated by a desire to promote and extend the British Empire and he spent much time in the organization of many schemes which promised little personal reward. Jones appreciated, of course, that any action he could take to enhance the power and prestige of Britain in Africa would almost certainly benefit his companies in the form of increased cargoes but he also appears to have acquired a genuine belief in the virtues of imperialism and it is impossible to separate his altruism from his self-interest in this context.

A typical example of a case of this type occurred in 1892. Lord Salisbury could not be persuaded that the threat being made by the French to the hinterland of Sierra Leone was serious. Jones was convinced that it was and supplied arms, via the Sierra Leone Coaling Company, to the local Africans, the Safas, who were fighting the French. He then sent Captain Williams, the agent of the coaling company, to make a treaty with the Safas under which he would have obtained permission to build roads and railways, coin money and tax the native population. Jones was very anxious that Britain should annex this territory and was quite prepared to surrender his own rights if this were done, but he felt he could not just stand by and let the French take over.[14] His support for the Safas was ended, however, when Lord

[13] See above, chapter 5, pp. 75–6.
[14] FO 84-2265.

Salisbury warned him that if he sent another mission it would be detained in Freetown under the Arms Restriction Ordinance.[15]

Alfred Jones was attracted to the Canary Islands for the sole purpose of establishing a coaling depot for his ships,[16] but he quickly became involved in other activities:

> I visited the Islands for the purpose of deciding on the feasibility or otherwise of establishing a coaling station for our African steamers. I was much struck by the poverty of the Old Spaniards who form the bulk of the population. They formerly existed by producing cochineal, and on the substitution of the aniline dyes the community was practically ruined. The cochineal had fallen from 10s. to 2s. a pound; the land was lying waste and the people sunk in an apathy of despair. Well observing the prolific character of the soil, I bought up what land I could and grew fruit on it. Then, as I knew that that was not nearly enough for the trade I could foresee, I went round to the farms and offered so much for all the fruit they could grow and, where necessary, made them advances and financed them generally. The consequence is that land has now gone up to £1,000 per acre, the Islands receive a million a year for fruit, and the people are prosperous and comparatively speaking contented for they more than pay their way.[17]

Jones received much praise from the inhabitants of the Canary Islands for his enterprise[18] and this encouraged him to do even more for he was a man who '... loves being loved ...'.[19] Of course, the promise and subsequent achievement of substantial returns from the bunkering facility and the banana trade were equally important but Jones was at his most content when approbation and profit went hand in hand. The expertise gained in the Canary fruit business led ultimately to Chamberlain's invitation to provide an alternative market for Jamaican bananas.[20] In this case Jones's commercial judgement indicated that the proposed service required an annual subvention of £60,000 but he eventually agreed to accept only £40,000. His motivation in firstly allowing himself to begin the operation and, secondly, to continue it when his original estimates were confirmed by experience, is extremely complex. The promise of a knighthood

[15] C. Fyfe, *A History of Sierra Leone* (Oxford University Press, 1963), p. 503.
[16] See above, chapter 5, p. 66.
[17] Great Thoughts, *A Napoleon of Commerce*, 18 June 1898.
[18] *El Liberal* (newspaper of Grand Canary), translated and reproduced in the *Journal of Commerce*, 16 March 1892.
[19] W. R. H. Caine, *The Cruise of the Port Kingston* (Collier, London, 1908), p. 9.
[20] See above, chapter 5, pp. 68–9.

was a large incentive but there can be little doubt that he genuinely wished to assist the Jamaican economy if he could. When the real cost became apparent Jones did not, therefore, attempt to renegotiate his agreement. The £400,000 lost in this trade was, perhaps, a price worth paying if it helped to ensure satisfactory relations with the British Government.[21]

The establishment of the Bank of British West Africa was a rather happier affair. The absence of banking facilities was, by 1890, beginning to prove a major hindrance to the expansion of trade. Jones was made aware of the difficulties by his Lagos agent and quickly made the appropriate arrangements.[22] The long-term consequences of this action were certainly beneficial for British interests as it did much to promote commerce. This, in turn, encouraged the Government to take a more optimistic view of its West African territories and helped to persuade it to adopt a more active role in their economic development. All this was, of course, extremely pleasing to Alfred Jones who also had the satisfaction of earning good profits from the bank as well as from the additional cargoes carried by his ships.

Another instance where an investment was prompted by mixed motives concerned the growing of cotton. Jones was anxious to make Britain independent of American cotton and was largely responsible for the founding of the British Cotton Growing Association in 1902.[23] He made it his business, therefore, to obtain the services of an expert from New Orleans to instruct West Africans in the growing of the crop.[24] He also corresponded with the Colonial Office and Kew Gardens[25] and did everything within his power to see that the crop was firmly established. This included the carriage of the cotton from the Coast to Britain free of charge for two years. By this stage in his life Jones's 'imperialistic' motivations were very strong, but it should be noted that once the crop became substantial in size it was rated very highly and provided very satisfactory returns.[26] The result of these efforts to encourage the growing of cotton in West Africa were only

[21] See above, chapter 6, p. 94.
[22] See above, chapter 4, pp. 56–8.
[23] W. F. Tewson, *The British Cotton Growing Association, Golden Jubilee 1904–1954*, 1954.
[24] CO 45686-01, letter from Elder Dempster & Co. to the Colonial Office, 1 April 1901.
[25] CO 45686-01, letter from Elder Dempster & Co. to the Colonial Office, 24 February 1902.
[26] RCSR, evidence given by Sir Ralph Moor, Q.7294–7297.

moderate. They were successful in that a new crop was developed for export to Britain and this assisted both the internal economy and the shipping lines. The scale of production, however, was so small in comparison with British demand that it completely failed to provide an alternative to the imports from the United States.[27]

In some areas a conflict occasionally arose between commercial expediency and what might broadly be described as the national interest. One such case was involved with the carriage of cargoes between West Africa and New York. Under the conference agreement made with Woermann[28] all these goods were carried at the same rate as the freight charged from Liverpool to the Coast. This had the effect of preventing any American shipping line from seeking to enter the trade but it also meant that American goods could undercut those from Britain. Jones could always claim that he created a market in the United States for African produce because it did not have to pay the full cost of transport, but his real motivation was to protect his shipping from American competitors and he was prepared to see British manufacturers suffer in consequence.

It is probable that Jones's most altruistic action was his support for the Liverpool School of Tropical Medicine. This was certainly inspired by a desire to help in the conquest of the many diseases that made West Africa such an unhealthy place. Of course it could be argued that in the long run there could be a commercial spin-off so that the lessening of disease would enable better work to be produced so profits would be enhanced and there was always the possibility that activities of this sort would result in political recognition via the honours list. In the beginning, at least, this does not seem to have been the case for Joseph Chamberlain's prime aim was to establish a school of tropical medicine in London and it was, to some extent, against his wishes that a second institution was organized at Liverpool.[29]

Jones started the project by providing £350 per annum for the initial three-year life of the School, but his real success was to follow for, in the twelve-year period up to his death, he raised no less than £120,000 from the business community.[30] It was because of Jones's insistence that Major (later Sir) Ronald Ross was appointed to head the

[27] See appendix, table 17, p. 144.
[28] See above, chapter 3, p. 44.
[29] Liverpool School of Tropical Medicine, *Historical Record 1898–1920* (University of Liverpool Press, 1920), pp. 4–5.
[30] A. H. Milne, op. cit., p. 84.

new school although at that time Ross's work on the mosquito was not fully accepted. Many people were doubtful of Ross and it was not until he received the Nobel prize in 1902 that Jones's judgement was vindicated. In the interval Ross led a number of expeditions to West Africa and these played a vital role in the reduction of malaria and other diseases; the provision of free passages by Elder Dempster and the assistance supplied by many merchants on the Coast were important factors in the success of these ventures.[31]

As Jones's status increased, so did the demands for his support of numerous causes. Few requests found him unresponsive but he naturally concentrated on those topics of personal concern. Thus he used his position as president of the Liverpool Chamber of Commerce to promote the City for he felt a great affection for Merseyside and, as an individual, he was always prepared to assist the church, though in his later life he could not be described as a regular attender. Jones gave much practical help to the local charities, particularly the hospitals, and to the university although he had only a limited faith in the value of extended academic study:

> Another thing of primary importance is that a man should start early. Many men waste years of their lives at expensive schools instead of working at the professions for which they are intended. Indeed, I will go so far as to say that after the age of sixteen any time spent otherwise than in the work of his profession a man is wasting. All the education necessary to the practical affairs of life can be obtained by that time.[32]

Jones felt on more congenial ground in promoting the cause of the Lancashire (and other) sea training homes. Like many similar shipowners he realized that it was unwise to rely on the 40,000 aliens who were helping to man the British mercantile marine at the turn of the century.[33] Consequently, he gave the sea training institutions every encouragement and was eventually rewarded by seeing the scheme prove an outstanding success. Orphans and the children of poor families were recruited, instructed, kitted-out and found positions without any cost to themselves. Thus many potential 'unemployables' were fitted for a useful career and then provided a valuable supplement to the sea-going labour force. It should be appreciated that in this, as in other causes, it was not Jones's financial support that was most prized: it was

[31] Liverpool School of Tropical Medicine, *Historical Record*, op. cit.
[32] *Daily News*, 14 December 1909, obituary of Sir Alfred Jones.
[33] A. H. Milne, op. cit., p. 36.

his ability to inspire the rest of the business community to fo.
where he led.

V

Some of Alfred Jones's contemporaries looked upon him as a mere
'money grubber' and thought that his appetite for work arose purely
to satisfy his greed. This is, surely, an incorrect assessment of his
character. Naturally when he was young and making his way in the
world he was anxious to acquire sufficient wealth to secure his, and his
family's, future but this phase soon passed and he was then driven by
other motives. His basic need does seem to have been to achieve success
in life and he was quite prepared to subordinate everything else to this
end, but the acquisition of money was only a small aspect of his
aspirations. Thus, as he continued to make further and further progress, his inspiration gradually changed and many other sides of his
personality were disclosed.

Jones considered that good relations with the Government were
essential to his wellbeing and he made great efforts to remain on
friendly terms, particularly with the Colonial Office. Jones held a very
high opinion of Joseph Chamberlain and maintained that he had done
more for British West Africa in twelve years than previous Colonial
Secretaries had done in fifty years.[34] Letters from Chamberlain to
Jones show their amicable relationship but it would seem that this was
based solely on a mutual desire to see West Africa as a prosperous part
of the British Empire. There would appear to be no truth in the
allegation that Chamberlain favoured Jones for personal reasons and
he refused to open Elder Dempster's new offices when Colonial House
was completed in 1905.[35] Chamberlain did put Jones's name forward
for his knighthood and it could be suggested that this should be
regarded as evidence of a partisan relationship.[36] It is more likely that
Chamberlain acted in his official capacity in a quite impartial way, for
Jones's work in Africa and in the School of Tropical Medicine was
quite sufficient, by the standards of the times, to justify a major honour
even without his assistance with the Jamaican fruit trade.

[34] A. H. Stockley, op. cit., p. 169. This shows that Stockley agreed with this view
of Chamberlain.
[35] Mocatta Papers, letter from Chamberlain to Jones, 7 October 1905.
[36] See above, chapter 5, p. 69.

Some confirmation of this view may be obtained from a letter from Chamberlain to Jones the year after he had been given his knighthood:

> ... I congratulate you on the success of your dinner and the recognition then afforded of your energy and active interest in all that concerns the prosperity of the West Coast Colonies.
> You may be sure that I shall continue heartily to co-operate with you in everything that can promote their welfare.[37]

A further shred of evidence is provided by a letter written by Jones to the Governor of the Gold Coast:

> ... I have been trying very hard to get Mr. Chamberlain to open the Coomasie Railway himself and he does not altogether reject the idea. I have told him that he could 'kill two birds with one stone' and open the Sierra Leone Mountain and the Coomasie Railways on the one visit and I have also told him that if he will go to the Coast I will accompany him. . . .[38]

The final word in this respect must go to Dr. Ronald Ross who records a surprise visit made by Mr. and Mrs. Chamberlain to Liverpool in October 1903:

> ... Lord Derby (the sixteenth earl) asked Jones, Boyce and myself to meet them privately at lunch at the Adelphi Hotel. The great minister, with his cigar and eye glass, was a plagiarism of his caricatures, and acidly disputed some of Jones' schemes for West Africa, until the latter said laughing: 'Well, Mr. Chamberlain, everyone knows that you snub us all but that Mrs. Chamberlain smooths us down again.'[39]

Jones also had to contend with Winston Churchill, then a somewhat youthful Under-Secretary for the Colonies, and it needed all his powers to convince him that he was genuinely concerned with the true interests of British West Africa. Churchill was satisfied that he knew enough about Jones to be able to support him but this did not mean that he was blind to his faults:

> I am particularly glad to see my friend, Sir Alfred Jones. (Hear, hear.) He is, as I have said, a candid man, and never so candid as when he tries to conceal his thoughts.[40]

[37] Nathan Papers, item 99, of the correspondence between Jones and Nathan. (This collection is held at Rhodes House Library, Oxford.) Copy of letter from Chamberlain to Jones, 21 August 1902.

[38] Nathan Papers, item 155-6, letter from Jones to Nathan, 11 April 1903.

[39] Ronald Ross, *Memoirs* (John Murray, London, 1923), p. 488.

[40] *Daily Post and Mercury*, banquet given at the Adelphi Hotel by the Liverpool Chamber of Commerce. Speech made by W. S. Churchill, 7 May 1906.

Jones's ability to persuade people to trust him was a m; was not always fully appreciated:

> . . . Am afraid that Jones has got on the right side of Winstor that the Niger Railway will be all the most costly in consequence. Why are not these officials honest or why are they such fools? Anybody but a rogue or fool would advertise for a tender to carry the railway material to Boro and Jebba just as they advertised for the supply of the material itself, and made public the prices at which the contracts were placed. Why are they not equally honest about freights?[41]

On this occasion John Holt was mistaken and the material for the construction of the Southern Nigerian Railway was carried at a very low rate indeed.[42] Nevertheless his comments are valuable in so far as they demonstrate that Jones was regarded as a man worthy of trust by people in authority. To a large extent this was a reflection of Jones's determination to see that the Colonial Office was constantly being reminded of his ideas, plans and progress. The best surviving evidence of this is supplied by the correspondence between Jones and (Sir) Matthew Nathan who was Governor of the Gold Coast from 1900 to 1903.[43] It includes nearly ninety letters written by Jones during this period (together with many enclosures) and covers a vast array of topics.

These include many queries about the provision of a site at Sekondi for a new coaling depot, pier and slipway, and the progress of a hotel being built at that port by Jones. The accommodation, timekeeping and service provided by his ships are equally prominent and there are many references to the proposed introduction of new crops such as coconut trees (for copra) and cotton. The work of the School of Tropical Medicine is frequently mentioned but Jones insists that he is perfectly happy with the arrangements on the Coast, and that he does not favour a commission of enquiry:

> As regards the Commission which Mr. Chamberlain suggested we should send out to the Coast, I have seen him several times lately and discussed this question. I said we had four good West African Governors and that I did not consider it would be at all nice for us to send out a Commission to criticize their work. You are on the spot and I am perfectly certain your heart is in the work.[44]

[41] Morel Papers, F.8-2, letter from Holt to Morel, 11 February 1908.
[42] See above, chapter 6, p. 83.
[43] An outline of Nathan's career is provided in *Who Was Who, 1929–1940*, p. 992.
[44] Nathan Papers, item 74, letter from Jones to Nathan, 24 October 1901.

It transpires from the correspondence that Jones was prepared to go
to great lengths to keep Nathan happy and he made every effort to
remedy any complaints. But in at least two ways he appears to have
gone beyond what might be regarded as a business relationship and
provided Nathan with personal assistance:

> As regards the ice we are taking out for you, I need scarcely tell you we are
> pleased to do this without charge, but in case we should run short of ice at
> any time, of course you will let us off easily. This is between ourselves:
> I have not told the pursers.[45]

Jones was also prepared to carry horses and ponies for Nathan at a
very low rate (30s. each from Lagos) but whether these were for the
Governor's own use or for some other purpose is not clear.[46] In return
for these favours Jones frequently requested Nathan to help named
individuals who were travelling to the Gold Coast on various business
or private affairs. Nathan usually obliged but once complained of the
improper characters who were sometimes taken out to the Coast.[47]
In spite of the minor perquisites that smoothed their paths, this was no
corrupt relationship. Each man was content to adopt a pragmatic
approach to each problem as it arose. Jones was anxious to remain on
friendly terms and this, clearly, suited Nathan but when the revision
of freight rates came up for discussion both fought hard for their own
interests until a compromise was eventually agreed.[48]

Alfred Jones had less friendly relations with Lord Lugard,[49] who in
1898 travelled out to the Coast in the s.s. *Benin*:[50]

> The ship is a small and very dirty one. The cold was intense. We had 'strong
> gales and squalls' for the first few days, but I did not feel the motion tho' I
> caught a violent cold. We reached Canary late in the evening of March 12th
> and I posted 25 letters. We had a very sumptuous dinner at the Metropole,
> which was provided by Jones, who has had a banquet for all our fellows
> passing thro' – and no one was up early next day to take our money. I have

[45] Nathan Papers, items 93–4, letter from Jones to Nathan, 12 April 1902.
[46] Nathan Papers, items 40–1, letter from Jones to Nathan, 17 June 1901.
[47] Nathan Papers, item 169, letter from Jones to Nathan, 9 February 1904.
[48] Nathan Papers, items 137–9 and 141–2.
[49] Frederick Lugard was in the service of the Royal Niger Company from 1894
to 1895 and returned to command the West African Frontier Force in 1898.
[50] *Benin*, of 2,223 gross tons, had been built in 1884 by Harland and Wolff at
Belfast. She was owned by the African Steam Ship Company.

written, however, asking for our bills and insisting on paying. I have no wish to be under an obligation to Jones even for a dinner.[51]

Lugard was especially annoyed when the *Benin* sailed for she had been stacked with coal to such an extent that it was level with the bulwarks:

This, of course, is in utter violation of the Board of Trade rules, which prescribe, I believe, a clear gangway from stem to stern. Thus our lives are risked, and not merely in order to carry a little extra cargo and make money, but because this coal is cheaper than that at Sierra Leone &c. It is wanted for her *return voyage*! and so we are subject to this filth and inconvenience of constant flying coal dust and our lives risked for Jones' pocket. The life boats are full of boxes and baggage. Willcocks is rampagious about it, and offered to bet the Captain he could not have a life-boat in the water in less than an hour! and now, worse of all, they have actually slung boats wrapped up in sacking (being taken out as cargo) on the life-boat davits, while the latter remain on deck full of luggage.
. . . Nothing, however, could exceed the civility of the Captain to us. We (W. & I) have a cabin each on the hurricane deck – he ordered a kennel for my dogs to be made and they run free on the ship. We daily have afternoon tea with him. This makes it very difficult to report the disgraceful condition of things, though I frankly told the Captain I should do so, and Willcocks swears he will write to *The Times*. . . .[52]

It is not known if Lugard or Willcocks ever took any action in respect of this voyage but it certainly did nothing to endear Jones to them. It seems that even before the *Benin* incident, Lugard was highly critical of the shipping monopoly[53] and this continued when he was High Commissioner for Northern Nigeria from 1900 to 1906. Lugard subsequently, after Jones's death, became Governor of Northern and Southern Nigeria and, in 1914, was appointed the first Governor-General of Nigeria.[54] If Alfred Jones had lived it seems probable that the two would have collided rather violently.[55]

[51] Margery Perham and Mary Bull (eds.), *The Diaries of Lord Lugard* (Faber and Faber, London, 1963), vol. 4, p. 358.
[52] Perham and Bull, op. cit., p. 364.
[53] Ibid, p. 364.
[54] Ibid, p. 16.
[55] In fact, in 1915, Sir Frederick Lugard became a member of the Committee on Edible and Oil-Producing Nuts and Seeds, op cit., and asked a number of extremely pertinent questions about the arrangements for the shipment of produce. See Q.2638–2661.

Arthur Henry Stockley met Jones by chance in 1888 and from then until Jones's death, twenty-one years later, he knew him as well as any other business colleague.[56] Stockley quickly became Jones's expert on the banana and was an extremely gifted man himself:

> ... As you say, our respective experiences with ALJ were out of the common run of business, and he was really a remarkable man who you could love and hate equally strongly at different times. I often think of your extraordinary relations with him. Of course you must remember that you yourself are a remarkable man. . . .[57]

Stockley had a great respect for Alfred Jones, but as he worked so closely with him he was aware of his weaknesses as well as his strengths:

> ... He was no man for details and was accustomed to taking chances. But as an illustration of what a peculiar man ALJ was to deal with it may be noted that when these details were raised (the need for refrigeration) he turned on me and said I had never told him it would be necessary to go to this heavy expense and he had supposed the fruit would carry under natural ventilation. . . .[58]
> However, ALJ soon cooled down as he generally did on such occasions. . . .[59]

Stockley subsequently had many arguments with Jones and in 1901 was largely instrumental in establishing Elder and Fyffes Limited somewhat against Jones's wishes.[60] Jones, however, took up the biggest share in the new company and eventually his estate benefited from Stockley's policies.[61] Jones, according to Stockley, always enjoyed extraordinary luck:

> ... he certainly had a flair for making money and also for spotting the right thing to go in for. But I cannot help thinking that his luck changed when he decided to take up the Chamberlain subsidy, as he seemed to have nothing but ill-luck with his new Imperial (Direct) Line. Some of it was unsound judgement, but certainly the hurricane and then the earthquake were two

[56] See above, chapter 5, p. 68.
[57] A. H. Stockley, op. cit., p. 238, letter from H. J. Ward, chairman of J. & E. Hall, Refrigeration Engineers, and formerly in Elder Dempster's employ as a ship's architect.
[58] Ibid., p. 34.
[59] Ibid., p. 35.
[60] Patrick Beaver, op. cit., p. 33.
[61] Ibid., p. 49.

terrible blows to face. I can sincerely say that after the experience he had in Kingston in 1907 I never had any further disputes or difficulties with him.[62]

Jones always had great confidence in himself and this became even more marked towards the end of his life. A visit to King Leopold II of Belgium, recorded by Ronald Ross, shows this to perfection:

> . . . The King, Jones and I were standing together and talking about the Canary Islands, where Jones had large interests. Jones, who was short, energetic and direct, exclaimed: 'We should work up those islands: your Majesty should go with me there.' The King, who was immensely tall, thin and regal (he spoke English perfectly) looked down at Jones, laughing, and said: 'What! I go with *you*, Sir Alfred Jones!' The latter was not a bit abashed, and when the conversation veered to sleeping sickness, cried: 'We have done a great deal in this line: your Majesty should follow us.' This really nettled the monarch, who exclaimed haughtily: 'It is for me to lead and you to follow, Sir Alfred Jones!' Jones never turned a hair. . . .[63]

At times, brash over-confidence of this kind made Jones appear insensitive and made him susceptible to flattery. This was possibly his chief weakness, although E. D. Morel thought he made many errors because of his low estimate of human nature and his belief that everyone had his price.[64] Yet Mary Kingsley, a shrewd judge of character, held Jones in high esteem. Perhaps, unlike Lugard, she had been more impressed with the standard of the vessel on which, in 1893, she first travelled out to the Coast:

> Dirt and greed were the vessel's most obvious attributes. The dirt rapidly disappeared, and by the time she reached the end of her trip out, at Loanda, she was as neat as a new pin, for during the voyage every inch of paint work was scraped and repainted, from the red below her Plimsoll mark to the uttermost top of her black funnel.[65]

Mary Kingsley remained on friendly terms with Jones for the rest of her brief life[66] and it was to him that she turned when she lay dying in South Africa. She had been nursing the wounded from the Boer War and was worried in case the authorities would not permit her to be

---

[62] A. H. Stockley, op. cit., p. 93.
[63] R. Ross, op. cit., p. 498.
[64] *African Mail*, 17 December 1909, obituary of Jones by Morel.
[65] Mary H. Kingsley, *West African Studies* (Macmillan, London, 1899), p. 5.
[66] Stephen Gwynn, op. cit., p. 133. Jones bought 120 copies of her first book and put them in his ships.

buried at sea off Simonstown. There was, in fact, no official objection but to cover this possibility she left instructions for her body to be consigned to Jones and asked him to see that she `was buried off Liverpool.[67]

VI

Ronald Ross, as the first director of the Liverpool School of Tropical Medicine, saw a great deal of Alfred Jones and his impressions were keenly observed and recorded:

> A Welshman, 54 years of age; rather short, dark, stout, with grey hair, moustache, and tuft below the nether lip, a straight look, ready laugh, and boundless energy. A Lloyd George of business, perhaps a Cleon. Always surrounded by shorthand secretaries to whom he would fling a letter in dictation while he was talking to you on some other subject; and generally followed by reporters and by several people who wanted 'half a minute' with him. He gave innumerable dinners and luncheons, and, before they were quite over rushed off, secretaries and all, to catch the train for London which he did just as it was moving away. I saw him dismiss a bore by putting a large banana into each hand of him, spinning him round and pushing him out of the door, both laughing. He found out what you had to say (or thought he did) in half a minute and then instantly proposed a special meeting of the Chamber of Commerce or a deputation to the Colonial Secretary, or some similar move. He gave endless tips and charities, and then complained laughingly that he was being being fleeced. . . .[68]

Ross seems to have provided a very accurate picture of the character Jones wished to present to the public. Ross, however, was closely bound up with his own affairs and could not be expected to appreciate the scale of Jones's business and philanthropic activities. These were better understood by Lloyd George, then President of the Board of Trade:

> Sir Alfred Jones is always a perplexity to me. He is my despair. He looks as if he had never done a day's work in his life, whenever I meet him, and as if he never intended to do one, and yet I know that his energy is only comparable to the Atlantic Ocean: ruthless and absolutely restless, in fact, he is not a man, but a syndicate. Let me assure you even Wales can only turn out one Sir Alfred in a generation. . . .[69]

[67] JHP, 16-8, letter from Dr. Gerard Corre of the military hospital, Simonstown, to Alfred Jones.
[68] R. Ross, op. cit., pp. 373–3.
[69] *Liverpool Journal of Commerce*, 15 December 1909, obituary of Jones.

At whatever meeting or conference he attended, or in any deputation in which he took part, Jones's grasp of the essential principles, if not the details, was so complete that he always emerged as the dominant figure. His superiority was particularly evident in Elder Dempster where he entirely overshadowed everyone else. This was not just a reflection of the realities of power: it was his ability to convince that obtained a sympathetic reception for his point of view.

It was in the consideration and planning of a new project that Jones excelled. He was painstakingly efficient in investigating a proposal, but once he had made up his mind he permitted nothing to sway him. His energy and enthusiasm tended to spend itself in initiating a new development and once it was running smoothly he was usually willing to delegate part of his authority so long as he retained supreme control. A policy of this kind depended ultimately on his ability to select first-class men and on their being prepared to serve him loyally. In this he seems to have been very successful but, although he expected his employees to really exert themselves in his interest, he was not willing to pay high wages. He always held that if their pay was no more than adequate at least they enjoyed great responsibility.

Jones's personal magnetism was an outstanding characteristic which was felt by all who came into contact with him.[70] It was, however, extremely difficult to define. His manner was virile and energetic but at the same time he was friendly and completely disarming. Allied to these traits were his undoubted intellect and powers of conversation and persuasion. He possessed an enormous faith in his own abilities from a quite early age, and as his career progressed, this was reinforced by the confidence bestowed by wealth and authority. With the sole exception of his entry into the Jamaican fruit trade everything that he had touched had blossomed forth, and apart from his unfortunate support for Leopold's policies in the Congo he had enjoyed an exceptional relationship with the press. In these circumstances, it may not be considered strange that Jones had a high regard for his own capacity and that he was sometimes overbearing and autocratic.

On the other hand, Jones was not without a sense of humour. On one occasion he offered a very junior clerk the pursership of his finest ship on its maiden voyage!

---

[70] *Shipping Gazette*, 14 December 1909, 'A Character sketch – By one who knew him.'

'Ask your father about it,' he replied to my eyes, that had opened wider. Father said: 'Take no notice of him – he's making fun of you. You're too young.' and that was the end of it.[71]

Jones was not quite so pleased when the joke was made at his expense. Arthur Stockley noticed an item in the *Daily Mail* to the effect that Sir Alfred had brought over fifty mongooses from Jamaica and that he was prepared to supply them for clearing out rats. Stockley then sent the following telegram to Jones: 'Just seen article in *Daily Mail* please send me six' and signed it 'Lipton'.

Jones was delighted and told his secretary to wire to Sir Thomas Lipton immediately: 'Very pleased you want six mongoose am advising Bristol to send them off at once.' Jones was most annoyed to receive another telegram a little later on: 'Do not want mongoose somebody been pulling your leg.' As Stockley found out when they next met, Jones was not amused.[72]

In the final analysis it was his joy in the exercise of power that drove Jones on. By 1900 he could certainly have retired with a handsome fortune, but to what purpose? His whole existence was bound up with his business affairs; his only other real interest was the satisfaction which he derived from his home. With the growth of affluence Jones had moved from the family house to a larger one in Cressington Park and then, in 1886, had moved again, this time to a substantial mansion standing in its own grounds in the Aigburth district of Liverpool. His sister, Mrs. Pinnock, and her two daughters moved with him and this pattern was broken only when his eldest niece married O. H. Williams in 1892. From then until his death Jones enjoyed a pleasant home background, but he neither sought nor delighted in any form of extravagance.

Perhaps his only unnecessary possession was his country cottage, Pendyffrin, at Llandulas in North Wales. Here he spent most of what leisure he allowed himself, for he loved its peace and beautiful surroundings.[73] In every other respect he appears to have been quite content to live in a moderate, albeit comfortable, style and he positively disliked ostentation for its own sake:

On Euston platform Sir Alfred asked me to lunch with him. We met about one o'clock at a table for two. At the table next to us sat a young swell, who,

[71] *West Africa*, 26 March 1938, 'In the Great Days of A.L.J.'.
[72] A. H. Stockley, op. cit., p. 75.
[73] A. H. Milne, op. cit., p. 104.

on being asked by the attendant what he would drink replied, 'Bring me a pint of your best champagne.' 'Waiter,' said Sir Alfred, 'bring me a bottle of lager; then to me, sotto voce, 'that's good enough for me.'[74]

The combination of a modest way of life and a substantial income made Jones a wealthy man but many of his contemporaries were somewhat surprised when he left only £600,000. As noted above,[75] the sale of his assets was conducted in such a way as to undervalue the estate quite considerably. Even taking this into account, however, it meant that Jones was controlling his vast commercial empire from a relatively small capital base. This he achieved by the use of a number of financial devices including the extensive use of debentures. Thus the British and African Steam Navigation (1900) Limited issued debentures worth £800,000 in 1900;[76] Elder Dempster Shipping Limited sold another £600,000 worth in 1899[77] and the African Steam Ship Company owed over £200,000 to its debenture holders in 1900.[78] Jones also made the fullest possible use of mortgage facilities and just about everything he owned was pledged to secure one loan or another.[79] In addition, the introduction of the deferred rebate system meant that Elder Dempster always had a sum equal to 10 per cent of nine months' freight receipts as an interest-free loan in their possession.[80] Jones retained control of the ordinary shares of his companies but was quite prepared to allow other individuals and firms to take part. In many cases, therefore, his original investment was a relatively small percentage of the capital employed, though nothing to match the extremely high gearing that was to characterize Elder Dempster when it became part of the Royal Mail Group after his death.[81]

VII

Late in December 1906 Alfred Jones took a large party of potential investors, businessmen, friends and Members of Parliament on a voyage to Jamaica. He promised that the cruise of the *Port Kingston*

[74] *Liverpool Courier*, 16 December 1909, 'The Passing Hour'.
[75] See chapter 5, pp. 76–7.
[76] See above, chapter 5, p. 63.
[77] See above, chapter 5, pp. 63–4.
[78] See above, chapter 3, p. 41; see also report of the African Steam Ship Company for the twelve months ending 31 December 1900.
[79] See *The Trade Makers*, op. cit., pp. 450–2.
[80] See above, chapter 3, p. 44.
[81] Davies and Bourn, *Lord Kylsant and the Royal Mail*, op. cit., pp. 109–10.

would prove to be of 'national, commercial and historic importance',[82] and so it might have proved but for the working of providence.

On 14 January 1907 a terrible earthquake devastated Kingston and thousands of people were killed. Jones was inside the Myrtle Bank Hotel when the tragedy occurred but, in spite of being trapped and having to crawl out through the debris, was able to escape without physical injury.[83] Indeed, he quickly organized every facility owned by Elder Dempster and his presence and energy did much to minimize the hardships of the survivors.[84]

On his return home it was noted by those who knew him best that he had changed. Jones was much quieter and more restrained[85] than before his unfortunate trip to the West Indies, and although he continued to busy himself in his usual way a gradual degeneration, both mental and physical, had set in.[86] Although a confident man in other ways, Jones had always been excessively nervous of travel[87] and it was partly for this reason (the other was the loss of time) that prevented him from ever returning to West Africa. Apart from his voyage on the *Port Kingston* he did manage to visit the Canary Islands and the Continent but he was never happy away from his office.

During his last year Jones was advised many times to take a rest but although he seems to have had some premonition of impending danger he refused to take even a fortnight's holiday.[88] Contemporary photographs show the extent of his deterioration[89] but he continued to work as hard as ever and made his usual visit to London during the last week in November. Jones caught a cold which he could not shake off on this journey, so when he returned home he felt far from well and did not leave the house for a couple of days. On 30 November Jones attended a previously arranged luncheon given by him in his capacity as president of the Liverpool Chamber of Commerce for Sir Hesketh Bell, the Governor of Northern Nigeria. He also called in his office on that day, but it was for the last time as he caught a fresh cold and

[82] W. R. H. Caine, op. cit., p. 1.
[83] *Journal of Commerce*, 15 December 1909, obituary of Jones.
[84] Ibid., p. 226.
[85] See above, this chapter, pp. 114–5.
[86] *The Times*, 14 December 1909, obituary of Jones.
[87] *Shipping Gazette*, 14 December 1909, obituary of Jones.
[88] *Liverpool Echo*, 14 December 1909, obituary of Jones.
[89] *Daily Mirror*, 15 December 1909, and *Journal of Commerce*, 15 December 1909. This reproduces a photograph of Jones taken in August 1909, when he was decorated by the Czar of Russia.

returned to 'Oaklands' with a severe chill. Two weeks later, on 13 December, he died from what was officially described as heart failure.[90]

Alfred Jones's career saw him rise from modest beginnings as a cabin boy to considerable power and wealth as the senior partner of companies which owned or controlled over a hundred ocean-going ships. In the process he did much to encourage the economic growth and trade of West Africa and thus helped to ensure that large areas of the Coast and its hinterland would remain as viable colonies under the British flag. To this must be added his work in restoring the Canary Islands to prosperity and his attempt to do the same for Jamaica, together with the consequence of this activity in providing a new and valuable addition to the basic diet of the working class. Jones's effort to make Britain less dependent on American cotton was only partially successful but the establishment of the Liverpool School of Tropical Medicine was to prove a considerable and lasting triumph. Jones was particularly proud of the school and of the achievements of the many missions sent to Africa and other tropical regions.

Jones has a further claim to fame and this lay at the base of all his aspirations. This was his faith in the future of West Africa. He was virtually alone, at one time, in seeing in the swamps of the mosquito-ridden Coast the promise of a vast imperial possession. He foresaw that the day would come when malaria would no longer be a major handicap and that the difficulties of communication would gradually be solved. Jones played a large part in overcoming both these drawbacks to viable growth and his foresight and enterprise gave him large financial returns. His real reward, however, was to see the transformation of British West Africa into a thriving economic development that promised a share in lasting prosperity to its inhabitants and appeared likely to enhance permanently the power of the British Empire.

Jones's imperialism and altruism were quite sincere but he was a man of his times and the expectation of profit acted as a tremendous spur to his activities. There can be little doubt that it was for this reason that Jones first entered into an agreement to provide a service to the Congo.[91] In the early 1890s this was simply one of many business ventures that promised a satisfactory return, but when it was alleged

[90] *Liverpool Daily Post & Liverpool Mercury*, 14 December 1909, 'Death of Sir Alfred Jones'.
[91] See above, chapter 5, pp. 65–6.

that the trade was based on intimidation and exploitation he steadfastly refused to withdraw. The basis of this criticism was that while the exports of the area were constantly rising, imports were stagnating at a very low level: the implication being that the labour force was being coerced, not paid.[92] Jones, of all people, was in a position to judge the truth of these accusations as his ships (together with Woermann's) were responsible for carrying all cargoes to and from the only port at Matadi. His failure to make a proper investigation or to act on the information at his disposal must, inevitably, lessen his stature in the eyes of posterity.

The reports of Belgian brutality were widely circulated and believed so it should have become clear to Jones at a fairly early stage that he ought to sacrifice his profits on this one, minor, route in the wider interests of his companies. This was not really a question of the objectivity of the horrific accounts themselves: if sufficient people believed them to be accurate then this should have been enough to have caused Jones to end his association with the trade. According to Morel, Jones was held back,

> ... partly by the material interests of the shipping line, partly by evil counsels and by that flattery from the highly-placed to which, like other men of his stamp, he was peculiarly accessible.[93]

Jones's motivation in this affair has never been fully understood and, in spite of Morel's assertions, may have been that he just refused to admit that his collaboration with King Leopold had been a mistake. In the event he not only continued to provide shipping services but also attempted to minimize the many adverse accounts of Belgian policy that appeared in the press. In turn this provoked much criticism of his activities and he had to endure considerable hostility from certain sections of the public.

In itself these difficulties made very little difference to Jones or, in fact, to those like E. D. Morel and Roger Casement, both ex Elder Dempster employees, who worked to reveal what they believed to be the true conditions that prevailed in the Congo Free State. Morel deplored Jones's opposition on this issue but felt it had only a very limited and temporary effect. He was convinced that the real tragedy lay in the failure of the reform movement to persuade Jones to be their leader:

[92] Brian Inglis, *Roger Casement* (Hodder & Stoughton, London, 1973), p. 55.
[93] E. D. Morel, 'Sir Alfred Jones', *African Mail*, 17 December 1909.

... at one time this man had it in his power more than any man, alive or dead, to bring home to the nation the full enormity of the Congo crime, not only as to its effects upon native life, but as to its deep-seated causes, its violation of economic laws, its destruction of the very edifice of normal Afro-European relationship. . . .

... I have always contended and I do not think that anyone fully acquainted with all the facts can truthfully deny it, that had Sir Alfred Jones come forward as the defender of the Congolese, instead of doing his best to block the movement for reform, tens of thousands of native lives would have been spared and the Congo tragedy would have been terminated long years ago.[94]

[94] Ibid.

Appendices

TABLE 1

Exports from British West Africa to the United Kingdom, 1854–1913

	1854	1884	1900	1913
Palm oil	40.2	53.9	40.7	39.5
Nuts for oil	3.0	25.9	12.5	15.4
Cocoa	—	—	—	9.9
Tin ore	—	—	—	8.3
Timber	36.4	—	14.4	8.2
Rubber	—	12.8	27.4	4.7
Other raw materials	—	—	—	4.3
Cotton	—	1.3	—	3.3
Manufactured articles	—	—	—	1.4
Grain, corn and maize	—	—	—	1.0
Gold	—	—	—	0.5
Ivory	0.6	1.1	1.2	0.3
Gum	2.5	1.9	0.5	0.1
Ginger	3.1	1.1	0.9	0.1
Wax	7.9	0.2	0.1	0.05
All other items	6.3	1.8	1.8	2.95
	100.0	100.0	100.0	100.0
Total values	£252,814	£1,099,256	£2,137,023	£5,173,553[1]

[1] Details of the trade of British West Africa with Britain are given in the *Annual Statements of the Trade of the United Kingdom with Foreign Countries and British Possessions*, published by Her Majesty's Stationery Office. A comprehensive list of the value and weight of the principal commodities is given, but due to changes in political boundaries it would be unwise to compare the individual totals of the separate colonies with earlier or later years. A further complication is caused by the fact that many of the commodities arriving in Britain were without a specific port of origin, and were shown as 'not particularly designated', and were thus not included in the totals of imports from British possessions. The best available guide to the intricacies of West African trade statistics is given in the Statistical Appendices, 1800 to 1914, provided in C. W. Newbury, *British Policy towards West Africa, Select Documents 1875–1914* (Oxford University Press, London, 1971).

TABLE 2

Earnings of Alfred Lewis Jones while employed by Messrs. Fletcher and Parr

	£	s.	d.		£	s.	d.
1860	6	10	0	1870	125	0	0
1861	13	0	0	1871	137	10	0
1862	26	0	0	1872	150	0	0
1863	32	10	0	1873	175	0	0
1864	40	16	8	1874	175	0	0
1865	67	10	0	1875	201	15	3
1866	75	0	0	1876	232	9	7
1867	80	0	0	1877	247	8	4
1868	106	5	0				
1869	125	0	0		2,016	14	10

A further £115 12s. 6d. was received as commission in 1878 although by then Jones had started his own company.

Source: Fletcher & Parr private journals in the author's possession.

TABLE 3

The African Steam Ship Company: Capital Structure

		£	£
1852	Nominal capital: 12,500 shares of £20 each		250,000
	Issued capital: 11,008 shares (£10 called up)	110,080	
	Amount paid in anticipation of further calls	22,762	
	Capital employed		132,842
1869	Further issue of 1,492 shares (£10 called up)		
1871	Nominal capital: 12,500 shares of £20 each		250,000
	Issued capital: 12,500 shares (£12 called up)	149,960	
	Amount paid in anticipation of further calls	18,702	
	Debentures issued	45,300	
	Balances retained in company	42,246	
	Capital employed		256,208
1872	Further issue of debentures to make total of	82,800	
1873	Further £2 per share called up (£14)		
1875	Further £2 per share called up (£16)		
1891	Nominal capital: 50,000 shares of £20 each		1,000,000
	Issued capital: 26,500 shares (£16 called up)	424,000	
	To be issued	135,500	
	Amount paid in anticipation of further calls	65,265	
	Debentures	83,000	
	Balance retained in company	279,692	
	Capital employed		987,457
1896	Nominal capital: 50,000 shares of £20 each		1,000,000
	Issued capital: 33,731 shares (£16 called up)	539,696	
	Amount paid in anticipation of further calls	98,276	
	Debentures issued	212,786	
	Balance retained in company	89,200	
	Capital employed		939,958
1909	Nominal capital: 50,000 shares of £20 each		1,000,000
	Issued capital: 33,731 shares (£20 called up)	674,620	
	Debentures issued	154,030	
	Balance retained in company	331,657	
	Capital employed		1,160,307

The African Steam Ship Company was incorporated by Royal Charter on 7 August 1852. Investment in this firm was undoubtedly encouraged by the limited liability status conferred by its Royal Charter. This was an uncommon form of commercial organization until the Limited Liability Acts of 1855 and 1856. Another, less desirable, consequence was that the African Steam Ship Company was not obliged to send annual returns to the Registrar of Companies. Hence no details of the general pattern of shareholdings have survived and the holdings of Alfred Jones have been obtained from other sources.

Details of the capital structure were secured from the annual reports of the directors of the company. The author has a complete set which covers the period from 1852 to 1923.

TABLE 4

British & African Steam Navigation Company: Capital Structure

		£
1868	Nominal capital: 400 shares of £500 each =	200,000
	Issued capital:	
	192 'A' shares (£275 called up) } 130 'B' shares (£120 called up) } = 322	68,400
6.4.1872	Change from 400 shares @ £500 to 320 shares @ £625. Nominal capital remained at	200,000
28.3.1881	Change from 320 shares @ £625 to 2,500 shares @ £100 (£90 called up). 156 shares not issued. Nominal capital =	250,000
23.4.1883	Became *limited* company. 15,000 shares @ £50. 11,720 taken up (£42 called up). Nominal capital =	750,000
19.3.1884	1,280 new shares issued (£25 called up) = 13,000 shares.	524,240
18.3.1885	New shares made equal to old by calling up £17 on them. Now 13,000 shares @ £42 called up =	546,000
15.6.1886	Nominal capital reduced from £750,000 (15,000 @ £50) to £600,000 (15,000 @ £40).	
16.2.1887	£5 per share returned, leaving 13,000 issued @ £35.	
16.3.1887	Nominal capital: 15,000 @ £40 =	600,000
	Issued capital: 13,000 @ £40 =	520,000
	Issued capital	
	(reduced): 13,000 @ £35 =	455,000
18.1.1888	£5 per share returned, leaving 13,000 issued @ £30.	
	Reduced issued capital: 13,000 @ £30 =	390,000
26.3.1890	Liability of £10 per share cancelled and each share divided into 3 new shares, now 45,000 @ £10 (39,000 issued and fully paid) =	390,000
1.3.1899	Articles of association changed.	
28.9.1900	Company voluntarily wound up. Liquidators were A. Elder, J. B. Mirrlees, John Wilson, Tom Davidson, J. Dempster, D. Murray.	

Source: File E.67206, dissolved at the Companies Registration Office, Edinburgh.

TABLE 5

Bank of British West Africa Limited

(File 40828, live at Companies House, London)

Formed:	30.3.1894.
Capital:	10,000 shares at £10 each = £100,000 (nominal).
Agreement:	26.7.1894 shows that the company owed Jones (£6,932), Davey (£1,732) and Sinclair (£1,732). They then received the following shares, each with £4 per share paid up: Jones – 1,733 Davey – 433 Sinclair – 433.
Directors:	Henry Coke Alfred Lewis Jones George W. Neville Owen Harrison Williams.
8.10.1900:	Capital increased to £250,000 by the issue of 15,000 shares at £10 each.
28.10.1907:	Capital increased to £1,000,000 by the issue of 75,000 shares at £10 each.
1957:	Name changed to Bank of West Africa Limited.
31.8.1966:	Name changed to Standard Bank of West Africa Limited.

TABLE 6

Bank of British West Africa Limited: Distribution of Shares

		1894	1895	1896	1897	1898	1899	1900	1901	1902	1907
E. Laurence	Merchant	50	50	50	50	50	50	50	50	50	50
D. H. Williams	Cotton broker	100	100	100	100	100	100	100	100	100	100
W. Ross	Clerk	1	1	1	11	1	11	10	10	10	—
F. Bond	Gentleman	50	50	50	100	50	100	100	100	100	—
H. Coke	Merchant	50	50	50	100	50	100	200	200	200	200
J. Pinnock	Merchant	100	100	100	100	100	100	100	100	100	—
J. Roxburgh	Cotton broker	50	50	50	80	50	100	100	100	100	130
A. L. Jones	Ship owner	1,733	1,628	1,628	1,648	1,648	1,648	1,723	1,820	2,161	4,739
W. J. Davey	Ship owner	433	433	433	433	433	433	433	433	433	520
A. Sinclair	Ship owner	433	433	433	433	433	433	433	433	433	—
G. W. Neville	Manager	—	100	100	100	100	100	100	150	150	100
Edward Jones	Manager	—	2	2	2	2	2	2	2	2	2
John Manning	Secretary	—	2	—	—	—	—	—	—	—	—
Leslie Murg	—	—	1	—	—	—	—	—	—	—	—
Mary Jones	—	—	3	3	3	3	3	3	3	3	3
		3,000	3,000	3,000	5,535	5,788	6,945	8,700	10,475	11,680	15,000

Source: File 40828, live at Companies House, London.

TABLE 7

Elders Navigation Collieries Limited

(File 65244, dissolved at Companies House, London)

Founded: 5.3.1900.

Directors: A. L. Jones
            W. J. Davey
            Raylton Dixon
            David Highgate
            David Jones
            William Dempster
            Laurence Jones.

Capital: 5,000 shares @ £10 each =   £50,000
            5% debentures   =   75,000
                                          _____
                                          £125,000
                                          _____

Jones received £124,930 by allotment of 4,993 shares, value £49,930, and the debentures, making a total of £124,930.

19.12.1910: Name changed to Elders Collieries Ltd.

20.4.1915: Name changed to Celtic Collieries Ltd.

1930:   Wound up.
            Colliery situated at Garth, Maesteg, Glamorgan.

TABLE 8

Elders Navigation Collieries Limited: Share Distribution

	1901	1902	1903	1904	1905	1906	1907	1908	1909	1910
A. L. Jones[1]	4,993	3,993	4,893	4,893	4,893	4,893	4,893	4,793	4,793	—
W. J. Davey[1]	1	1,001	101	101	101	101	101	101	101	—
R. Dixon	1[2]	1	1	1	1	1	1	1	1	1
D. Highgate	1	1	1	1	1	1	1	1	1	1
D. Jones	1	1	1	1	1	1	1	1	1	1
W. Dempster	1	1	1	1	1	1	1	1	1	1
L. Jones	1	1	1	1	1	1	1	1	1	1
J. Craig	1	1	1	1	1	1	1	1	1	101
	5,000	5,000	5,000	5,000	5,000	5,000	5,000	5,000	5,000	—
O. H. Williams	—	—	—	—	—	—	—	—	—	100 (Ex A.L.J.)
Elder, Dempster & Co.	—	—	—	—	—	—	—	—	—	4,794 (Ex A,J,L., W.J,D.)
										5,000
										—

[1] Directors.
[2] Lady Dixon.

Source: File 65244, dissolved at Companies House, London.

TABLE 9

Elders and Fyffes Limited

(File 70123, live at Companies House, London)

Formed: 9.5.1901.

Directors: A. L. Jones, ship owner   H. Wolfson, fruit merchant
A. H. Stockley, fruit merchant   J. M. Leacock, fruit merchant
A. R. Ackerley, fruit merchant   E. C. Barker, fruit merchant
R. Ackerley, fruit merchant

Registered
office: 9/12 Bow Street, London.

Capital: £150,000 in 150,000 shares of £1 nominal, divided into 'A', 'B'
and 'C' shares. £160,000 in Debenture Stock issued 10.6.1901.

Trustees: Owen Harrison Williams, Alfred Lloyd Barrell.

The company took over the business in certain spheres of Messrs. Elder,
Dempster & Co. and of Messrs. Fyffe, Hudson & Co. Ltd. Alfred Jones was to
be chairman as long as he remained a director but neither he nor W. J. Davey
were to be paid for services as chairman or director.

Satisfaction of debentures	Increase of capital
£20,475 repaid on 30.6.1902	10. 2.1903 +122,460 = 272,460 total
10,000 ,, ,, 16.9.1902	16. 2.1904 + 77,540 = 350,000
10,000 ,, ,, 1.7.1903	23.12.1904 +100,000 = 450,000
10,000 ,, ,, 30.6.1904	30. 8.1913 +550,000 = 1,000,000
10,000 ,, ,, 30.6.1905	
10,000 ,, ,, 30.6.1906	
10,000 ,, ,, 30.6.1907	
10,000 ,, ,, 30.6.1908	

Mortgages on ships

12. 5.1904. Mortgage of £50,000 to Barclay & Co. satisfied on 11.2.1905
13. 2.1905.   ,,   ,,   75,000 ,,   ,,   ,,   ,,   ,,   30.9.1905
2.10.1905.   ,,   ,,   75,000 ,,   ,,   ,,   ,,   ,,   23.8.1906

(Also borrowing on the s.s. *Miami*, s.s. *Matina*, s.s. *Manichee*)

Elders and Fyffes Limited: Share Distribution

	1901	1901	1902	1903	1903	1905	1905	1908	1908	1909	1909
A. L. Jones	70,500	70,505	70,505	55,449	—	83,254	1	55,503	27,752	20,000	27,752
W. J. Davey	23,493	23,495	23,495	13,479	—	20,237	1	13	6,752	13	6,746
A. H. Stockley	2,000	2,000	2,000	5,998	4,000	9,006	6,006	10,008	5,004	10,008	5,004
A. H. Ackerley	2,000	2,000	2,000	2,998	1,000	4,501	1,502	4,004	2,001	4,002	2,001
R. Ackerley	2,000	2,000	2,000	1,998	—	2,999	1	2,000	1,000	2,000	1,000
'A' shares	99,993	100,000	100,000								
H. Wolfson	2,000	2,000	2,607	—	21,644	1	32,497	21,665	10,833	21,665	10,833
J. W. Leacock	22,000	2,000	2,607	—	21,644	1	32,496	21,665	10,832	21,665	10,832
E. C. Barker	2,000	2,000	2,606	—	21,643	1	32,496	21,665	10,832	21,665	10,832
Wolfson, Leacock, Barker	42,180	42,180	42,180	—	—	—	—	—	—	—	—
L. Wolfson	1,820	1,820	—	—	—	—	—	—	—	—	—
'B' shares	50,000	50,000	50,000								
A. L. Jones	4	A. Preston		16,900	12,100	31,509	31,100	67,229	37,500	67,229	37,500
W. J. Davey	1	J. Jones		12,520	11,700	22,520	19,700				
A. H. Stockley	1	B. Parmer		11,350	10,300	21,350	14,300	25,150	10,500	25,150	10,500
A. R. Atcherley	1	M. Keith		9,500	9,116	20,600	19,784	18,606	—	18,606	—
	—	C. Hubbard		8,600	8,000	9,500	9,116	22,384	18,000	22,384	18,000
	7	F. Hart		6,521	6,000	14,521	11,000	16,521	9,000	16,521	9,000
Subscribers	—			145,313	127,147	240,000	210,000				
				272,460		450,000					
R. Clark								100		100	
Williams & Ross								13,479		13,479	
Robertson & Hughes (Bankers)								—		35,503	
								300,000	150,000	300,000	150,000
								450,000		450,000	

TABLE 10 – *continued*

Elders & Fyffes Limited

	1910 Fully paid	1910 Partly paid
'A' shares		
A. L. Jones	—	—
W. J. Davey	—	—
A. H. Stockley	10,008	4,904
A. R. Ackerley	4,002	2,001
R. Ackerley	2,000	1,000
'B' shares		
H. Wolfson	21,665	10,833
J. W. Leacock	21,665	10,832
E. C. Barker	21,665	10,832
Wolfson, Leacock & Barker	—	—
L. Wolfson	—	—
A. Preston	67,229	37,500
J. Jones	—	—
B. Palmer	25,150	10,500
M. Keith	18,616	—
C. Hubbard	22,384	18,000
F. Hart	16,521	9,000
R. Clark	100	—
Robertson & Hughes (Bankers)	—	—
R. Miller	—	100
Sir P. Bates	—	—
Elder Dempster & Co. Ltd.	68,995	34,498
	300,000	150,000
	450,000	

18.12.1907: Agreement made with the United Fruit Co. of New Jersey re bananas.

4.10.1913: New shares issue of £550,000 in £1 shares taken up by United Fruit Company.

Dec. 1913: This return shows that Elder Dempster's had sold their 68,995 fully paid and 34,498 partly paid shares to A. Preston of the United Fruit Company.

Source: File 70123, live at Companies House, London.

TABLE 11

Imperial Direct West India Mail Service Co. Ltd.

(File 72110, dissolved at Companies House, London)

Formed: 9.12.1901.

Capital: 50,000 shares @ £10 = £500,000.

Agreement: 31.12.1901. Between A. L. Jones and W. J. Davey, and the new company. This provided for the sale to the company of the undermentioned ships valued at £475,000 plus £25,000 for goodwill:

Port Royal	*Port Antonio*	*Port Maria*
Port Morant	*Montrose*	*Garth Castle*
Delta		

In return Jones received £250,000 in cash and 25,000 shares at £10 each – a total of £500,000.

Mortgages: 14.1.1902. 1st mortgage of £250,000 4½% debentures.
(Trustees: Sir Edward Laurence, Charles McArthur, J. S. Harwood-Rowe.)

16.3.1904. Addition of *Port Kingston*.

1937. Wound up.

TABLE 12

Imperial Direct West India Mail Service Co. Ltd.: Share Distribution

	1901	1902	1903	1904	1905	1906	1907	1908	1909	1910	1911
A. L. Jones[1]	18,672	18,672	18,672	8,672	8,672	8,672	8,672	8,672	8,472	—	—
W. J. Davey[1]	6,224	6,224	6,224	6,224	1,224	1,224	1,224	1,224	1,224	5,000	—
H. R. Dixon[1]	100	100	100	100	100	100	100	100	100	100	100
Sir W. H. Wills	1	1	1	1	1	1[2]	1	1	1	1	1
A. Elder	1	1	1	1	1	1	1	1	1	1	1
P. Napier Miles	1	1	1	1	1	1	1	1	1	1	1
John Dempster	1	1	1	1	1	1	1	1	1	1	1
British & African Steam Navigation Co.	—	—	—	10,000	10,000	10,000	10,000	10,000	10,000	10,000	—
E.D. Shipping Ltd.	—	—	—	5,000	5,000	5,000	5,000	5,000	5,000	5,000	—
John Craig	—	—	—	—	—	—	—	—	100	100	100
H. W. Davey	—	—	—	—	—	—	—	—	100	—	—
O. H. Williams	—	—	—	—	—	—	—	—	—	100	100
Elder, Dempster & Co. Ltd.	—	—	—	—	—	—	—	—	—	9,696	24,596
Other	—	—	—	—	—	—	—	—	—	—	100
Totals	25,000										25,000

[1] Directors.
[2] Became Lord Winterstoke.

TABLE 13

Elder Dempster Shipping Limited

(File 61912, dissolved at the Public Record Office, London)

Formed: 3.5.1899.

Capital: 100,000 shares @ £10 = £1,000,000.

Agreement: 5.5.1899. This provided for the purchase of the undermentioned ships for £1,100,000, i.e., £600,000 in cash and 50,000 shares @ £10 = £500,000.

Montcalm	*Montclair*	*Monteagle*
Montenegro	*Monterey*	*Montfort*
Montpelier	*Mount Royal*	*Monarch*
Andori	*Ashanti*	*Banana*
Regama	*Iokoja*	*Milwaukee*
Yola	*Yoruba*	

Schedule:

Owners or nominees	*Amount in shares and cash*		*Numbers of each share*
A. L. Jones and Davey	48,990 and	£489,900	
A. L. Jones	250	2,500	
W. J. Davey	250	2,500	
A. Sinclair	250	2,500	
R. Dixon	250	2,500	
A. Elder	3	30	
J. Dempster	3	30	
J. Craig	2	20	
D. Jones	1	10	
H. D. Bateson	1	10	
	50,000	500,000	
E.D. & Co.		600,000	
		£1,100,000	

139

TABLE 13 – *continued*

Elder Dempster Shipping Limited

Mortgages:

18. 5.1899	Trust deed: £600,000 debenture stock @ 4½%.
	Trustees: Sir Edward Laurence, Charles MacArthur, John Sutherland Harwood-Banner.
2.10.1901	s.s. *Bida*, s.s. *Hausa*.
27.12.1902	s.s. *Llandulas*, s.s. *Nyanga*, s.s. *Abeakuta*.
12. 5.1903	s.s. *Melville*
4. 1.1904	s.s. *Etalia*, s.s. *Memman*, s.s. *Lycia*.
3. 3.1904	s.s. *Canada Cape*.
3. 5.1904	s.s. *Porto Novo*.
30. 5.1904	s.s. *Muraji*.
20. 7.1904	s.s. *Zanzeru*.
18. 3.1905	s.s. *Benue*.
28.12.1905	s.s. *Dahomey*, s.s. *Angola*.
20. 2.1906	s.s. *Port Morant*.
26. 6.1906	s.s. *Coaling*.
12. 7.1906	s.s. *Patani*.
3.10.1906	s.s. *Falaba*.
28. 3.1907	s.s. *Ashogbo*.
14. 9.1907	s.s. *Sobo*.
30.12.1907	s.s. *Forcados*, s.s. *Lagos*.
20. 2.1909	s.s. *Jamaica*.
24. 6.1909	s.s. *Badaga*, s.s. *Monrovia*.
21. 5.1910	Name changed to Elder Line Limited.

In 1914 the African Steamship Company held 48,740 of the 50,000 shares.
In 1919 the African Steamship Company held 49,246 of the 50,000 shares.
In 1922 the new share issue of 50,000 were all retained by the African Steamship Company.
In 1929 the African Steamship Company held 98,996 of the 100,000 shares.
11.6.1936. The company was wound up.

TABLE 14
Elder Dempster Shipping Limited: Share Distribution

(File 6912, dissolved at the Public Record Office, London)

	1899	1900	1901	1902	1903	1904	1905	1906	1907	1908	1909
Jones & Davey	48,990	48,990	48,990	48,990	48,990	15,990	15,990	15,990	15,990	15,990	16,240
A. L. Jones	250	250	250	250	250	250	250	250	250	250	250
W. J. Davey	250	250	250	250	250	250	250	250	250	250	250
A. Sinclair	250	250	250	250	250	—	—	—	—	—	—
R. Dixon	250	250	250	250	250	250	250	250	250	250	250
A. Elder	3	3	3	3	3	3	3	3	3	3	3
J. Dempster	3	3	3	3	3	3	3	3	3	3	2
J. Craig	2	2	2	2	2	2	2	2	2	2	2
D. Jones	1	1	1	1	1	1	1	1	1	1	1
Bateson	1	1	1	1	1	1	1	1	1	1	1
Jones, Davey & Sinclair	—	—	—	—	—	5,000	5,000	5,000	5,000	5,000	—
Harland & Wolff	—	—	—	—	—	7,000	7,000	7,000	7,000	7,000	7,000
O. H. Williams	—	—	—	—	—	250	250	250	250	250	250
Sir C. Furness	—	—	—	—	—	10,000	10,000	10,000	10,000	10,000	10,000
Webb & Vaisey	—	—	—	—	—	2,000	2,000	20,00	2,000	2,000	2,000
British & African S.N. Co.	—	—	—	—	—	9,000	9,000	9,000	9,000	9,000	9,000
Irvings Shipping	—	—	—	—	—	—	—	—	—	—	2,000
O. H. Williams & Ross	—	—	—	—	—	—	—	—	—	—	2,500
H. W. Davey	—	—	—	—	—	—	—	—	—	—	250
W. Dempster	—	—	—	—	—	—	—	—	—	—	1
Totals	50,000										50,000

Note: 1914: 48,748 shares held by the African Steamship Co.
1919: 49,246 shares held by the African Steamship Co.
1920: 50,000 shares (new issue) also held by the African Steamship Co.
1929: 98,996 shares held by the African Steamship Co.
Company wound up, 11 June 1936

TABLE 15

Elder, Dempster and Company Limited

(File 108502, dissolved at Companies House, London)

Formed: 31.3.1910.

Directors: Lord Pirrie, Sir Owen Phillips.

Capital:

500,000 of £1 cumulative preference shares	=	£500,000
400,000 of £1 ordinary shares	=	400,000
10,000 of £1 management shares	=	10,000
		910,000
5% of debenture stock		1,000,000
		£1,910,000

Liverpool managing directors: John Craig
Owen Harrison Williams
David Jones
James Henry Sharrock (accountant)
Edwin Bicker-Caarten (secretary).

Allocation of shares to estate of Sir A. L. Jones

'Sale to the company of the business and goodwill of Elder, Dempster and Company, The Grand Canary Coaling Company, the Teneriff Coaling Company and the Sierra Leone Coaling Company, and of the profits and assets mentioned in an agreement dated 2.4.1910.'

Total payments under this agreement were:

Cash	£200,000
Debenture stock	200,000 (part of £1 million)
Preference shares	100,000
	£500,000

Agreement dated 2 April 1910 between Owen Harrison Williams, and Lord Pirrie and Sir Owen Phillips.

TABLE 16

Sale of the Beaver Line in 1903

Elder Dempster and Company sold their Canadian interests to the Canadian
Pacific Line for the sum of £1,417,500. This included provision for 'goodwill'
and the following vessels, but note that part of the fleet, formerly used on the
Canadian service, was retained by Elder Dempster and used for other purposes:

Vessels transferred to Canadian Pacific

	Built	Gross tons
Montreal	1900	6,870
Montezuma	1899	7,345
Milwaukee	1897	7,323
Montcalm	1897	5,505
Monteagle	1899	5,498
Montfort	1899	5,519
Mount Royal	1898	7,064
Mount Temple	1901	7,656
Monterey	1898	5,455
Montrose	1897	7,094
Lake Champlain	1900	7,392
Lake Erie	1900	7,550
Lake Manitoba	1901	8,852
Lake Michigan	1902	7,000

Source: F. C. Bowen, *History of the Canadian Pacific Line* (Marston & Co., London,
1928), pp. 84–5.

TABLE 17

Raw cotton imports into the United Kingdom (£)

	British West Africa	United States	Egypt	Total
1896	—	27 million	6 million	36 million
1900	938	30	9	40
1904	15,099	40	11	54
1908	66,780	39	13	55
1912	122,092	55	20	80
1916	259,451	60	19	84
1919	554,053	125	50	190

Source: *Annual Statements of the Trade of the United Kingdom*, HMSO.

TABLE 18

Will of Sir Alfred Lewis Jones

As Sir Alfred Jones had never married, his next of kin were his sister, Mrs. Mary Isobel Pinnock, and his two nieces – Mrs. Florence Mary Williams and Miss Blanche Elizabeth Pinnock – and these were the main beneficiaries. To his sister he left £1,500 plus an annuity of £2,500 per annum. She also received all the household goods at 'Oaklands', Aigburth, where she had kept house for Jones, and the use of this residence during her lifetime. Mrs. Williams received £20,000 upon trust for life, and Miss Pinnock was left £30,000 on the same basis. There were also several bequests to friends, and provision was made for servants and clerks. The residue of the estate was then to be formed into a trust fund to help worthy causes – mainly those with a West African bias. The total value of the estate was originally estimated at £674,259 but was later re-sworn to £583,461. As will be imagined, it was largely tied up in various companies and as many of the assets were mortgaged it was a complicated matter to settle.

The estate was not finalized until 1928. By then it was stated that over £325,000 had been distributed to charitable and other institutions. Included in the scheme were provision for research work in tropical diseases, for technical education for the local people of West Africa and for the relief of poor relatives and old employees. The administration of the will involved the investigation of over 11,000 claims to legacies by clerks who had been in Sir Alfred's employ although only 800 were admitted, costing £70,000.

For full details of the will, see: A. H. Milne, *Sir Alfred Lewis Jones*, K.C.M.G. See also *West Africa*, 12 May 1928, p. 580.

TABLE 19
Family Tree of Sir Alfred Jones

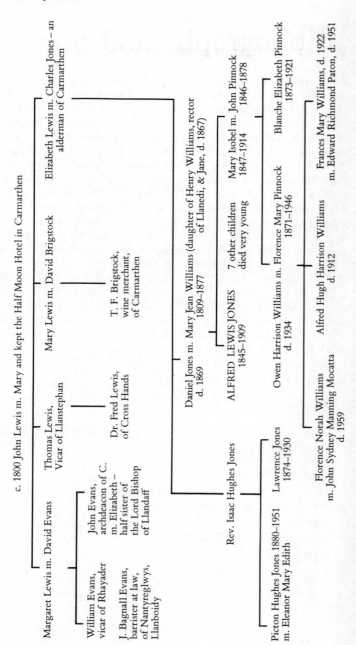

c. 1800 John Lewis m. Mary and kept the Half Moon Hotel in Carmarthen

Bibliography and Sources

Manuscript Sources

1. PARLIAMENTARY MANUSCRIPTS

Foreign Office Papers in the Public Record Office, London
FO 83/1238 (General West Africa); FO 84/1882 (Appendix to Government Gazette of 1888; Description of Benin River); FO 84/1916 (1888), FO 84/1917, FO 84/1919, FO 84/1929, FO 84/2094, FO 84/2157 (1891) (These papers deal with the opposition of the steamship companies to the extension of the charter of the Royal Niger Company); FO 84/2265 (1892) (Expedition to Sierra Leone financed by Alfred Jones); FO 2/85 (Confidential memo. of conversation held between Alfred Jones, Bond and MacDonald at the Foreign Office on 8 November 1895).

Colonial Office Papers in the Public Record Office, London
CO 147/98–99–100–101–102–103 and 136: These cover West Africa in general including the importation of silver, the issue of notes, differential duties on spirits and local purchases of cement.

CO 537/10: Supplementary correspondence. Secret despatches 1884–1909. These include the correspondence of the West African Frontier Force as well as many miscellaneous items.

CO 537/11: Miscellaneous Departments, 1884 to 1909. This covers correspondence in respect of the Admiralty, the Treasury, the War Office, the Colonial Office (Miscellaneous and Individuals).

CO 537/12–13–14–15 and 16: Foreign Office, 1884 to 1899. Negotiations with France over Niger and other boundaries in West Africa, and Slave Trade Conference.

Colonial Office Papers in the Colonial Office Library, London
African No. 250: Correspondence 1877 to 1884. Appointment of joint British and French Commission to define the boundary at Assinee.

Africa West No. 592: Correspondence 1892 to 1899. The currency of the West African Colonies.

Africa West No. 616: West African Currency Committee. Report, Minutes of Evidence and Appendices. Note evidence of Alfred Jones, pp. 25–30. Also letters from Bank of British West Africa and the Liverpool Chamber of Commerce.

Africa West No. 645: (Confidential) 1900 to 1903. Further correspondence relating to the currency of the West Africa Colonies.

Africa West No. 745: 1902 to 1905. Correspondence regarding Cotton Growing in West Africa.

Africa West No. 835: 1906 to 1907. Further correspondence re Cotton Growing in West Africa.

Africa West No. 979: (Confidential) 1907 to 1910. Correspondence re proposed Note Issue in West Africa.

2. PRIVATE MANUSCRIPTS

Elder Dempster Lines Manuscripts
Elder Dempster Lines Limited, now part of Ocean Transport and Trading Limited, hold most of the remaining records of the African Steam Ship Company, Elder Dempster and Company and Elder Dempster and Company Limited. As a result of the changes in company structure which followed the Royal Mail crash, and because of the damage sustained during the wartime blitz on Liverpool, few items have survived but many gaps have been filled from the archives of J. T. Fletcher (Shipping) Limited – formerly Fletcher and Parr – where Alfred Jones was employed as a shipping clerk during the 1860s and 1870s.

The John Holt Papers
These are an invaluable guide to the merchanting aspects of West African history and cover the period from *c.* 1870 to the present day. They have been well catalogued by Dr. J. E. Flint and are now kept at the Rhodes House Library in Oxford. The relevant files are as follows:

Box 6, File 1. Instructions to the agents of the African Association.
2. African Association, 1889–92.
3. African Association, 1893–1922.
4. West African Trade Association, 1897–1910.
5. Letters from Jones, Dempster, Elder, Davey.
6. Letters from Jones and shipping documents.
7. Testimonial to Jones.
8. Letters from James Knott re proposed new shipping company to West Africa.
9. Letters from Furness, Withy and Henry Tyrer re proposed new shipping line.
11, 6. Letters from Jones re School of Tropical Medicine.
12, 1. Letters from Messrs. Fletcher and Parr.

13,   2. Testimonial to Captain Davies.
14,   4. Letters from John Holt to Thomas Holt.
16,   8. Letters re death of Mary Kingsley.
17,   3. Letters from Jones and Lord Scarbrough.
18, 10. Letters from E. D. Morel.
21, 1–5. Miscellaneous correspondence.
24, Pamphlets 62. Monopolist System of Shipping (Morel).
          65. History of Nigerian Marine.
          75. Trading Monopolies in West Africa (Morel).
          94. Cotton Growing Association.
Letter Book 26/3a. Flimsy copies of John Holt's outward letters.

The papers of James Deemin, who acted as Senior Agent for Holts in West Africa during this period, have been catalogued by the present author and now form part of the Holt archives at Rhodes House Library, Oxford.

The Guinea Gulf Line Manuscripts

The papers of the Shipping Department of John Holt and Company (Liverpool) Limited, the John Holt Line Limited, and the Guinea Gulf Line Limited, have been collected under the above heading and were kindly made available to me by Mr. Douglas Mather, the former chairman of the firm.

The Mocatta Papers

Mrs. Florence Norah Mocatta of Hoylake, Wirral, is the great niece of Sir Alfred Jones. She has in her possession the remaining private papers of Sir Alfred. These include only a small number of letters and telegrams but also of value is the scrapbook of Florence Mary Pinnock (Jones's niece) compiled while she was living at her uncle's home. Other items of interest include a short, handwritten, biography of Jones by his sister, Mrs. Isobel Mary Pinnock, many family photographs and a detailed 'Book of Obituary'.

The E. D. Morel Papers

This huge collection of the letters and documents of E. D. Morel is now kept at the British Library of Political and Economic Science, London School of Economics. The relevant files are as follows: Box F. 8/1. Letters from Alfred Jones; Box F. 8/2. Letters from John Holt.

The Nathan Papers

Nathan, Governor of the Gold Coast from 1901 to 1904, conducted an extensive correspondence with Alfred Jones during this period. This collection is now held at Rhodes House Library in Oxford.

The Niger (and Royal Niger) Company Papers

These are now kept at Rhodes House Library, Oxford, having been presented by the Earl of Scarbrough. The relevant files are: MSS. Afr. S.95, Vol. 7. Transport; Vols. 11, 12 and 13. Miscellaneous.

Henry Tyrer Manuscripts
Henry Tyrer and Company Limited operated chartered vessels to West Africa during the Alfred Jones era and made many attempts to encourage other lines to enter the West African shipping trade. A number of important papers concerning this firm were made available to me by the late Mr. Frederick Cutts who also gave me the benefit of his seventy years' experience in the trade. The Company's archives are currently being reorganized by its Chairman, Mr. Charles Harrison, and will eventually be stored at its Head Office in Liverpool.

United Africa Company Papers
These papers are held at United Africa House, Blackfriars Road, London. The general index gives details of items kept on behalf of the UAC and of its constituent firms including the Niger Company, Millers, the African and Eastern Trade Corporation – successors to the African Association – and Swanzys.

3. COMPANY FILES

The following files of live companies are kept at Companies House, 55–71 City Road, London:

Ref. No. 40828 Bank of British West Africa Limited.
      70123 Elders and Fyffes Limited.
      51851 John Holt and Company (Liverpool) Limited.
    112584 West Africa Lighterage and Transport Company Limited.

The following files of dissolved companies are also kept at Companies House, London, though they will eventually be transferred to the PRO:

Ref. No. 41742 Ocean Transport Company Limited.
      65244 Elders Navigation Collieries Limited.
      72110 Imperial Direct West India Mail Service Company Limited.
    132775 Alfred L. Jones Trust and Estate Company Limited.

The following files of dissolved companies are kept at the Public Record Office, London:

Ref. No. 54838 Beaver Line Associated Steamers Limited.
      61912 Elder Dempster Shipping Limited.
      61912 Elder Line Limited.
      65211 Laird Brothers Limited.
      73475 Elders and Fyffes (Shipping) Limited.
    105490 Beaver Shipping Company Limited.
    108502 Elder Dempster and Company Limited.
    125828 Elder Dempster (Grand Canary) Limited.
    125829 Elder Dempster (Tenerife) Limited.

The following files of dissolved companies are kept at the Companies Registration Office, 102 George Street, Edinburgh:

BIBLIOGRAPHY AND SOURCES

Ref. No. E.67206 British and African Steam Navigation Company Limited.
E.67206 British and African Steam Navigation Company (1900) Limited.

4. UNPUBLISHED WORKS

Sir Alfred Jones and the Development of West African Trade (M.A. thesis by P. N. Davies, University of Liverpool, 1964).
A British Merchant in West Africa in the Era of Imperialism (Ph.D. thesis by Miss Cherry Gertzel, dealing with John Holt in the Bodleian Library, Oxford).
Anglo-German Commercial Rivalry in West Africa, 1884–1918 (Ph.D. thesis by A. Olorunfemi, University of Birmingham, 1977).
The Rise and Development of Legitimate Trade in Palm Oil with West Africa (M.A. thesis by N. H. Stilliard, University of Birmingham, 1938).
Glasgow and Africa, Connexions and Attitudes, 1870–1900 (Ph.D. thesis by W. Thompson, University of Strathclyde, 1970).
The History of the United Africa Company Limited to 1938. This was written anonymously by a senior member of the staff and was based on the recollections of the older employees. It has now been largely superseded by the work of F. Pedler (see below).

Printed Sources

1. GOVERNMENT PAPERS
Parliamentary Papers, 1842, vol. XI, p. 573.
Memorandum for the *Committee on West African Trade and Slavery*, submitted by MacGregor Laird.
Parliamentary Papers, 1865, vol. V, (412), p. iii. Proposed withdrawal from West Africa.
Committee on the Currency of the West African Colonies, Minutes of Evidence, C. 2984, 1899.
West African Currency Committee, Report, Cd. 6426, 1912.
Edible and Oil Producing Nuts and Seeds Committee, Cd. 8248, 1916.
Annual Statements of the Trade of the United Kingdom with Foreign Countries and British Possessions.
Annual Reports for the Gold Coast.
A Handbook of Empire Timber, Department of Scientific and Industrial Research, London, HMSO, 1945.

2. BOOKS
R. G. Albion, *Seaports South of Sahara*, New York, 1959.
A. Anderson (D. MacPherson), *Annals of Commerce*, vol. VI, London, 1805.
W. Ashworth, *An Economic History of England, 1870–1939*, London, 1960.
W. B. Baikie, *Narrative of an Exploring Voyage up the Rivers Kwora and Bi'nue (commonly known as the Niger and Tsa'dda) in 1854*, London, 1856.
P. T. Bauer, *West African Trade*, London, 1954.

151

P. Beaver, *Yes! We have some. The Story of Fyffes*, Stevenage, 1976.

J. W. Blake, *European Beginnings in West Africa, 1454–1578*, London, 1937.

F. C. Bowen, *History of the Canadian Pacific Line*, London, 1928.

Sir A. Burns, *History of Nigeria*, 6th Edition, New York, 1963.

W. R. H. Caine, *The Cruise of the Port Kingston*, London, 1908.

Sir Julian Crossley and John Blandford, *The D.C.O. Story*, London, 1975.

K. G. Davies, *The Royal African Company*, London, 1957.

P. N. Davies, *The Trade Makers, Elder Dempster in West Africa*, London, 1973.

P. N. Davies (Ed.), *Trading in West Africa*, London, 1976.

K. O. Dike, *Trade and Politics in the Niger Delta, 1830–1885*, London, 1956.

D. Ellison (Ed.), *Cox and the Ju Ju Coast*, St. Helier, 1968.

J. D. Fage, *An Introduction to the History of West Africa*, London, 1955.

C. E. Fayle, *Seaborne Trade*, vol. I, London, 1920.

J. E. Flint, *Sir George Goldie and the Making of Nigeria*, London, 1960.

R. Fry, *Bankers in West Africa (The Story of the Bank of British West Africa Limited)*, London, 1976.

C. Fyffe, *A History of Sierra Leone*, London, 1962.

S. Gwynn, *The Life of Mary Kingsley*, London, 1932.

J. D. Hargreaves, *Prelude to the Partition of West Africa*, London, 1963.

J. D. Hargreaves, *West Africa Partitioned*, London, 1974.

R. J. Harrison-Church, *West Africa*, London, 1966.

A. C. G. Hastings, *The Voyage of the Dayspring*, London, 1926.

G. K. Helleiner, *Peasant Agriculture, Government and Economic Growth in Nigeria*, Homewood (Illinois), 1966.

C. R. Holt (Ed.), *The Diary of John Holt*, Liverpool, 1948.

A. G. Hopkins, *An Economic History of West Africa*, London, 1973.

B. S. Hoyle and D. Hilling (Eds.), *Seaports and Development in Tropical Africa*, London, 1970.

T. J. Hutchinson, *Narrative of the Niger, Tshudda and Benue Exploration, 1855*, London, 1966.

B. Inglis, *Roger Casement*, London, 1973.

H. A. Innis, *A History of the Canadian Pacific Railway*, London, 1923.

Mary Kingsley, *West African Studies*, London, 1899.

A. W. Kirkaldy, *British Shipping. Its History, Organisation and Importance*, London, 1914.

M. Laird and R. A. K. Oldfield, *Narrative of an expedition into the interior of Africa by the River Niger in the steam vessels Quorra and Alburkah in 1832, 1833 and 1834*, 2 vols., London, 1837.

Charlotte Leubuscher, *The West African Shipping Trade, 1909–1959*, Leyden (Holland), 1963.

Liverpool School of Tropical Medicine, Historic Record, 1898–1920, Liverpool, 1920.

Christopher Lloyd, *The Navy and the Slave Trade*, London, 1949.

J. R. McCulloch, *Dictionary of Commerce*, London, 1882.

BIBLIOGRAPHY AND SOURCES

Allister MacMillan, *The Red Book of West Africa*, London, 1920.
Allan McPhee, *The Economic Revolution in British West Africa*, London, 1926.
E. W. Marwick, *William Balfour Baikie*, Orkney, 1965.
D. Marx Junior, *International Shipping Cartels*, New Jersey, 1953.
M. F. Maury, *The Physical Geography of the Sea*, 6th Edition, London, 1856.
G. E. Metcalfe, *Great Britain and Ghana, Documents of Ghana History*, 1807–1957, London, 1964.
A. H. Milne, *Sir Alfred Lewis Jones, K.C.M.G.*, Liverpool, 1914.
C. W. Newbury, *British Policy towards West Africa, Selected Documents 1786–1874* (London, 1965) and *Selected Documents 1875–1914* (London, 1971).
W. T. Newlyn and D. C. Rowan, *Money and Banking in British Colonial Africa*, London, 1954.
S. D. Neumark, *Foreign Trade and Economic Development in Africa*, Stanford, 1963.
R. Oliver and J. D. Fage, *A Short History of Africa*, Harmondsworth, 1962.
F. J. Pedler, *Economic Geography of West Africa*, London, 1955.
F. J. Pedler, *The Lion and the Unicorn in Africa (The United Africa Company, 1787–1931)*, London, 1974.
Margery Perham and Mary Bull (Eds.), *The Diaries of Lord Lugard*, London, 1963.
Sir Alan Pim, *The Financial and Economic History of the African Tropical Territories*, London, 1940.
J. H. Plumb and C. Howard, *West African Explorers*, London, 1955.
Howard Robinson, *Carrying British Mails Overseas*, London, 1964.
R. E. Robinson and J. Gallagher with Alice Denny, *Africa and the Victorians*, London, 1961.
Ronald Ross, *Memoirs*, London, 1923.
E. C. Smith, *A Short History of Naval and Marine Engineering*, London, 1937.
J. Russell Smith, *The Ocean Carrier*, London, 1908.
S. G. Sturmey, *British Shipping and World Competition*, London, 1962.
W. F. Tewson, *The British Cotton Growing Association (Golden Jubilee, 1904–1954)*, issued by the Association, 1954.
R. H. Thornton, *British Shipping*, London, 1959.
C. Wilson, *The History of Unilever*, vols. I and II, London, 1954.
C. Wilson and W. Reader, *Men and Machines* (A History of D. Napier and Son, Engineers, Limited), London, 1958.

3. PRIVATELY PUBLISHED PAPERS
P. N. Davies, *A Short History of the Ships of John Holt and Company (Liverpool) Limited and the Guinea Gulf Line Limited*, published privately by the Company, Liverpool, 1965.
A. H. Stockley, *Consciousness of Effort, The Romance of the Banana*, printed for private circulation, 1937.
Merchant Adventure, published privately by John Holt and Company (Liverpool) Limited, Liverpool, 1948.

153

Compagnie Maritime Belge (Lloyd Royal), house history published by the Company, Antwerp, 1948.
A Short History of the German Africa Lines, published privately by the Deutsche Afrika-Linien, Hamburg, 1967.
List of Iron, Steel and Wood Vessels built at the Birkenhead Iron Works (Laird's shipyard), Willmer Brothers, Birkenhead, 1894.
Ocean Highways, an illustrated souvenir of Elder Dempster and Company, Liverpool, 1902.

4. ARTICLES
A. A. Cowan, 'Early Trading Conditions in the Bight of Biafra', *Journal of the Royal African Society*, October 1935.
P. N. Davies, 'The African Steam Ship Company', in J. R. Harris (Ed.), *Liverpool and Merseyside*, London, 1969.
P. N. Davies, 'The Impact of the Expatriate Shipping Lines on the Economic Development of British West Africa', *Business History*, vol. XIX, no. 1, January 1977.
P. N. Davies, 'Group Enterprise: Strengths and Hazards'. To be published by Liverpool University in a *Festschrift* entitled *Business and Businessmen* in honour of Professor F. E. Hyde, October 1977.
P. N. Davies and A. M. Bourn, 'Lord Kylsant and the Royal Mail', *Business History*, vol. XIV, no. 2, July 1972.
B. Drake, 'Continuity and Flexibility in Liverpool's Trade with Africa and the Caribbean', *Business History*, vol. 18, no. 1, January 1976.
H. S. Goldsmith, C.M.G., 'MacGregor Laird and the Niger', *Journal of the African Society*, vol. XXXI, no. CXXXV, October 1932.
R. G. Greenhill, 'The State under Pressure – the West Indian Mail Contract, 1905', *Business History*, vol. XI, no. 2, July 1969.
D. Hilling, 'The Evolution of the Major Ports of West Africa', *Geographic Journal*, vol. 135, part 3, September 1969.
A. G. Hopkins, 'Economic Imperialism in West Africa, Lagos, 1880–1892', *Economic History Review*, vol. 21, no. 3, December 1968.
R. S. Irving, 'British Railway Investment and Innovation, 1900–1914', *Business History*, vol. XIII, no. 1, January 1971.
A. L. Jones, 'Autobiography', *MAP Magazine*, 28 December 1901. Reproduced in P. N. Davies, *Trading in West Africa*, op. cit.
W. D. McIntyre, 'British Policy in West Africa – the Ashanti Expedition, 1873–4', *Historical Journal*, vol. 5, no. 1, 1962.
S. B. Saul, 'The British West Indies in Depression, 1880–1914', *Journal of Inter-American Economic Affairs*, vol. 12, no. 3, Winter 1958.

Index